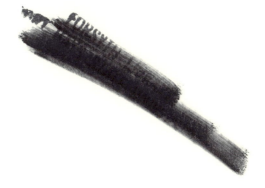

The Bank of the United States and the American Economy

Recent Titles in
Contributions in Economics and Economic History

Opening the West: Federal Internal Improvements Before 1860
Laurence J. Malone

Oil and Coffee: Latin American Merchant Shipping from the Imperial Era to the 1950s
René De La Pedraja

The American Peasantry
Southern Agricultural Labor and Its Legacy, 1850–1995: A Study in Political Economy
Ronald E. Seavoy

Keynes: A Critical Life
David Felix

Treasure from the Painted Hills: A History of Calico, California, 1882–1907
Douglas Steeples

Ecology and the World-System
Walter L. Goldfrank, David Goodman, and Andrew Szasz, editors

Latin American Merchant Shipping in the Age of Global Competition
René De La Pedraja

Maritime Sector, Institutions, and Sea Power of Premodern China
Gang Deng

Charting Twentieth-Century Monetary Policy: Herbert Hoover and Benjamin Strong,
1917–1927
Silvano A. Wueschner

The Politics of Economic Restructuring and Democracy in Africa
Obioma M. Iheduru

Keynesian and Monetary Approaches to Managing Disequilibrium in Balance of Payments
Accounts
*Augustine C. Arize, Theologos Homer Bonitsis, Ioannis N. Kallianiotis, Krishna
Kasibhatla, and John Malindretos, editors*

Energy and the Rise and Fall of Political Economy
Bernard C. Beaudreau

The Bank of the United States and the American Economy

Edward S. Kaplan

Contributions in Economics and Economic History, Number 214

GREENWOOD PRESS
Westport, Connecticut • London

Library of Congress Cataloging–in–Publication Data

Kaplan, Edward S.
    The Bank of the United States and the American economy / Edward S.
Kaplan.
      p. cm.—(Contributions in economics and economic history,
ISSN 0084–9235 ; no. 214)
    Includes bibliographical references and index.
    ISBN 0–313–30866–7 (alk. paper)
    1. Bank of the United States (1791–1811)—History. 2. Bank of the
United States (1816–1836)—History. 3. United States—Economic
conditions—To 1865. I. Title. II. Series.
HG2525.K36   1999
332.1′1′0973—dc21   99–15390

British Library Cataloguing in Publication Data is available.

Library of Congress Catalog Card Number: 99–15390
ISBN: 0–313–30866–7
ISSN: 0084–9235

First published in 1999

Greenwood Press, 88 Post Road West, Westport, CT 06881
An imprint of Greenwood Publishing Group, Inc.
www.greenwood.com

Printed in the United States of America

The paper used in this book complies with the
Permanent Paper Standard issued by the National
Information Standards Organization (Z39.48–1984).

10 9 8 7 6 5 4 3 2 1

To the memory of John Edwin Fagg, my professor at New York University

Contents

Preface   ix

1. The Need for a National Bank   1

2. Alexander Hamilton and the First Bank of the United States   19

3. The Period between the First and Second Banks   37

4. The Creation of the Second Bank of the United States   49

5. The Second Bank and the Panic of 1819   67

6. Nicholas Biddle and the Second Bank   79

7. The Jacksonians and the Second Bank   97

8. The Bank War   121

9. The Last Years of the Second Bank   141

10. Conclusion   151

    Bibliography   165

    Index   169

Preface

This book tells the story of the First and Second Banks of the United States and how they functioned within the American economy. These Banks, acting as national and central banks, helped the government in its early years through wars and economic instability. Their necessity was proven during their absences. When the Continental Congress refused to renew the charter of the First Bank in 1811, enough economic chaos prevailed afterward to cause the chartering of a Second Bank in 1816. When its charter expired in 1836, the country suffered through numerous economic crises, due mostly to an inelastic money supply. This problem was finally resolved with the creation of the Federal Reserve Banking system in 1913.

The seeds of the Bank of the United States were planted during the American Revolution, when the Continental Congress realized that it lacked the funds to finance the war against Great Britain. After much haggling, in 1781, Congress created the country's first national bank, the Bank of North America, under Robert Morris. The bank proved successful in financing the remainder of the war and in helping the confederated government with its finances.

Alexander Hamilton had supported the concept of a national bank as early as the American Revolution. He and Morris had exchanged ideas concerning the role of a national bank in society, and when Morris created the Bank of North America, he found Hamilton to be an enthusiastic supporter. When the Bank of North America became a private bank prior to the Constitutional Convention, Hamilton had pushed for a national bank that would serve the new government.

The chartering of the First Bank of the United States in 1791, for a period of twenty years, created a semipublic institution where the government owned twenty percent of the stock. The Bank acted as a fiscal agent for the government and became a depository for all public money. Hamilton had never meant it to become a central bank, but later it acted as such by imposing restraints on lending. In this role it served the nation's economic welfare. However, it also attracted numerous enemies. In its early years, the Bank's opponents claimed that it was unconstitutional, and though it had functioned well, and Secretary of the Treasury Albert Gallatin had supported it, the Bank's charter was not renewed in 1811.

It was mostly the inability to finance the War of 1812 that created a demand for the Second Bank of the United States. In 1791, it was the Federalists who had supported it, whereas the Jeffersonian Republicans had opposed it, mostly on constitutional grounds. In 1816, it was a complete turnabout in all respects: the Federalists from the New England and Middle Atlantic states wanted no part of the Bank, though many of the Jeffersonian Republicans in the South became its supporters. Though there was some opposition on constitutional grounds in 1816, the Bank's main opponents were primarily businessmen and state bankers in the Northeast.

The Second Bank of the United States started out badly, due to the poor management by its first president William Jones and the Panic of 1819. However, its most prosperous years came under Nicholas Biddle, who had succeeded Langdon Cheves, the Bank's second president, in January 1823, and remained at the Bank's helm, until its charter expired in March 1836.

Under Biddle's leadership, the Bank's best years were from 1823 to 1828. The new president proved innovative and conservative, as he performed central banking duties, such as regulating the money supply and expanding credit. The Bank had dominated the exchanges, protected the investment market, worked closely with the government, and gave the nation a better currency. It was only after 1828 that the Bank encountered problems, for which it had mostly itself to blame. It became involved in the speculation mania of the early 1830s, as its loans increased more rapidly than its available specie.

The election of Andrew Jackson as president in 1828 marked the beginning of the end of the Bank. Jackson, a hard money advocate, disliked banknotes and banks in general, and despised Biddle and the Second Bank in particular. He had refused to support rechartering the Bank under any circumstances. The Bank war began when Biddle asked Congress to renew the Bank's charter in spring of 1832, four years prior to its expiration. This action made the renewal a political issue and challenged the president, who was running for reelection that year. Jackson accepted the challenge by vetoing the bill and winning reelection. The president then destroyed the effectiveness of the Bank by removing the government funds from its vaults in 1833.

Though the Bank's charter expired in 1836, Biddle had it rechartered in Pennsylvania as a state bank. He continued as president of the United States Bank of Pennsylvania until his retirement in 1839.

The United States Bank of Pennsylvania had suffered through the Panics of 1837 and 1839. Unfortunately, the Bank was not strong enough to survive the effects of the 1839 downturn, and two years after Biddle's retirement, it closed its doors for good.

1

The Need for a National Bank

The financial problems of the colonies during the American Revolution were directly related to the absence of a national bank. In this chapter, we trace the history of money and banking in the new United States from the colonial period just before the American Revolution through the Confederation, 1777 to 1787. It was during this time that state governments controlled the power of the purse, as they alone had the right to levy taxes. Both the national government, known as the Continental Congress, and the state governments could issue paper money which led to severe inflation and a lack of confidence in the financial system. This made it difficult for the Congress to establish credit to finance the Revolutionary War, and it threatened the very survival of the new nation. This could have been avoided if a national banking system had been put into place immediately after the Declaration of Independence. However, it was not until 1781 that the Bank of North America came into existence, and by that time, the economy was on the verge of collapse. Fortunately, men like Robert Morris and Alexander Hamilton were able to step into the breach and lead the new nation through its most critical time.

THE SHORTAGE OF SPECIE IN
THE COLONIES

A shortage of specie in the colonies before the American Revolution was due to several reasons. It was very expensive to import, and Great Britain prohibited specie exports to the colonies as well as the minting of coins in the colonies.[1] Though there was an inadequate supply of hard money to meet the needs of shopkeepers on the eve of the Revolution some Spanish, Portuguese, and Dutch coins entered the colonies as a result of the West Indian trade.[2] For example, South Carolina in 1701 used nine varieties of silver and gold coins as money, brought mostly from the West Indies as a result of a favorable balance of trade with that area. However, the most popular of all coins used in the colonies was the Spanish dollar, more frequently called the "Piece of Eight" because it was divided into eight bits. The American dollar was based upon the "Piece of Eight" as two bits equaled a quarter.[3] Pirates, those scoundrels of the high sea, actually helped provide the colonies with coin when they visited the port cities of North America. Some merchants welcomed them with open arms as they spent their money freely on food, drink, and women. Most of these pirates came from the West Indies, the Red Sea, Madagascar, and the Indian Ocean.[4]

Though Parliament had passed laws at the request of creditors of Great Britain and the colonies to prohibit the use of most paper money, pound sterling notes issued in England were permitted to circulate. These notes were used for all transactions, including the payment of taxes. The British government also allowed provincial legislatures to issue paper money called "promises to pay," and some of these bills also included a specified interest to be paid at a future date.[5]

Notwithstanding the shortage of money, people proved enterprising by using bills of exchange or making entries into book accounts. Colonists used credit transactions with each other and with agents and purchasers. These transactions met the daily, monthly and yearly needs to purchase supplies, equipment, land, livestock, and slaves and to sell their products and services. People extended credit to others and were repaid in kind, in paper money or by note or book account that its owner could use in settling another debt he owed to a third party.[6]

Bills of exchange were used on a regular basis by the American colonists. It was a form of credit where transactions were conducted at great distances without having to send cash. For example, merchant A in the colonies would buy goods from merchant B in the West Indies. Merchant A would send merchant B a promise to pay called a bill of exchange and in return would get his merchandise. Merchant B would use the bill to purchase goods from merchant C who lived closer to A, and C would send the bill to A for cash.[7]

Bills of exchange were used throughout the colonial period, and they were supplemented with bank credit. For example, in 1686, the Massachusetts colony granted a charter to a private bank to issue banknotes. This bank made loans either in specie or in bank notes which circulated as paper money.[8] Though a number of other colonies also used banks for the same purpose, they had little influence on the overall size of the money supply. It should be noted that these lending institutions were not really banks as we define them today—they did not take deposits but only made loans.[9]

It is always tempting to compare the widespread use of credit in the colonial period with the present day. However, it should be remembered that the colonists were forced to use credit because of a shortage of both specie and paper money. Today many people use credit to spend beyond their means.

FINANCING THE AMERICAN REVOLUTION

The most important problem facing the Continental Congress in 1775 was financing the American Revolution. Governments can raise funds by taxing, borrowing, and printing. From an economic point of view taxing is the best way to raise funds, because it can be done without causing inflation like printing or cause interest rates to rise like borrowing. However, the Continental Congress was not granted the power to levy taxes, as the states feared that it would abuse the power and become like the British government that they were now rebelling against. Therefore, the right to tax was only given to the states, and the Congress would have to depend on the states to send their share of tax money to the central government. Unfortunately, as states were shy about taxing their citizens, this method of raising funds proved, for the most part, inadequate.[10]

Continental Currency

Between 1775 and 1781, paper money was used almost exclusively to finance the war. This continental currency consisted of bills of credit that were issued in anticipation of tax revenue from the states with which they might be redeemed. However, the tax collections were so few that people lost hope that the continentals could be exchanged for specie, and what was to be a temporary dependence on paper became permanent.[11] As early as 1776, the continental bills began to decline in value, and by the end of 1779, a total of $241 million of these bills had been issued with their value set at about two cents on the dollar.[12] In an attempt to halt the depreciation of the continental currency, the Congress adopted a resolution that became known as the forty-for-one funding measure in March 1780. It called for all old bills to be exchanged at forty paper dollars to one dollar in specie. As quickly as the old bills were returned, new bills were to be issued, valued at one dollar in specie. Though it failed to stop the depreciation, it reduced the national debt in terms of specie from $200 million to about $5 million. By 1781, paper currency had declined drastically in relation to gold and silver. For example, wheat cost over 600 shillings in continental currency, but only six shillings in specie, and by the end of 1781, it took one hundred paper dollars to buy one dollar in specie.[13]

What the colonists experienced was demand pull inflation—too many dollars chasing too few goods. In January 1778, delegates from the New England and the Middle Atlantic states met in New Haven, Connecticut, to recommend price controls. They decided that prices on certain manufacturing goods should not go higher than seventy-five to one hundred percent of their levels in 1774. Although certain states such as Connecticut, Pennsylvania, New York, and New Jersey agreed to abide by these recommendations, they proved ineffective and were repealed by June 1779.[14] As the Congress failed to reduce the amount of paper currency in circulation, prices of most commodities increased dramatically. Iron prices shot up 111 percent in one month in 1781. Short supplies were responsible for the high prices of sugar and salt. Wheat prices in Pennsylvania more than tripled and many farmers in that state refused to accept continental currency for their produce. It is interesting to note that the British army in Pennsylvania had no trouble buying produce and meat from these same farmers for gold and silver.[15]

The depreciation of the continental currency and the inflation that followed cannot be blamed solely on the Continental Congress. The states also bore responsibility for financing the war. They also printed their own money, sold Tory estates, and introduced state import duties. The distress within the states paralleled that of the central government. Joseph Reid, president of the Executive Council of Pennsylvania, spoke for many state officials when he wrote to General George Washington that:

It is difficult for your excellency to form a competent Judgment of the Difficulties and Embarrassments with which the procuring Supplies is attended. The Confidence of the People in Paper Money is so shaken that the Produce of the Country is furnished to the Commissioners with much reluctance, and even of this Money we have but a very incompetent Sum when compared with the Amount and Value of the Supplies. Credit may be said to be at an End; the innumerable Certificates granted by the Quarter Master and the Commissary Departments and by the Authority of the state having extinguished all Confidence.[16]

The states had problems with their own currency and did not want the responsibility of issuing continental funds.

In March 1780, the Congress began replacing old money with $10 million of new currency. It was to be backed by the states and to bear interest. As old notes were redeemed by state treasuries, they were to be replaced by the new issue. However, merchants in Philadelphia refused to cooperate with the Congress. They could make more money depreciating the currency by raising their prices even though the state governments tried to regulate them. For example, the Pennsylvania legislature asked the leading merchants to form an association to stop the depreciation of the continental currency which was then selling for 75:1. Merchants temporarily agreed to stabilize at that ratio, which pleased both the assembly and the Congress. However, as soon as the merchants returned to work they quickly doubled the specie prices of their articles, causing a further depreciation of the continental currency. Other merchants, looking to profit, took advantage of the current situation and held scarce goods, waiting for their prices to rise. All this created a new rich class of merchants called "profiteers."[17] Charles Calomiris, the economic historian, placed the blame for the rapid depreciation of the continental currency directly on the states. He declared that the failure of the states to support the currency fully or to vest the Congress with the power to tax was the primary cause of depreciation. By the middle of 1781, continentals had stopped circulating and were kept from that time on as a speculative store of value. Specie imports and new state bill issues became the media of exchange.[18]

Borrowing

Though borrowing began as early as 1776, it was not until 1781 that it was used as a major source of funding. It was difficult to convince wealthy people to make loans to an unstable government, and most colonists did not have the capital for investment in government bonds or certificates. France, America's most important ally, was reluctant to help until the United States demonstrated that it could win a major victory against the British army. The victory of American forces at the Battle of Saratoga, in October 1777, was a major turning point in the war. France, Spain, and Holland were now ready to support the American Revolution through loans, and, in the case of France, military aid as well.[19]

In October 1776, the Congress offered four percent interest for $5 million in certificates. However, most wealthy merchants, who could afford to lend their money, waited until the interest rates increased to six percent. Loan offices were opened in each state with a commissioner in charge of its operation. Because no certificates were issued for under $300 only wealthy people could afford to buy them.[20] Interest-bearing certificates were also issued by purchasing agents of the army. In return for goods supplied to the armed forces, the agents of the services would give certificates of indebtedness for the value of the goods received.[21]

Foreign loans from 1776 to 1780 came mostly from France. It began with a gift of 1 million livres in 1776. Eighteen million livres were borrowed in 1778, 10 million in 1781, and 6 million in 1783. France had loaned the United States over $6 million by the end of the war. Spain loaned an additional $248,000, mostly in cash and supplies, whereas most loans from Holland came after the war and during what became known as the "critical period," from 1783 to 1787. By the end the war, the United States had borrowed a total of $67 million, with a specie value of $11.5 million based on the June 1780 index. Based on percentages, both foreign and domestic loans accounted for about thirty-five percent of all war funding compared with fifty-nine percent in paper money.[22]

Requisitions

In November 1777, the Congress had asked for a total of $5 million to be apportioned among the states. The states would provide cash, loans, and commodities of all sorts, including food, clothing, and wagons for transportation. At first the states were all too eager to help fight Great Britain. However, as the war continued into the 1780s the states had less money to give because they refused to continue taxing their citizens; they also had a difficult time trying to transport food due to its perishable nature. Requisitions played a small role in the funding process, accounting for only $4 million or six percent of total funding.[23]

Agriculture and Industry

The agricultural community in the New England and in the Middle Atlantic states benefited from the war. Most of the food crops, such as corn, wheat, barley and oats, were in great demand by the Continental army, the French troops, and the fleet. The increased demand for most farm commodities resulted in higher prices and inflated land values. The state of Connecticut was the major source of meat and grain, and farmers near American, French, or British forces were paid well. In fact, most farmers preferred dealing with the French and British troops, who paid for their goods in specie rather than the worthless continental.[24] The continued success of the farmer was due to the fact that most of the crops that he grew were for domestic consumption and, therefore, were not threatened by the British coastal blockade. This was not the case in the Southern colonies where the chief commercial crops—tobacco, rice and indigo—were all exported. The farmer also prospered because the cost of production and living expenses did not rise as rapidly as farm prices.[25]

Unlike agriculture, commerce suffered during the early years of the American Revolution. Though the Congress opened American ports to all nations except England in April 1776, the British blockade of the northern seaboard towns reduced commercial activity. The fishing industry was crippled and shipbuilding was temporarily stopped. The British occupation of Boston, Philadelphia, and Newport made it almost impossible for those states to conduct trade. Many colonists who could not find work in the shipping industry turned to privateering. This questionable way of making a living became so lucrative that it even took manpower away from the farming industry.[26]

The Condition of the Continental Army

The Congress had to fight the war without money and without the power of force over the states or its citizens. Though volunteers quickly responded to the call of arms, most believed that the war would be quickly won. However, the complaints of the soldiers about the poor pay, inadequate clothing, and the scarcity of supplies began to increase as the war dragged on from year to year. Alexander Hamilton, a volunteer for duty and a captain of the Provincial Company of Artillery, constantly bombarded the Continental Congress with letters begging for supplies and for money with which to pay the soldiers. Hamilton saw firsthand what was happening in the economy as purchasing power declined and prices rose to all time highs. He understood the importance of a strong central government that could tax and a national bank that could provide the necessary funds to the government in emergency situations. If France had not provided the United States with a substantial loan in 1779, the revolt would have failed from bankruptcy.[27]

Quartermaster General Timothy Pickering declared in October 1780 that no supply magazines had been furnished for the winter. The army stationed at West

Point lived on a day-to-day basis. General Anthony Wayne, who commanded the forces in Pennsylvania, begged for clothing supplies. He even offered to have his troops repair their own clothing if the Congress would only send the needle and thread.[28] However, the worst conditions existed in the South where General Nathanael Greene assumed command. He wrote George Washington in December 1780 that: "Nothing can be more wretched and distressing than the condition of the troops, starving with cold and hunger, without tents and camp equipage. Those of the Virginia line are literally, naked; and a great part totally unfit for any kind of duty, and must remain so until clothing can be had from the northward."[29]

The officers, who for the most part felt compassion for their men, demanded special concessions in the way of pay. Though they received a pay increase in 1776, they demanded half pay for life after the war was over. This was not an unusual practice in the European armies. General Washington at first opposed the idea, but he soon realized that he needed his officers to keep the army intact, and asked the Congress to comply to these demands. In 1778, the Congress agreed to give those officers, who remained for the duration, half pay for seven years from the war's end. Not wanting to leave out noncommissioned officers, the Congress gave them a bounty of one year's pay equal to eighty dollars. However, the officers refused to yield on the lifetime pay issue, and as more and more of them resigned, the Congress finally granted them half pay for life in October 1780.[30]

HAMILTON'S EARLY BANK PLANS

The Bank Plan of 1779

As early as November 1779, Hamilton was concerned about the depreciation of the continental currency, as the new issue was losing its value as fast of the old, wrote his friend Robert Morris to propose his bank plan. He realized that the government needed the support of the wealthy people or the so-called "moneyed men" to provide a permanent paper credit and to get that backing a national bank was necessary. He spoke about how the Bank of England came to the rescue of the British government. It was established in 1694 to raise money for King William's War against the French. Almost immediately the Bank started to issue notes in return for deposits. These notes became a means of exchange because they promised to pay the bearer the sum of the note on demand. The Bank of England was able to unite public authority and faith with private credit and provide the funds necessary to run the business of government and carry out its wars during a critical time in British history. Hamilton believed that if England could create a national bank to end its financial difficulties then the United States could do the same.[31]

In his letter to Morris, Hamilton proposed that the bank should be chartered for a test period of ten years with a initial capitalization of $200 million. Part of this stock would be a foreign loan of $10 million. The government would be a partner in the bank by guaranteeing one-twentieth of the subscription money to the stockholders and would share half of the stock and profits of the bank. Repayment of the investment at the end of the charter was to be guaranteed by the government in Spanish dollars in the ratio of 20:1—a Spanish dollar in November 1779, the time of this proposal, was worth 38.5 continental dollars. The government would receive the privilege of borrowing two million pounds annually at four percent, and private borrowers would pay six percent. Certificates of bank stock would be negotiable and would circulate as additional currency. Though the bank would be managed by a private board of trustees chosen by the shareholders, a government board would inspect the bank's operations.[32]

In the final paragraph of his letter to Morris, who would become the Superintendent of Finance when the Articles of Confederation were finally ratified in 1781, Hamilton expressed confidence in his national bank proposal. He wrote: "It stands on the firm footing of public and private faith. It links the interest of the State in an intimate connection with those of the rich individuals belonging to it. It turns the wealth and influence of both into a commercial channel for the mutual benefit, which must afford advantages not to be estimated."[33]

Though the plan was a quick fix and would undergo considerable change later, and the idea itself did not originate with Hamilton (he was modeling his institution on the Bank of England), this was the first time that a bank for governmental purposes had been proposed in America. Hamilton should be given credit for understanding that the problem during this period was raising enough money to finance the war. To persuade the wealthy to invest, he had to offer them something in return. The national bank proposal in 1779, as described above, would mean a profit to the rich of about one hundred percent return on their original investment after ten years, without taking the effect of inflation into account.[34]

The Bank Plan of 1781

In 1779, Hamilton's proposal for a national bank was an impossible dream. The states were jealous of any centralized authority that could challenge their newfound power under the Articles of Confederation. They certainly would not accept a national bank that would deprive them of control over their own money. In 1780 Hamilton continued to write some of his close friends, like James Duane, a fellow New Yorker and a delegate to the Congress, about the establishment of a national bank. He wrote Duane that the only way the government could establish paper credit was to convince the "moneyed classes" in the United States that it was worth their while to invest in the government through the bank.[35] Hamilton told Duane that even though the wealthy in this country were not nearly as well off as the "moneyed classes" in England, it was still possible to create the bank with less funds. The capital, according to Hamilton, was not the issue; it was getting the support of the Continental Congress. He had little hope that the

Congress would realize the importance of a national bank. He said, "The Bank of England underwrites public authority and faith with private credit; and hence we see what a vast fabric of paper credit is raised on a visionary basis. Had it not been for this, England would never had found sufficient funds to carry on her wars."[36]

On April 30, 1781, Hamilton wrote once again to Robert Morris, who had just been appointed to the post of superintendent of finance in February. He hoped to convince Morris to support his new bank plan, which called for a capitalization of 3 million pounds backed by landed security. A subscriber of six to fifteen shares at five hundred pounds a share should pay one-half in specie and the other half in landed security. The shortage of specie in the colonies forced Hamilton to consider land as security. Later he would oppose any kind of land banks—banks that used real estate as security for the issuance of bank notes. (Land banks accepted mortgages on land as collateral for subscriptions to its stock and would deal largely with loans based on land as security instead of bills of lading, commercial paper, and promissory notes. Its clientele would come from the agrarian and debtor classes. Farmers and small merchants were suspicious of all specie banks and bankers.) Any subscription greater than fifteen shares should be paid one-third in specie, one-sixth in foreign bills, and one-half in landed security. Because there was no confidence in continental currency, banknotes would be paid in pounds, shillings, and pence.[37]

Hamilton told Morris that the new national bank should be given a charter for thirty years and have the power to make contracts with foreign governments for the supply of its armies and fleets in the United States. Of course, the new bank would also contract with the Congress to supply the American army. The Congress was to receive a loan of 1.2 million pounds at eight percent; a sinking fund of 110,400 pounds per year was to be established for twenty years payment. The bank would be managed by twelve directors, eight chosen by the stockholders and four by the Congress.[38]

Hamilton was very direct with the new superintendent of finance when he emphasized the immediate need for a national bank. He declared

In my opinion we ought not to hesitate because we have no other resource. The long and expensive wars of King William had drained England of its specie, its commerce began to droop for want of a proper medium, its taxes were unproductive and its revenues declined. The Administration wisely had recourse to the institution of a bank and it relieved the national difficulties. We are in the same and still greater want of a sufficient medium; we have little specie; the paper we have is of small value and rapidly descending to less; we are immersed in a war for our existence as a nation for our liberty and happiness as a people; we have no revenues nor no credit. A bank if practicable is the only thing that can give us either the one or the other.[39]

THE HAMILTON-MORRIS RELATIONSHIP

Alexander Hamilton held a high regard for Robert Morris's ability in the field of finance. When Morris was chosen by the Congress to the position of superintendent of finance in February 1781, he assured Morris that he was by far the best person to restore the finances of the United States. Even though Hamilton praised Morris's integrity and competence, he was quick to give the new superintendent of finance advice on how to do his job. For example, in April 1781, a month before Morris officially accepted his position, Hamilton told him that the only way to stop the depreciation of the continental was to restore public confidence in the economy by creating a national bank.[40] Hamilton explained to Morris that the major economic crisis facing the United States resulted almost exclusively from a collapse of the credit of the Continental Congress, and not from a general economic exhaustion. Hamilton knew at the time that Morris was planning to create a national bank, but he was concerned that Morris might change his mind due to the opposition in the states against any such venture. Hamilton told Morris that most of the opposition to the bank came from ignorance about its function, and that if people knew that the tendency of a national bank was to increase public and private credit, expand industry, agriculture, and bring true wealth and prosperity to the nation, they would gladly support the venture.[41]

Morris not only welcomed Hamilton's thoughts on the financial problems of the nation, he actually supported most of his ideas on restoring the credit of the country, including the national bank. In fact, to show his respect for Hamilton, Morris appointed Hamilton's good friend, Gouverneur Morris (the two men were not related) of New York as assistant superintendent of finance.[42] In August 1781, shortly after Morris assumed his post, Hamilton once again praised Morris, declaring that he had high hopes that Morris would restore the public credit of the nation, given the support of the Congress. Hamilton was ecstatic that Morris had already proposed a plan for a national bank to the Congress, and pointed out that if this were done four years ago, the United States could have avoided the depreciation of the currency.[43]

ROBERT MORRIS AND THE
BANK OF NORTH AMERICA

By the end of 1780, the Congress had declared the country bankrupt—the public treasury was empty and the currency had collapsed. Continental currency was valued anywhere from $500 to $1,000 for one silver dollar, and prices had skyrocketed.[44] The problem of finance had now taken center stage, and the Congress looked to Robert Morris for help. Morris had been a member of the Congress until he resigned his seat in 1778 to concentrate on his business as an international merchant and an owner of privateers. He proved very successful at selling goods at high prices on both sides of the Atlantic.[45]

In June 1780, Morris had established the Bank of Pennsylvania, the first active bank in the United States. To accomplish this, he had to raise 300,000 pounds, most of which he received from business associates and friends; to show his own commitment, he contributed 10,000 pounds of his own money.[46] This was not the national bank that Hamilton had wanted, but it did serve the purpose of purchasing supplies for American troops until it was replaced by the Bank of North America. It is interesting to note that Thomas Willing would serve as president of both the Bank of Pennsylvania and later the Bank of North America.[47]

In the spring of 1781, Robert Morris was elected by the Congress to the post of superintendent of finance, a newly created executive office. However, he refused to accept the position until the Congress agreed to give in to his demands. For example, he wanted the right to continue his own private business while in office, appoint all officers in his department, and have the right to appoint or dismiss anyone in government who would be connected with the spending of money—he wanted total financial control over the government. After lengthy discussions from April to May, Morris was granted the authority that he had demanded, and he officially took his post on May 14, 1781.[48]

Morris faced an almost impossible task as superintendent of finance in restoring public credit. His chief concern was providing the Congress with the funds to stay in existence, and his first proposal was the organization of a bank. Only three days after taking office, he submitted his own national bank proposal to the Congress. It was a much less ambitious plan than that proposed by Hamilton only two weeks before. For example, the Morris plan called for a subscription of only $400,000 whereas Hamilton's plan called for a 3 million pound subscription. The $400,000 subscription would be split up into shares of $400 each to be paid in gold and silver.[49] Morris had realized that the amount of the subscription was very small but, on May 26, he told Hamilton that once the bank was finally established he hoped to increase its capitalization. His reasoning was that the more the capitalization there was at the beginning, the more difficult it would be to find the money, and the greater the chance the whole project would fail.[50]

Though some in the Congress wanted a bank owned and operated by the government, Morris's plan called for government support, but not control. The bank would be run by twelve directors, and its president would be selected from among them; the superintendent of finance would have the right to examine the affairs of the bank and have access to all its books and papers. The number of shares held by the shareholders determined how many votes they controlled—one share equaled one vote.[51] Banknotes were to be issued which would be payable on demand, and these notes "shall by law be made receivable in the duties and taxes of every state in the union, and by the treasury of the United States, as specie."[52]

Though Congress had passed a resolution approving the Bank of North America as a national bank on May 26, 1781, Morris had problems finding the capital to put the bank into operation—it was difficult finding men of property interested in the bank.[53] The new superintendent of finance used his friends and business partners to help sell the bank stock. He even sent agents to the army to sell subscriptions to both the officers and enlisted men, but the armed forces had little money to spare on the purchase of stock.[54]

Morris, desperate for capital for his new bank, decided to use $86,800 in stock in the Bank of Pennsylvania, which had been in existence for only eighteen months, as the initial private capital for the Bank of North America. After this was agreed to at a stockholders' meeting in the spring of 1781, the Bank of Pennsylvania was officially replaced by the Bank of North America.[55]

It would not be until September 1781, after John Laurens had returned from Europe with nearly half a million dollars in cash that he had borrowed for the Congress, that Morris would finally have the money he needed to establish the bank. As superintendent of finance he had control of all monies, and he decided to use $250,000 of it to buy 633 shares of the bank's stock.[56]

On November 1, 1781, the subscribers met to elect the twelve directors, and the directors chose a good friend and business partner of Morris, Thomas Willing, to be the bank's president. A charter was written and approved by the directors on December 22, 1781, and it was presented to Congress. The ordinance of incorporation met opposition mostly because there were questions on whether the Articles of Confederation granted such a power. It was never specifically mentioned in the Articles that a bank could be formed. However, after Morris pleaded with the Congress on how important the bank was to the credit of the United States, it finally passed the ordinance on December 31, 1781. Shortly afterward, it opened its doors on the North Side of Chestnut Street, West of Third in Philadelphia, which was then the financial capital of the United States.[57]

Morris looked upon the bank as his major achievement of the American Revolution. He clearly detailed how the bank would help the nation; he hoped that it would last as long as the United States, and declared that it would "prove the means of saving the liberties, lives, and property of the virtuous part of America."[58] He claimed that the government, in receiving credit and monies, would derive great advantages from the bank. In a letter to Franklin in July 1781, Morris described the bank's most important function. He wrote, "I mean to render this a principal pillar of American credit, so that as to obtain the money of individuals for the benefit of the union, and thereby bind those individuals more strongly to the general cause by ties of private interest."[59]

Morris believed that the issuance of notes by the Bank of North America would solve the depreciation problem, because the notes would replace all other currency. People of the United States would demand these notes because they were backed by the bank, and he hoped that they would circulate at par.[60] Morris continued to stress that he was creating a private bank under government auspices that would serve the government as a national bank. He said that "the public will have much connexion with the bank, and at times deposit considerable sums of money in it, and always be availing themselves of its credit."[61] Also he firmly believed that private investors would rush into the project because it would benefit them. He stated, "It is not doubted but every subscriber will increase his capital in the bank so soon as he finds not only the national advantages it will produce, but sees clearly his private interest advanced beyond his most sanguine expectations.[62]

Like Hamilton later, Morris viewed the bank as the institution that could unite the states and their people. He said

It will facilitate the management of the finances of the United States. The several States may, when their respective necessities require and the abilities of the bank will permit, derive occasional advantages and accommodations from it. It will afford to the individuals of all States a medium for their intercourse with each other and for the payment of taxes more convenient than the precious metals and equally safe. It will have a tendency to increase both the internal and external commerce of North America, and undoubtedly will be infinitely useful to all the traders of every State in the Union.[63]

The Bank of North America was granted charters in Pennsylvania and Massachusetts. However, its most important work was conducted during the period from 1781 to 1784 when Morris was superintendent of finance. During that period, he borrowed about $1.25 million from the bank to provide the government with needed funds. The Bank discounted bills of exchange drawn on Morris as superintendent, and when the Bank's directors decided that enough money had been loaned to the Congress, Morris sold $200,000 par value of the government's shares in the Bank for $300,000 and lowered the debt by that sum. The next year he sold the remainder to Dutch investors. By the time Morris retired from office in November 1784, the debt of the Congress to the Bank had been paid and the Congress was no longer a stockholder.[64]

After Morris resigned as superintendent of finance, the Pennsylvania Assembly repealed the Bank of North America's charter in September 1785. This was mostly due to politics and jealousy among many of Morris's enemies. The growing wealth and power of the Bank created a climate of fear and hatred of Morris. Many wealthy merchants believed that Morris had too much money at his command. For example, shortly after the official news of peace, the Bank's directors announced a dividend of 6.5 percent for six months since January 1783. During the next six months, the dividends rose to eight percent, making a total of 14.5 percent on the capital stock for the year of 1783. In 1784, the Bank had declared dividends of fourteen percent on its stock.[65]

It is interesting to note that in the same year that the Bank of North America lost its charter, James Wilson, the most important lawyer in the state of Pennsylvania, published his *Consideration on the Bank of North America*, in which he argued that the Congress had the power to charter banks.[66] The constitutionality of a national bank was to become an issue, once again, when Hamilton created the Bank of the United States in 1791.

On March 7, 1787, the state of Pennsylvania renewed the Bank of North America's charter for fourteen years. The Bank continued to flourish throughout the nineteenth century, and in 1929, it became part of the East Pennsylvania Banking and Trust Company.[67]

The Bank of North America became the most important part of the program to restore public credit during the Period of the Confederation. It helped expedite daily transactions and provided an active currency to replace the worthless continental. It helped to attract private funds and credit used by the government to run its programs.

THE BANK OF NEW YORK

In February 1784, Hamilton's brother-in-law, John B. Church, a major shareholder in the Bank of North America, wrote Hamilton about starting a specie bank in New York state. Hamilton favored the idea, and both men agreed that they wanted a bank that would primarily do business with merchants and businessmen, with capital made up of money, bonds, and commercial paper, not mortgages or other interest on land. Its starting capital would be $500,000 in gold or silver, a thousand shares of $500 each.[68] That same month, Hamilton and Church met with a group of merchants and chose Hamilton's old friend General Alexander McDougall as chairman of the new bank while Hamilton served as a director. The bank's charter was drawn up at the organizational meeting on March 15, 1784, and it was called the Bank of New York.[69]

Hamilton and Church had competition from Robert R. Livingston, a large upstate landowner who had petitioned the New York state legislature to grant a charter for a land bank.[70] Hamilton, who now opposed land banks, spoke before the legislature on behalf of his specie bank. Unlike Church, who only thought of the bank as a profit making business, Hamilton stressed how the Bank of New York could serve both the state and the nation by lending money to the government and funding infant industry and commerce. However, the legislators were suspicious of all kinds of banks, and they refused to incorporate either the Bank of New York or the land bank.[71] Nonetheless, the Bank of New York opened for business as a private bank in June 1784, and it was finally incorporated in New York state in March 1791, after Hamilton had become secretary of the treasury. It is the only bank, before the Constitution, that exists today under the same name.[72] The Bank of Massachusetts, also formed in 1784, was the only other bank in the United States before the Constitution; it merged in 1903 with the First National Bank of Boston.[73]

THE ECONOMIC CRISIS LEADING
TO THE CONSTITUTION

The Bank of North America provided the government with currency to help finance the American Revolution, but it failed to deal adequately with the economic crisis that followed it. This was partly due to the return to power of its political enemies, both in the Congress and in the state of Pennsylvania; partly due to the heavy loans to some of its friends; and partly due to the failure of the nationalists, those favoring a strong central government, to obtain revenues for the Congress.[74]

The major problem after the war was that the central government or the Congress had a debt of $40 million and little revenue. It had no power to levy taxes or regulate commerce. These powers existed only with the states, and each state followed its own economic policy. Because there was a shortage of specie after the war due mostly to a high demand for foreign goods, the debtor class in many states, particularly farmers, demanded the unlimited printing of paper money. However, the state governments, run mostly by creditors, refused to issue paper money, fearing that it would cause inflation and that they would be paid back in cheaper dollars.[75] Instead, many states raised poll, property, and excise taxes to reduce their state debts. All these taxes were based on the benefit principal and not on the ability to pay principal of taxation and fell heavily upon the poor. For example, in Massachusetts one-third of farm income was taken in poll and real estate taxes, and because many debtors could not meet their obligations, their farms and livestock were sold off.[76]

Seven states, including Rhode Island, had passed paper money acts by 1786. The Rhode Island legislature controlled by the debtor interest made paper money legal tender for all public and private debts. However, many merchants refused to accept the paper bills and this led to the famous court case of *Trevett vs. Weeden*. Weeden had refused to accept the paper money from Trevett at par value. The opinion of the court was that the forcing act, making people accept paper bills, was unconstitutional. However, it said nothing about the constitutionality of paper money.[77]

In 1786, the Massachusetts House of Representatives passed a paper money act which led to a feeling of jubilation among the debtor classes. However, after its defeat in the state senate, Daniel Shays led a rebellion against the authorities.[78] Shays, a veteran of the American Revolution, returned home, and waited for his military pay. In the meantime, his farm income fell while his taxes increased, and when he protested, like so many other farmers in the western counties of Massachusetts, nobody seemed to care. Instead, farm foreclosures occurred in alarming numbers, and farmers were sent to jail for nonpayment of debt. In the winter of 1786-1787, Shays led some two thousand western farmers in defiance against the government of Massachusetts. They closed the courts, burned records, and took back foreclosed property. The state militia, under General Benjamin Lincoln, eventually ended the rebellion, but not before it alarmed Americans in every part of the United States.[79]

Though Shays's rebellion, more than any single event, had shown the weakness of the present government under the Articles of Confederation, and had quickened the call for a new form of government, the actual process of revising or replacing the existing government began in 1785 when Maryland and Virginia signed an agreement over navigation rights on the Potomac River and the Chesapeake Bay. After Maryland had decided to include Pennsylvania and Delaware, the nationalists in Virginia proposed a meeting of all the states at Annapolis in September 1786 to discuss commercial problems. However, when only five delegates arrived at Annapolis, Hamilton and Madison determined that it was a waste of time to continue a meeting that would just deal with commercial problems. Both men saw that the real problem confronting the new nation was the weakness of the current central government. Therefore, they decided to call for a convention of all the states to meet in Philadelphia in May 1787, for the express purpose of revising the Articles of Confederation. This eventually led to the establishment of the Constitution and a new era in American history.[80]

NOTES

1. Charles W. Calomiris, "Institutional Failure, Monetary Scarcity, and the Depreciation of the Continental," *Journal of Economic History* 48 (1988): 47.

2. Alice Hanson Jones, *Wealth of a Nation to Be: The American Colonies on the Eve of the Revolution* (New York: Columbia University Press, 1980), p. 132.

3. Gilbert C. Fite and Jim E. Reese, *An Economic History of the United States* (Boston: Houghton Mifflin Company, 1973), p. 50.

4. Ibid.

5. Calomiris, "Institutional Failure, Monetary Scarcity, and the Depreciation of the Continental," p. 47; Jones, *Wealth of a Nation to Be*, p. 133.

6. Jones, *Wealth of a Nation to Be*, p. 153.

7. Fite and Reese, *An Economic History of the United States*, p. 20.

8. Ibid., p. 52.

9. Ibid.

10. Merrill Jensen, *The New Nation: A History of the United States during the Confederation, 1781-1789* (New York: Alfred A. Knopf, 1967), pp. 29-30; Fite and Reese, *An Economic History of the United States*, p. 107.

11. Clarence L. Ver Steeg, *Robert Morris Revolutionary Financier* (Philadelphia: University of Pennsylvania Press, 1954), p. 43.

12. Fite and Reese, *An Economic History of the United States*, p. 108; Ver Steeg, *Robert Morris*, p. 46.

13. Ver Steeg, *Robert Morris*, p. 46; Fite and Reese, *An Economic History of the United States*, p. 108.

14. Fite and Reese, *An Economic History of the United States*, p. 110.

15. Ibid., pp. 108-109.

16. Ver Steeg, *Robert Morris*, pp. 46-47.

17. Jensen, *The New Nation*, pp. 40-41; Fite and Reese, *An Economic History of the United States*, p. 109.

18. Calomiris, "Institutional Failure, Monetary Scarcity, and the Depreciation of the Continental," pp. 59-61.

19. Jensen, *The New Nation*, p. 37.

20. Ibid., p. 38.

21. Ver Steeg, *Robert Morris*, pp. 43-44.

22. Jensen, *The New Nation*, pp. 38-39; Ver Steeg, *Robert Morris*, p. 45.

23. Ver Steeg, *Robert Morris*, pp. 44-45.

24. Ibid., p. 53.

25. Ibid., p. 50.

26. Ibid.

27. Robert Hendrickson, *Hamilton I* (New York: Mason/Charter, 1976), p. 224.

28. Ver Steeg, *Robert Morris*, p. 47.

29. Ibid., p. 48.

30. Jensen, *The New Nation*, pp. 31-32.

31. Harold Syrett, ed., *The Papers of Alexander Hamilton*, Vol. 2 (New York: Columbia University Press, 1961), p. 414.

32. Ibid.; Hendrickson, *Hamilton I*, p. 230.

33. Hendrickson, *Hamilton I*, p. 230.

34. Ibid.

35. Ibid., p. 264.

36. Ibid.; Syrett, ed., *The Papers of Alexander Hamilton*, Vol. 2, p. 414.

37. E. James Ferguson, ed., *The Papers of Robert Morris, 1781-1784*, Vol. 1 (Pittsburgh, PA: University of Pittsburgh Press, 1973), pp. 46-54; John Holdsworth and Davis R. Dewey, *The First and Second Banks of the United States* (Washington, DC: Government Printing Office, 1910), pp. 9-10.

38. Ferguson, ed., *The Papers of Robert Morris*, Vol. 1, p. 54.

39. Ibid., p. 43.

40. Syrett, ed., *The Papers of Alexander Hamilton*, Vol. 2, p. 606.

41. Ibid., pp. 616-618.

42. Hendrickson, *Hamilton I*, p. 341.

43. Syrett, ed., *The Papers of Alexander Hamilton*, Vol. 2, pp. 673-674.

44. Eleanor Young, *Forgotten Patriot: Robert Morris* (New York: Macmillan Company, 1950), p. 88.

45. Jensen, *The New Nation*, p. 57.

46. John F. Chown, *A History of Money from AD 800* (London: Routledge, 1996), p. 160.

47. Young, *Forgotten Patriot*, p. 87.

48. Jensen, *The New Nation*, pp. 55-57.

49. Ver Steeg, *Robert Morris*, p. 66.

50. Syrett, ed., *The Papers of Alexander Hamilton*, Vol. 2, pp. 645-646.

51. Ver Steeg, *Robert Morris*, p. 66.

52. Ibid.

53. Ibid., p. 67.

54. Jensen, *The New Nation*, p. 62.

55. Ferguson, ed., *The Papers of Robert Morris*, Vol. 1, pp. 72-73.

56. Jensen, *The New Nation*, p. 62.

57. Ibid.

58. Ibid., p. 61.

59. Ver Steeg, *Robert Morris*, p. 67.

60. Ibid., p. 68.

61. Ibid., p. 66.

62. Ibid.

63. Ibid., p. 86.

64. Jensen, *The New Nation*, p. 63.

65. Ibid., pp. 63, 228; Harold Syrett, ed., *The Papers of Alexander Hamilton*, Vol. 3 (New York: Columbia University Press, 1962), pp. 626-627.

66. Syrett, ed., *The Papers of Alexander Hamilton*, Vol. 3, p. 627.

67. Chown, *A History of Money*, p. 160.

68. Hendrickson, *Hamilton I*, pp. 434-435.

69. Ibid., p. 435.

70. Ibid.

71. Ibid., p. 437.

72. Ibid.

73. Chown, *A History of Money*, p. 160.

74. Jensen, *The New Nation*, p. 63.

75. Fite and Reese, *An Economic History of the United States*, p. 115.

76. Ibid.

77. Ibid.

78. Ibid.

79. Hendrickson, *Hamilton I*, p. 445.

80. Ibid., pp. 442-446.

2

Alexander Hamilton and the First Bank of the United States

The Constitution went into effect and the new nation was secure after New Hampshire became the ninth state to ratify on June 21, 1788. Early in 1789, George Washington was elected the first president of the United States, and he immediately began the process of selecting his cabinet. The question was who would get the job as secretary of the treasury. According to Bishop William White, brother-in-law of Robert Morris, the superintendent of finance during the confederation, Washington had asked Morris "What are we to do with this heavy debt?" Morris replied, "There is but one man in the United States who can tell you; that is Alexander Hamilton. I am glad you have given me the opportunity to declare to you, the extent of the obligations I am under to him."[1] Morris knew Hamilton well, as they corresponded on a regular basis, and Hamilton also served under him as collector of continental revenue for New York. With Morris's recommendation, Washington appointed Hamilton to become the nation's first secretary of the treasury. The act establishing the Treasury was passed on September 2, 1789, and Hamilton was commissioned nine days later on September 11th.[2]

HAMILTON'S PLAN FOR AMERICA

Both Hamilton and Secretary of State Thomas Jefferson had a vision of the future of America. Jefferson had a preference for an agrarian society; he believed that the strength of the new nation was entrusted to the vast majority of independent farmers. Jefferson stated that farming was the Lord's work, and those who made a living this way were closest to God. On the other hand, the secretary of state pointed to the factory system in Europe which encouraged rulers to engage in tyranny to control underpaid workers. Most manufacturing centers in Europe were a source of corruption and poverty, and Jefferson did not want to see them take root in the United States. He remained suspicious of high finance and public debt and was opposed to the speculators, the creditors, and the wealthy bank stockholders who benefitted from a public debt. He perceived bankers as greedy moneylenders, having no stake in the general prosperity, whose only interest was in becoming rich.[3]

Though Hamilton recognized the importance of agriculture in America, he wanted the United States to look toward manufacturing and industry for its future prosperity. The secretary of the treasury declared that industry would free the nation from foreign dependence and put it on an equal footing with the great nations of the world. He pointed to Great Britain as America's model, wanting to encourage, as soon as possible, strong commercial ties between the two governments.[4] Hamilton's program could be summed up in the three reports that he sent to the Congress for approval. They were the "Report on the Public Credit," November 1789; the "Report on a National Bank," December 14, 1790; and the "Report on Manufactures," December 1791.

When Hamilton took office, he soon discovered that the United States owed over $54 million. Most of this debt was incurred to pay the soldiers during the American Revolution and was originally held by patriotic citizens. However, by 1790, many merchants and speculators had purchased the debt at much less than its face value during the critical period of the 1780s. They were betting that times would improve and that they could make a large profit. Many Americans, including James Madison of Virginia, felt that current holders of the debt should not be paid face value. However, Hamilton, in his "Report on Public Credit," took the opposite position, declaring that the national government pay the entire national debt, both foreign and domestic, at its face value. He also wanted the national government to assume all the debts of the states. His reasoning for the complete funding of the national debt was very simple. He knew that the United States would need to borrow large amounts of money in to create the capital base to industrialize like Great Britain. If it failed to meet all its debt obligations, it would never be able to attract future investment. In assuming the debts of the states, Hamilton was attempting to show the dominant economic power of the national government over the states.[5]

The "Report on Manufactures" came one year after the "Report on a National Bank," which will be discussed below under its own heading. Hamilton was convinced that the extractive-commercial economy of the United States had to be developed. He called for the federal government to stimulate the rise of manufacturing in America. Specifically, he wanted a protective tariff to replace the tariff for revenue which was already in place. Hamilton contended that if the government wanted Americans to invest in new industry and manufacturing, it had to protect these investments in their infant stages. The secretary of the treasury also called for the government to support a system of roads and canals. Unfortunately, Hamilton, who was killed in a duel with Aaron Burr in 1804, would not see most of his ideas on manufacturing come to fruition.[6]

it drove our forefathers to this country? Was it not the ecclesiastical corporations and perpetual monopolies of England and Scotland? Shall we suffer the same evils to exist in this country, instead of taking every possible method to encourage the increase of emigrants to settle among us? For, if we establish the precedent now before us, there is no saying where it shall stop."[19] Jackson saw the Bank of the United States as an ally to the mercantile interest and did not see how it could possibly help the farmers. He claimed that it would increase the debt of the country, and he called it a "monopoly of the public moneys" that would infringe on the charter of the Bank of North America. When Representative William Smith of South Carolina made a motion to have the bill recommitted to check it for defects, Jackson was one of seven southerners to support it. The motion was defeated by a vote of thirty-four to twenty-three.[20]

However, the main argument against the bank was not economic, but political and legal. Was Hamilton's proposal for a national bank constitutional? Representative James Madison of Virginia, an ardent opponent of the bank in 1791, began his comprehensive argument against it on February 2, 1791, by declaring that the Constitution did not give the government the right to incorporate a bank. He said that "he well recollected that a power to grant charters of incorporation had been proposed to the General Convention and rejected."[21] If the bank was chartered, the federal government would be disregarding the limitations of its powers and interfering with the rights of the states. Madison was worried about a possible conflict between the states' interests and the federal interests. He said that a national bank issuing notes on a national basis "would directly interfere with the rights of the states to prohibit as well as to establish Banks, and the circulation of (state) bank notes."[22] Madison said the bank proposal

was condemned by the silence of the Constitution; was condemned by the rule of interpretation arising out of the Constitution; was condemned by its tendency to destroy the main characteristic of the Constitution; was condemned by the expositions of the friends of the Constitution whilst depending before the public; was condemned by the apparent intentions of the parties which ratified the Constitution; was condemned by the explanatory amendments proposed by Congress themselves to the Constitution; and he hoped it would receive its final condemnation by the vote of this House.[23]

The construction of the Constitution and not the bank had become the major issue for Madison.

Proponents of the First Bank of the United States rested their case on the power given in the Constitution in Article I, section 8, which enabled Congress to borrow money and lay and collect taxes. They promoted the bank both as a private commercial bank and as a public or national bank, but not as a central bank. It would serve as a fiscal agent to the treasury, issue a uniform national paper currency, and furnish credit to the government. Representative Fisher Ames, the chief spokesman for the proponents of the bank, claimed that banks were known to be useful to the private economy and government. He said, "Congress may do what is necessary to the end for which the Constitution was adopted, provided it is not repugnant to the natural rights of man." Because the bank essentially served this purpose by making payments for and promptly supplying funds to government, the Congress had the power and duty to create the bank.[24] Representative Elias Boudinot of New York, another defender of the bank, stated that most of the opposition was not against the bank itself, but to the act of incorporation. He urged his colleagues to consider the advantages of the bank during a war, when the government would have to borrow large amounts of capital and could not obtain it from individuals or small banks.[25]

After a week's debate, the bill was passed on February 8, 1791, by a vote of thirty-nine to twenty. Thirty-three of the thirty-nine affirmative votes came from New York, New Jersey, and Pennsylvania, and fifteen of the twenty negative votes were from Virginia, the Carolinas, and Georgia. One South Carolina vote favored it and one Massachusetts vote was against it. If we look at the vote based on party lines, eleven Republicans voted for and six Federalists voted against.[26]

When the bill was sent to President Washington, he took more than two weeks to sign it. Not knowing if it was constitutional, he asked the opinion of Jefferson, Hamilton, and Attorney General Edmund Randolph, his three most prominent cabinet members. It wasn't that the president didn't know where they all stood on the bank, but he wanted their opinions in writing so he could study them and make up his own mind. It is interesting to note that Washington waited for both Randolph and Jefferson to submit their opinions that the bank was unconstitutional and then sent them to Hamilton for his reply.[27]

Both Randolph and Jefferson, in their reply to Washington, insisted emphatically that the word *necessary* in the clause of the Constitution giving power to the government "to make all laws *necessary* and proper for carrying into execution the enumerated powers" did not give the power to create a bank. Jefferson told the president that the bank might be a convenience, but he was positive it was not a necessity. He asked

Can it be thought that the Constitution intended that, for a shade or two of convenience, more or less, Congress should be authorized to break down the most ancient and fundamental laws of the several states, such as those against mortmain, the laws of alienage, the rules of descent, the acts of distribution, the laws of escheat and forfeiture, the laws of monopoly? Nothing but a necessity invincible by any other means can justify such a prostration of laws which constitute the pillars of our whole system of jurisprudence.[28]

Jefferson also claimed that the bank was a monopoly because it stipulated an exclusive right of banking under the national authority. He was very concerned that the incorporation of a national bank would give it the power to make laws paramount to those of the states.[29]

Hamilton realized that his response to Randolph and Jefferson's critique of the bank had to be convincing for Washington to sign the banking bill. His position was

That every power vested in a government is in its nature sovereign, and includes, by force   ·

of the term, a right to employ all the means requisite, and fairly applicable to the attainment of the ends of such power; and which are not precluded by restrictions and exceptions specified in the Constitution; or not immoral, or not contrary to the essential ends of political society . . . there are implied, as well as express powers, and that the former are as effectually delegated as the latter.[30]

Hamilton conceded that the authority to create a corporation was not included in the enumerated powers of Congress. However, it was conferred by implication of the right of Congress "to make all laws necessary and proper for carrying into execution the foregoing powers vested by the Constitution in the Government of the United States, or in any department or officer thereof."[31]

Hamilton replied to Jefferson's concern that the national bank would become a monopoly and would prevent the existence of state banks. He contended that the national banking bill did not prohibit states from erecting as many banks as they pleased, and, therefore, it did not create a monopoly.[32]

Washington, after reading Hamilton's reply on the constitutionality of the First Bank of the United States, signed the bill into law on February 25, 1791. Hamilton had several factors that favored him over Randolph and Jefferson. He convinced the president that the bank was important in helping the government to borrow money. He was perceived as very knowledgeable on money and banking matters. Since 1779, he had presented his banking plan four times and was one of the founders of the Bank of New York. However, most important, he had convinced Washington that the purpose of the Constitution was to establish a workable government.[33]

THE ORGANIZATION AND OPERATION OF
THE FIRST BANK OF THE UNITED STATES

The First Bank of the United States opened on December 12, 1791, in Philadelphia. Originally, it occupied Carpenters' Hall on Chestnut between Third and Fourth streets; however, in 1797, it moved around the corner on Third between Chestnut and Walnut streets.[34]

The capital stock of the Bank consisted of $10 million, which was divided into 25,000 shares of $400 each. Of the $10 million, $2 million was set aside for the government and the other $8 million was available to the public. These subscriptions were payable within two years, twenty-five percent in specie (gold and silver coins) and seventy-five percent in six percent-funded debt of the United States. The specie served as bank reserves, and the debt allowed for a capital structure large enough to justify the issuance of bank notes.[35]

The subscribers of the Bank's stock were mostly merchants, professionals, politicians, and speculators in public securities. Thirty members of the Congress had subscribed to the Bank, which was more than a third of all the membership and half or more of the number that had voted for the Bank. The Massachusetts bank, New York State, and Harvard College were also subscribers. It is interesting to note that when subscriptions were first taken in the summer of 1791, the entire $8 million that was available to the public was gone within an hour.[36]

The government's purchase of $2 million of the Bank's stock was done in a most perplexing manner. The government drew for the $2 million on the U.S. commissioners who were then selling government securities in Amsterdam. It then deposited the drafts with the Bank, and drew against the deposit to pay for the stock. It would seem that the stock purchase was with the funds borrowed in Europe. However, the government did not want the drafts cashed and the specie actually shipped from Europe because it would only have to be shipped back again to be used for other purposes. So the government borrowed the $2 million from the Bank and used the amount to take up the drafts on the commissioners. The end result was that the government had $2 million of bank stock and at the same time was in debt to the Bank for $2 million, though theoretically the money that was owed to the Bank had not been used to buy the stock, but instead to restore the funds in Amsterdam which had been used for that purpose.[37]

The Bank was chartered for twenty years, and during that time, no similar bank could be established. The debts of the bank, exclusive of deposits, would not be allowed to exceed the amount of its stock. In October 1791, the stockholders held a meeting to elect the directors. They voted in a diminishing ratio based on the number of shares each held.[38] All the directors had to be stockholders and citizens of the United States. Twenty-five directors were chosen: nine from Pennsylvania, seven from New York, four from Massachusetts, and one each from Connecticut, Maryland, Virginia, North Carolina, and South Carolina. Thomas Willing, a director of the First Bank of the United States and the president of the Bank of North America, was now chosen to be the first president of the new bank. He served from 1791 to 1807 and was succeeded by David Lennox who was president for the remaining four years of the Bank's existence.[39]

Though the Bank was privately run by the directors, it acted as a fiscal agent of the treasury. It made payments of interest on the public debt, received subscriptions of government securities, paid the salaries of government officials, helped collect the customs bonds, and dealt in the foreign exchange market for the treasury. It was the principal depository of government funds, and it could issue a uniform currency that aided the national government in making its payments. Upon request, this privately owned and publicly operated commercial bank had to open its books to the secretary of the treasury for inspection, not exceeding once a week.[40]

It was interesting to note that Hamilton had borrowed from the Bank of England Act in 1694 when he developed his plan for the First Bank of the United States in 1791. For example, there was a similarity in the sections dealing with the redemption of notes in specie. Both the Bank of England and the First Bank of the United States redeemed its notes in gold upon demand. The charter of both banks prohibited debts in excess of the capital, and would not allow trade in commodities nor financial aid to the government without the approval of the legislature or the parliament.[41]

The First Bank of the United States acted as both a creditor and a debtor to the government. It held government deposits as well as debt; however, its government deposits were greater than its debt, as the government's fiscal operations reduced the outstanding national debt by about fifty percent between 1804 and 1812. The Bank's holdings of the federal debt dropped from $6.20 million to $2.23 million, over the same period, and eliminated the Bank's function as a financier of government credit.[42]

The first loan, which the Bank made to government, as mentioned above, was in connection with its subscription of capital. In May 1792, when the government needed money to finance one of its numerous Indian wars, Hamilton contracted with the Bank for a loan of $400,000 at five percent.[43] In 1794, Secretary of the Treasury Oliver Wolcott, who succeeded Hamilton, entered into negotiations with the Bank for a $1 million loan. Unfortunately for the government, the Bank, which had made too many previous loans, would only lend $800,000 at six percent at the time. At the end of 1792, its first fiscal year, the Bank had loaned the government more than $2,500,000. This indebtedness increased to $6,200,000 at the end of 1795. Within four years from the time the Bank had opened, the government had borrowed nearly two-thirds of the Bank's capital.[44]

The First Bank of the United States used its public position carefully. Compared with the state banks, it paid modest dividends while the market value of its stock showed little appreciation. On the other hand, the state banks showed enormous profits, and its stock values soared.[45] From the beginning, the First Bank of the United States cooperated with the state banks. The First Bank's directors appointed a committee to confer with a similar committee of the Bank of North America once a week. Neither bank had wanted to interfere with the other's business. The two banks made settlements and exchanged notes daily, and when the Bank of Pennsylvania was created in 1793, it became part of this arrangement. By 1796, the three banks adopted uniform rules regarding discounts and other matters.[46]

Similar cooperation existed between the New York branch of the First Bank of the United States and the Bank of New York until economic problems drove a wedge between the two banks. A financial crisis occurred in Europe in 1796 that forced the Bank of England to suspend specie payment; its effects were felt in America. The Bank of New York had loaned the treasury $200,000 by giving it deposit credit for the said amount. However, the treasury wanted these funds deposited in the First Bank of the United States, so the New York office of the Bank of the United States received the checks the treasury drew and became the creditor of the Bank of New York. The First Bank of the United States demanded payment in specie. However, the Bank of New York did not have the funds and turned to Hamilton, one of its founders, to intercede with Oliver Wolcott, the new treasury secretary. Wolcott assured the Bank of New York of assistance, but at the same time gave it a lecture about having enough specie on hand to meet the demands of its depositors. He said in regard to raising the specie, "I think, however, that they must principally rely on the sale of stock, and in my opinion, any sacrifice ought to be preferred to a continuance of temporary expedients." Wolcott sounded just like a central banker.[47]

When Alexander Hamilton presented his plan for a national bank, it did not include branch banking. In fact, he specifically opposed the idea, believing that it would divide the bank and weaken it. He also believed that branches of the Bank of the United States would be perceived by the state banks as rivals. This was especially true after Congressman Ames suggested to Hamilton that the new national bank, through branching, should take over the four state banks then in existence. Ames saw no need for the Bank of New York, the Bank of North America, the Bank of Massachusetts and the Bank of Maryland. He wrote Hamilton in July 1791 that "I have had my fears that the state banks will become unfriendly to that of the United States. Causes of hatred and rivalry will abound. The state banks may become dangerous instruments in the hands of state partisans."[48] When the majority of directors voted for branches before the main office opened in Philadelphia, Hamilton wrote on November 25, 1791, that "the whole affair of branches was begun, continued, and ended, not only without my participation but against my judgment."[49]

It was interesting to note that though the First Bank of the United States had a total of eight branches, the first four opening in 1792 in Boston, New York, Baltimore, and Charleston, followed by a branch in Norfolk, Virginia, in 1800, in Washington and Savannah in 1802, and in New Orleans in 1805, none of the existing state banks became branches of the national bank. The local business communities supported the state banks and refused to allow them to become branches of the First Bank of the United States.[50]

Shortly after the establishment of the branch in Savannah, the state of Georgia levied a tax on it. After the First Bank of the United States refused to pay, state officials carried off $2,004 in silver from the Savannah vaults. The bank then sued the state, but the Supreme Court in the *Bank of the United States vs. Deveaux* in 1809 ruled in favor of the state on the grounds of jurisdiction. The question as to whether the Bank of the United States was constitutional would have to wait until *McCulloch vs. Maryland* in 1819.[51]

THE FIRST BANK OF THE UNITED STATES AS A CENTRAL BANK

Neither Hamilton nor anybody else ever believed that the First Bank of the United States would become a central bank. By definition, a central bank is able to control the money supply or credit of the nation. When the Bank was created, Hamilton saw it primarily as a government depository and a creditor of the government. However, as it turned out, the Bank was also the general creditor of the other state banks. It not only had the account of the government, but the receipts of the government that were primarily in the notes of state banks, and most of these notes were deposited in the First Bank of the United States. Therefore, currency transactions with the state banks were inevitable. For example, if the First Bank felt that credit restraint was in order, it simply presented the state banknotes for redemption in specie. If the state banks did not have the specie, they would have to suspend their operations. On the other hand, if the First Bank wanted to ease credit and expand the money supply, it delayed the return of the notes to the state banks.[52] The mood of the state banks toward credit control of the First Bank varied. The conservative banks that made few loans and paid their debts accepted credit control. However, the speculative and reckless banks resented the power exercised by the First Bank, and waited for the opportunity to destroy it.[53]

THE FAILURE TO RECHARTER THE
FIRST BANK OF THE UNITED STATES

When Jefferson became president of the United States in 1801, he continued to denounce the First Bank and made attempts to weaken it. For example, in 1804, the new administration decided to leave the banking business and sold all its Bank stock for a profit.[54] At the same time, the president decided to deposit some government funds in state banks, because the charter of the First Bank contained no stipulation that all the government's funds had to be deposited with it. Jefferson was worried about what American citizens would think about depositing so much of the government's money in an institution where a great deal of the stock was held by foreigners. (In 1809, seventy-five percent of its stock was held by foreigners.) The president wrote his secretary of the treasury, Albert Gallatin, a defender of the First Bank, that "the consideration is very weighty that it is held by citizens while the stock of the United States bank is held in so great a proportion by foreigners."[55]

In January 1808, three years before the expiration of the charter, the stockholders sent a memorial to Congress that declared it "a duty to the Government and to the commercial world as well as to themselves to submit the expediency of protracting the duration of their charter." They asserted that the termination of the First Bank's charter would "impair the fiscal machinery provided by the bank for the collections and payment of public funds, while the withdrawal of $10 million of banking capital would produce serious embarrassment to the trade and commerce of the country."[56] To sway the Congress into early rechartering, this memorial or petition discussed the financial advantages the government had received from the Bank. It stated that during the thirteen years that the government had been a stockholder, it had profited through the difference between its loan from the Bank at six percent and the dividends on its stock which averaged about eight percent; when it finally sold its stock, it realized a profit of over $650,000. According to the stockholders, the Bank proved indispensable in helping the government in maintaining the public faith and credit both at home and abroad by advancing loans amounting to millions of dollars at between five and six percent.[57]

It was both premature and unwise for the stockholders of the First Bank to bring the issue of rechartering to the attention of the Congress in 1808. In fact, Gallatin had written the Bank's president, Thomas Willing, in November 1807 and asked that he wait until after the next presidential election to make the issue of recharter as nonpolitical as possible.[58] Gallatin, a Republican, became the First Bank's staunchest ally in the Jefferson administration. As a result, he would encounter more opposition from his own party than Hamilton had met in 1791 at the hands of the opposition.

Both the House and Senate refused to act on the memorial to recharter the First Bank until 1810. In January of that year, the memorial was referred to a House committee which reported in favor of renewal on February 19th.[59] On April 7, 1810, a bill was presented to continue the existing Bank for another twenty years. Gallatin, however, made some modifications in the charter, such as having the Bank pay a bonus of $1,250,000 to the government. In addition, the Bank would loan the government, upon three months' notice, a sum of money no greater than $5 million at no more than six percent interest. The Bank also was to pay the government three percent on all its deposits above $3 million for a whole year. The bill was debated by the Committee of the Whole on April 13, 1810, but never came to a vote.[60]

The second memorial to the Congress was submitted by the directors of the First Bank on December 10, 1810, only three months prior to the expiration of the charter. This petition was very similar to the first, as it stressed the Bank's services and benefits to the government and predicted economic chaos if the charter was not renewed.[61] This time the directors based their urgency for recharter on the grounds that the First Bank of the United States played the role of a central bank. They asserted that the Bank had been a "general guardian of commercial credit and by preventing the balance of trade in the different States from producing a deficiency of money in any, has obviated the mischiefs which would have been thereby produced. It has fostered and protected the banking institutions of the States, and has aided them when unexpectedly pressed."[62]

In January 1811, the memorial was discussed actively in both chambers of the Congress. On January 24th, it was "postponed indefinitely" in the House by a vote of sixty-five to sixty-four.[63] However, on February 5, 1811, a bill to amend and renew the charter was proposed in the Senate where Henry Clay of Kentucky attacked it passionately. Though the directors of the Bank described it as a central bank, they purposefully omitted the word "central." However, Clay had recognized the First Bank's central banking potential and demanded that it use restraint rather than license. He stated that the Bank was originally chartered as a national bank, for the express purpose of helping the treasury in its fiscal functions and nothing more. He declared

It is a mockery worse than usurpation, to establish [the institution] for a lawful object, and then extend to it other objects which are not lawful. You say to this organization, we cannot authorize you to discount—to emit paper—to regulate commerce. No! Our book has no precedents of that kind. But then we can authorize you to collect the revenue, and, while occupied with that, you may do whatever else you please![64]

The bill in the Senate was debated for ten days and centered mainly on two questions: the constitutionality and the expediency of the bank. The constitutional question was the same as ever. Simply put, the Constitution did not explicitly allow for the incorporation of the Bank. As far as expediency was concerned, the Bank's enemies declared that it was unnecessary because it did little for the federal government that the state banks could not do. More important, they pointed out that of the majority of stockholders, about seventy-five percent, were foreigners, and this imposed a "burdensome and degrading tribute on the country."[65]

Both Gallatin and Jonathan Fisk, an upstate New York Republican, challenged the arguments against the Bank. Gallatin asserted, as Hamilton had in 1791, that the Constitution did not prohibit the incorporation of a national bank. He stated that the Bank was very useful to the government. It kept the public moneys safely, and it transferred government payments efficiently and aided in the collection of revenues. It supplied short-term funds to the government, making it unnecessary for an increase in the permanent debt outstanding. Though Gallatin admitted that the state banks could manage the government's funds without difficulty, he explained that the First Bank of the United States was a safer place than the state banks because it was responsible for all the deposits in its separate branches.[66] Gallatin even had an answer to those who criticized the foreign ownership of the bank. The secretary of the treasury warned that if the Bank were liquidated, the foreign holdings of $7,200,000 would have to be paid to the foreign stockholders; however, if the charter was renewed, only the dividends of about 8.5 percent would be sent abroad.[67]

Fisk elaborated on the expediency of the Bank by demonstrating what it meant to the economy. He showed that the exports of the country in 1791, when the Bank was established, were only $18 million, and this had increased to $76 million in 1804. The reason for this dramatic rise in export revenue was due, in large part, to the increased activity of capital created and promoted by the First Bank of the United States. Fisk warned the Bank's opponents that because the bulk of the country's trade was now conducted on a paper medium, with specie having virtually disappeared, if the First Bank's charter was not renewed, as much as one-third of the $50 million in circulating medium, in the country, would be checked, and all paper credit would receive a "mortal blow."[68]

After hearing the arguments for and against the renewal of the First Bank's charter, the Senate vote on February 20, 1811, was seventeen to seventeen. Vice-president George Clinton, a foe of Gallatin and Madison, cast the deciding vote against renewal of the charter.[69]

It is interesting to note who some of the supporters and opponents of the Bank were in 1811. In 1791, it was primarily the Federalists, under Hamilton, who supported the new institution; the Republicans, like Jefferson and Madison, vehemently opposed it. By 1811, many Republicans who were then in power became advocates of renewal and some Federalists opposed it. There was a crossing of party lines when it came to voting on the Bank. Note that Clay, a Republican, as mentioned above, opposed the renewal of the charter; he was to become a leading proponent of rechartering the Second Bank of the United States during the 1832 election.[70] Though Jefferson did not like the First Bank—he did not like banks in general—he came to accept its existence. In a letter to John Adams in 1814, he recognized his antibank reputation. He said, "My zeal against those institutions was so worn and open at the establishment of the Bank of the United States that I was derided as a maniac by the tribe of bank mongers."[71] Madison, the Bank's first opponent, now supported its existence on the grounds that it had been recognized by the Congress for the past twenty years. In his opinion, a precedent was now established for the renewal of the charter, making the constitutional question irrelevant. As treasury secretary, Gallatin also had some influence on Jefferson and Madison.[72]

Did the state banks and trade organizations support renewal of the First Bank's charter? Two of the leading experts on early banking history in the United States take opposing viewpoints. Professor John Holdsworth stated that in general state banks and trade organizations supported the renewal of the First Bank's charter. The directors of the Bank of New York petitioned the Congress in January 1811 on behalf of renewal. The four state banks in Philadelphia—the Bank of Pennsylvania, the Bank of North America, the Bank of Philadelphia, and the Farmer and Mechanics' Bank—supported a resolution that declared that "general duties and inconvenience will attend the cessation of so great a monied institution."[73] A manufacturers and mechanics trade delegation and a group of merchants, both from Philadelphia, spoke on behalf of the First Bank. They worried that without the Bank, the economy would suffer a shortage of credit that would lead to a major recession.[74] On the other hand, Professor Bray Hammond took the position that the business community and state banks were opposed to the charter renewal whereas the agrarian interests supported it.[75] Whether you supported or opposed the recharter often depended on your vested interest rather than whether you were a farmer or a businessman. For example, Clay, who voted against the recharter, was closely associated with the business community and had vested interests in two Kentucky banks. Senator Samuel Smith of Maryland, a rich banker and merchant, also voted against recharter.[76] Entrepreneur John Jacob Astor of New York had no use for the First Bank of the United States because it had refused him credit and had closed his account. He was also an investor in state bank stock.[77]

The vote against the First Bank in the House of Representatives and the Senate was by one vote. Unfortunately, the Bank's enemies did a better job of getting their message across than the Bank's supporters. The Bank's directors showed little passion for politics. Aside from hiring an ineffective lobbyist, they did little else to help save the Bank. They seemed to want the whole thing to end quickly so they could find other ways to make money. The Bank's stockholders were more a liability than an asset, as many of them were foreigners and mostly from Great Britain. Keep in mind that the charter renewal was being discussed at the same time that the United States was having problems with Great Britain that would lead to the War of 1812. The American press and public were very critical of the British policy of impressment—the forceful removal of sailors from U.S. ships. The opponents of renewal used the anti-British feeling to their benefit when they referred to the First Bank as the British bank.[78]

The First Bank of the United States asked Congress for a two-year extension to liquidate its assets. This request went to Clay's committee and was denied on constitutional grounds. Clay asserted that because the original charter was unconstitutional, the extension of it would also be unconstitutional. The Bank branches were sold to the organizers of new local banks.[79] The First Bank closed for business on March 3, 1811, and trustees were appointed to liquidate its assets. On March 14, 1811, they petitioned the Pennsylvania legislature for a state charter which was denied.[80] Shortly afterward, Stephen Girard, the First Bank's largest stockholder, gained control of the Bank's operations, and by December 11, 1811, he moved his investment into a local bank which was called the Bank of Stephen Girard. In May 1812, he bought the Philadelphia office of the First Bank of the United States and operated it as an unincorporated financial institution.[81]

NOTES

1. Broadus Mitchell, *Alexander Hamilton: The National Adventure, 1788-1804* (New York: Macmillan Company 1962), pp. 21-22.

2. Ibid., pp. 22-23.

3. Mansel G. Blackford and K. Austin Kerr, *Business Enterprise in American History* (Boston: Houghton Mifflin Company, 1986), pp. 74-75.

4. Ibid., p. 75.

5. Raymond H. Robinson, *The Growing of America: 1789-1848* (Boston: Allyn and Bacon, Inc., 1973), p. 3.

6. Ibid.

7. Mitchell, *Alexander Hamilton*, p. 88.

8. Harold Syrett, ed., *The Papers of Alexander Hamilton*, Vol. 8 (New York: Columbia University Press, 1965), pp. 218-219.

9. Ibid., p. 219.

10. Adam Smith, *The Wealth of Nations*, ed. Edwin Cannan (New York: Random House, Modern Library Edition, 1937), p. 304.

11. *Annals of Congress*, 1st Cong., 2d Sess., 1790, "Report on a National Bank," pp. 2082-2111.

12. Smith, *Wealth of Nations*, p. 308.

13. Mitchell, *Alexander Hamilton*, pp. 90-91.

14. Ibid., p. 91.

15. Harold Syrett, ed., *The Papers of Alexander Hamilton*, Vol. 7 (New York: Columbia University Press, 1963), p. 406.

16. Bray Hammond, *Banks and Politics in America from the Revolution to the Civil War* (Princeton, NJ: Princeton University Press, 1985), p. 115.

17. Mitchell, *Alexander Hamilton*, p. 94.

18. *Annals of Congress*, 1st Cong., 3d Sess., 1791, p. 1919.

19. Hammond, *Banks and Politics in America*, p. 116.

20. Ibid.; Mitchell, *Alexander Hamilton*, p. 94.

21. Mitchell, *Alexander Hamilton*, p. 95.

22. *Annals of Congress*, 1st Cong., 3d Sess., 1791, p. 1897; Hammond, *Banks and Politics in America*, p. 115.

23. Hammond, *Banks and Politics in America*, p. 116.

24. *Annals of Congress*, 1st Cong., 3d Sess., 1791, p. 1904; Mitchell, *Alexander Hamilton*, p. 96.

25. Mitchell, *Alexander Hamilton*, p. 97.

26. Hammond, *Banks and Politics in America*, p. 117.

27. Mitchell, *Alexander Hamilton*, pp. 98-99.

28. Hammond, *Banks and Politics in America*, p. 117.

29. Harold Syrett, ed., *The Papers of Alexander Hamilton*, Vol. 8 (New York: Columbia University Press, 1965), p. 110.

30. Ibid., p. 98.

31. Mitchell, *Alexander Hamilton*, p. 101.

32. Syrett, ed., *The Papers of Alexander Hamilton*, Vol. 8, p. 110.

33. Mitchell, *Alexander Hamilton*, pp. 99-100.

34. Hammond, *Banks and Politics in America*, pp. 125-126.

35. Richard H. Timberlake, *Monetary Policy in the United States: An Intellectual and Institutional History* (Chicago: University of Chicago Press, 1993), p. 6.

36. Hammond, *Banks and Politics in America*, p. 123.

37. Ibid., pp. 123-124.

38. Mitchell, *Alexander Hamilton*, p. 92.

39. Hammond, *Banks and Politics in America*, p. 125.

40. Ibid., p. 208; Timberlake, *Monetary Policy in the United States*, p. 6; Syrett, ed., *The Papers of Alexander Hamilton*, Vol. 7, p. 406.

41. Syrett, ed., *The Papers of Alexander of Alexander Hamilton*, Vol. 7, p. 237; Hammond, *Banks and Politics in America*, pp. 129-130.

42. Timberlake, *Monetary Policy in the United States*, p. 9.

43. John Holdsworth and Davis R. Dewey, *The First and Second Banks of the United States* (Washington, DC: U.S. Government Printing Office, 1910), pp. 42-43.

44. Ibid., p. 45.

45. Timberlake, *Monetary Policy in the United States*, p. 9.

46. Holdsworth, *The First and Second Banks of the United States*, pp. 40-41.

47. Hammond, *Banks and Politics in America*, pp. 200-201.

48. Ibid., p. 126.

49. Ibid.

50. Ibid., p. 127.

51. Ibid.

52. Timberlake, *Monetary Policy in the United States*, p. 10.

53. Hammond, *Banks and Politics in America*, p. 199.

54. Irwin Unger, *These United States* (Englewood Cliffs, NJ: Prentice Hall, 1989), p. 193.

55. Holdsworth, *The First and Second Banks of the United States*, p. 69.

56. Ibid., p. 72; Hammond, *Banks and Politics in America*, p. 209.

57. Holdsworth, *The First and Second Banks of the United States*, p. 73.

58. Hammond, *Banks and Politics in America*, p. 209.

59. Holdsworth, *The First and Second Banks of the United States*, p. 78.

60. Ibid., pp. 78-79.

61. Holdsworth, *The First and Second Banks of the United States*, pp. 80-81.

62. Timberlake, *Monetary Policy in the United States*, p. 10.

63. Hammond, *Banks and Politics in America*, p. 210.

64. *Annals of Congress*, 11th Cong., 3d Sess., 1811, pp. 212-213.

65. Hammond, *Banks and Politics in America*, pp. 215-218.

66. Timberlake, *Monetary Policy in the United States*, p. 11.

67. Holdsworth, *The First and Second Banks of the United States*, p. 75.

68. Ibid., p. 91.

69. Holdsworth, *The First and Second Banks of the United States*, p. 97.

70. Hammond, *Banks and Politics in America*, p. 210.

71. Holdsworth, *The First and Second Banks of the United States*, p. 67.

72. Hammond, *Banks and Politics in America*, p. 210.

73. Holdsworth, *The First and Second Banks of the United States*, p. 83.

74. Ibid., p. 87.

75. Hammond, *Banks and Politics in America*, p. 212.

76. Ibid., p. 211.

77. Ibid., p. 213.

78. Ibid., pp. 223-224.

79. Ibid., p. 225.

80. Holdsworth, *The First and Second Banks of the United States*, pp. 98-100.

81. Hammond, *Banks and Politics in America*, p. 226.

3

The Period between the First and Second Banks

From March 1811, when the First Bank of the United States closed its doors, until January 1817, when the Second Bank began its operations, the country was without a national bank. The immediate effect was that the treasury had to find other banks to deposit its funds to conduct business. The absence of a national bank could not have come at a worse time. By June 1812, the Congress would declare war on Great Britain, and the country would be in dire need of money to finance the conflict. The demise of the First Bank led to financial chaos from 1811 to 1816, which was exacerbated by the War of 1812, and this paved the way for the chartering of the Second Bank of the United States.[1]

THE GROWTH OF THE STATE BANKS

Shortly after the termination of the First Bank of the United States, Treasury Secretary Albert Gallatin offered his resignation, but President James Madison refused to accept it. Madison viewed Gallatin as indispensable to his administration and never blamed him for failing to convince the Congress on the necessity of recharter. Nevertheless, Gallatin remained pessimistic and despondent about the future of the economy after the dissolution of the First Bank. He lacked the confidence that the state banks could fill the role of the national bank as early as January 1811 when he wrote Senator William H. Crawford, a Republican from Georgia and a supporter of the bank. He told the senator that people and business have confidence in the Bank of the United States to collect revenue and to provide loans to keep the economy viable. He contended, "The public moneys are safer by being weekly deposited in banks, instead of accumulating in the hands of collectors, is self evident. The question, therefore, is whether a bank incorporated by the United States, or a number of banks, incorporated by the several States, be most convenient for those purposes."[2] According to Gallatin, the national bank was much better suited for this purpose because of its organization—it was responsible for the money deposited in all of its branches whereas the state banks were only held liable for the sums in its own hands.[3]

Gallatin believed that state banks would prove poor substitutes for a national bank, as the treasury would be unable to turn to them for emergency loans. Frequently, the government would be forced to negotiate with many different banks, which would prove time-consuming, and government funds, which had been always kept in the national bank, now would be transported from place to place, which could cause delay and security problems.[4]

Between 1811 and 1816, the number of state banks increased from eighty-eight to 246.[5] Many of these banks were organized with no restrictions or guidelines. For example, a problem that concerned the secretary of the treasury was that few state bank charters contained the requirements that the issuing bank had to redeem its notes on demand, or that a specie reserve should be held for possible redemption.[6]

The War of 1812 brought a great demand for credit, and the notes of the state banks were vastly expanded, causing serious inflation and eventual specie suspension, which will be discussed later. Gallatin stated that between 1811 and 1816, banknote circulation increased from $28 million to $68 million, and he blamed this situation on the absence of a national bank. He said:

The creation of new state banks was a natural consequence of the dissolution of the Bank of the United States. And, as is usual under such circumstances, the expectation of great profits gave birth to a much greater number than was wanted . . . That increase took place on the eve of and during a war which did nearly annihilate the exports and both the foreign and coasting trade. And, as the salutary regulating power of the Bank of the United States no longer existed, the issues were accordingly increased much beyond what the other circumstances already mentioned rendered necessary.[7]

For Gallatin, the regulator of bank credit no longer existed as the supply of bank credit increased, especially in the western states, where capital was in great demand, to purchase new land and to make internal improvements.[8]

Due to inflation and specie suspension, the values of state banknotes changed from state to state. This disorder of the currency had a negative influence on the operations of treasury imports, as foreign countries sought ports, such as Philadelphia and Baltimore, where currency had lost its value. These ports thrived at the expense of Boston and New York where the money still retained its value. In 1814, the treasury attempted to seek loans from the state banks, but due to the plethora of state banknotes in circulation, the money had little value. It was estimated that the direct loss to the government, from the worthless state banknotes received from 1814 to 1817, was more than $5 million.[9]

In 1814, the banking situation had deteriorated to such an extent that it caught the attention of Thomas Jefferson, who in a letter to John Adams said:

I have ever been the enemy of banks; not of those discounting for cash; but of those foisting their own paper into circulation, and thus banishing our cash. My zeal against those institutions was so warm and open at the establishment of the bank of the U.S. that I was derided as a Maniac by the tribe of bank-mongers, who were seeking to filch from the public their swindling and barren gains. But the errors of that day cannot be recalled. The evils they have engendered are now upon us, and the question is, how are we to get out of them? Shall we build an altar to the old paper money of the revolution, which ruined individuals but saved the republic, and burn on that all the bank charters present and future, and their notes with them? For these are to ruin both republic and individuals. This cannot be done. The Mania is too strong. It has siesed by it's delusions and corruptions all the members of our governments, general, special and individual. Our circulating paper of the last year was estimated at 200. millions of dollars. The new banks now petitioned for, to the several legislatures, are for about 60. millions of additional capital, and of course 180. millions of additional circulation, nearly doubling that of the last year; and raising the whole mass to near 400. millions, or 40. for 1. of the wholesome amount of circulation for a population of 8. millions circumstanced as we are: and you remember how rapidly our money went down after our 40. for 1. establishment in the revolution. I doubt if the present trash can hold as long. I think the 380. millions must blow all up in the course of the present year. Should not prudent men, who possess stock in any monied institution, either draw and hoard the cash, now while they can, or exchange it for canal stock, or such other as being bottomed on immoveable property, will remain unhurt by the crush? . . . You might as well, with the sailors, whistle to the wind, as suggest precautions against having too much money. We must scud then before the gale, and try to hold fast, ourselves, by some plank of the wreck. God send us all a safe delivrance.[10]

FINANCING THE WAR OF 1812

Trade and Taxes

President Madison asked the Congress for a declaration of war against Great Britain in June 1812. This conflict, as expected, increased American expenses while it decreased its revenues. Many congressmen, however, remained unconcerned about the financing of the war because they believed it would be over within weeks. As it turned out, the War of 1812 lasted until December 1814, two and a half years, and the United States was totally unprepared to deal with its financing.[11]

Before the Jefferson Embargo of December 1807, which destroyed American commerce, the United States had profited immensely by the Napoleonic Wars in Europe. From 1803 to 1807, commerce had doubled in the United States, helping to produce its first half-dozen millionaires. However, as a result of the embargo, exports in 1808 were only one-fifth as large as those of 1807, and imports were cut in half. Imports recovered slowly during the next few years, but declined again by 1811 and continued their downward spiral until, in 1814, they were only one-tenth of what they were in 1807. Thus, customs duties, the major source of federal revenue before the War of 1812, could not be depended on to finance the war, as it had reached a low point of $6 million in 1814.[12]

It was interesting to note that Gallatin, who had been secretary of the treasury since 1801, did not foresee the need for tax increases in 1808 when war with Great Britain or France seemed inevitable. He said in his annual report in December 1808 that "no internal taxes, either direct or indirect, were contemplated even in the case of hostilities carried against the two great belligerent powers."[13] Gallatin had $14 million in the treasury at the end of 1808, and even though he knew that this sum would be dissipated quickly, he could borrow from the First Bank of the United States and avoid tax increases.[14] However, in Gallatin's annual report in December 1811, he now changed his mind on taxes as he asked Congress to restore some of the internal taxes which had been abolished in 1802. The treasury secretary, knowing that the members of the House Ways and Means Committee did not want to pass any new tax bill, told them that if the First Bank of the United States had been rechartered, there would be no need for additional taxes.[15] Needless to say, Congress did not want an economics lesson from the secretary of the treasury, who was already an unpopular figure in the House of Representatives; it refused to consider the tax bill in 1812.[16] Finally, in the summer of 1813, Madison called the Congress into special session and insisted on a tax bill. Congress responded by enacting a direct tax of $3 million to be assessed for the first time in 1814. Taxes were levied on refined sugars and distillers of spirituous liquors, as well as auctions and stamps. In September 1814, the Congress doubled the 1813 tax and made it effective in 1815 and in 1816 when they imposed another $3 million in taxes on the American people.[17] These taxes were levied with reluctance, and only after the treasury was reduced to a state of poverty. Representative Alexander Hanson, a Federalist from Maryland, described the state of the treasury in these words:

So completely empty was the Treasury and destitute of credit that funds could not be obtained to defray the current ordinary expenses of the different Departments. The Department of State was so bare of money as to be unable to pay even its stationery bill. The Treasury was obliged to borrow pitiful sums, which it would disgrace a merchant in tolerable credit to ask for. The Paymaster was unable to meet the demands for paltry amounts—not even for $30. In short it was difficult to conceive a situation more critical and perilous than that of the government at this moment, without money, without credit, and destitute of the means of defending the country.[18]

Loans

Treasury Secretary Gallatin had underestimated the revenue need for the war. He determined that if the war lasted four years, the government would only need to borrow $50 million. As it turned out, the war lasted only two and a half years, and it raised the national debt from $45 million to $123 million—a rate of more than $30 million a year, about three times his estimate.[19]

Gallatin needed to find money quickly to fund the war as the treasury was in danger of collapse. What made his task difficult was that the circulating capital of the United States was concentrated in the large cities chiefly north of the Potomac where there was a strong antiwar sentiment. For example, twenty-five percent of the capital for potential loans came from New England where the people wanted no part of Madison's war. They were still smarting over the Embargo Act of 1807, which crippled their economy. Even the citizens of New England, who would have made loans to the government, found themselves with a specie shortage. A large importation of foreign goods into the eastern states in 1809 and trade in British government bills of exchange caused a drain on specie in the New England area.[20]

The failure to recharter the First Bank of the United States meant the immediate loss of $7 million to the treasury. That money was invested in the stock of the Bank by foreigners, and it left the country in 1811. If the money had remained in the Bank of the United States, it would have doubled the resources of the government at a very critical time. Gallatin had limited success in borrowing from state banks when the war came. Those in New York, Philadelphia, and Baltimore responded to the government, but in making these loans, they exceeded their resources and had to enlarge their issue of paper money, causing inflation and raising the cost of the government loans.[21]

The total bond issue authorized by the Congress from 1812 to 1814 was for $61 million. The first part of the $61 million loan was made in March 1812 only three months before the declaration of war. The Congress, believing a war with Great Britain would be brief, determined it only needed an $11 million loan to meet a probable deficit and new expenditures for an enlargement of the army, erection of fortifications, and construction of ships. This loan bore six percent interest, and none of it could be sold under par. Though the bonds that secured the loan were to mature in twelve years, there were few early subscribers. On April 28, 1812, a little more than five weeks after the initial subscription, *The New York Evening Post* declared, "Let those who are for the war subscribe—let those who dread it, avoid doing so, as they value all they hold dear." Within two weeks of the comment in the newspaper, $6 million of the $11 million was taken—$4 million by the banks and $2 million by individuals.[22]

After the war began in June 1812, it soon became apparent that the government would have to borrow additional money. On February 8, 1813, a loan for $16 million was offered to the public at bids below par, and it would never have been placed if it had not been for the cooperation of David Parish and Stephen Girard of Philadelphia and John Jacob Astor of New York. They agreed to take $8 million or half of the offering in expectation of a good profit and to help the government finance the war.[23] It was interesting to note that there was less financial support for this second loan. The government could not obtain the cooperation of any strong banking institutions, especially in the antiwar northeastern states. The New England states, individuals and banks together, contributed only $3 million of all money borrowed by the end of 1814.[24]

In analyzing the loans made by the government from 1812 to 1814, of the $61 million authorized by the Congress, only $45 million had been sold, and less than

$8 million of that had been sold at par; the discounts varied from twelve to twenty percent.[25] In 1814, an offering of $25 million brought the government only $10 million. The House Ways and Means Committee in 1830 calculated the total loss to the government in disposing of its loans during the period from 1812 to 1816. It estimated that for loans of over $80 million, the treasury received only $34 million as measured in specie.[26]

Treasury Notes

The loan program discussed above was insufficient in supplying the government with the immediate funds to wage a war against Great Britain. Recognizing the need to maintain liquidity, on June 30, 1812, the Congress authorized the first issue of $5 million in treasury notes to be redeemable within one year. They were issued as nonmoney, interest-bearing debt, but people and banks could and did use them as currency. The interest rate on the treasury notes in 1812 was 5.4 percent per year, and they were redeemable in one year.[27] The notes were legal tender for payments of all duties and taxes to the United States, for all government purchases from the private sector, and for all private transactions. Because most of these notes were issued in denominations of one hundred dollars or more (the 5.4 percent interest was paid on denominations of twenty dollars or more), their use as currency was limited to major purchases. Many bought these notes, legal tender that paid interest, as additions to their portfolios. Though they were redeemable in specie in June 1813, creditors continued to hold them as investments long after their maturity date.[28]

The success of the 1812 issue led the Congress to put additional treasury notes into the economy from 1813 to 1815. Though these notes paid the same interest rate and also matured one year from the date of issuance, they were not as popular as the first issue, and there were fewer takers. Of the additional $30 million in treasury notes authorized by the Congress after 1812, only $17 million were actually circulated, and only a small part of this sum was in circulation at any one time.[29] However, after specie suspension occurred, these notes depreciated rapidly and were mostly used to pay taxes. Nonetheless, the treasury notes proved useful to the government in the first year of the war, as the banks took these notes and gave the government the gold and silver it needed to meet its expenses.[30]

SPECIE SUSPENSION

In June 1814, the British landed troops on the Patuxent River and marched from Maryland to Washington with little opposition. The Congress, the president and many of the dignitaries had already fled the city when the British arrived in August 1814 to burn the capitol, the White House, and almost all of the city's public buildings. The panic that occurred caused runs on the banks for specie, and all the banks in Washington and Baltimore immediately suspended payment in specie.[31] This suspension spread to the banks in New York, Philadelphia, New Jersey, Virginia, Ohio, and Kentucky. Only the banks in New England and the Bank of Nashville in Tennessee continued to make payments in specie. However, about eighteen country banks in the New England area occasionally used suspension as an excuse not to make specie payments.[32]

It should be noted that the suspension of specie payments did not affect the other operations of the banks, and all the banks stayed open. Nonetheless, the effects of suspension sent shock waves throughout the country. State banks would neither pay in specie nor accept each other's notes at par, and the country lacked a medium of exchange. Banknotes began to sink under discounts varying "not only from time to time, but at the same time from state to state and in the same state from place to place."[33] Currency was worth a hundred cents on the dollar in New England, ninety-three cents in New York and Charleston, eighty-five cents in Philadelphia, and seventy-five to eighty cents in Baltimore. The New England states would only accept the notes of New England banks or specie for payment of debts. In November 1814, new Treasury Secretary Alexander Dallas was forced to declare to the holders of government securities in Massachusetts that the treasury was unable to pay interest on the national debt held in that section, because the government lacked both the specie and New England banknotes with which to pay.[34]

The suspension of specie payment had devastating effects on the government. It was now forced to receive its revenues in state bank paper and treasury notes of all degrees of depreciation if it wanted to collect taxes and imposts due it. Congress had made no provision for the treasury to make allowances for the discounts, and the government was unable to use the notes of one state in another state. Nor could the treasury notes be used to pay debts, for by law they were issued at par, but were now depreciated in the open market. After the war, Dallas was prohibited by law from accepting depreciated banknotes and could not withdraw funds from some of the banks in which the government had kept accounts.[35]

Gallatin had stated that if the First Bank of the United States had existed specie suspension would not have occurred. Specie payment was resumed after the formation of the Second Bank of the United States in 1816, and then only after the Congress declared that specie or notes of specie-paying banks would be accepted for the payment of all public debts.[36]

THE BEGINNINGS OF THE SECOND BANK

The contributions of six men stand out in the movement toward a Second Bank of the United States. They were:

1. John Jacob Astor, who came from Germany as a poor immigrant and built a great

fortune in the fur trade, maritime commerce, and New York real estate businesses. It is interesting to note that Astor did not support the rechartering of the First Bank (see chapter 2).

2. David Parish, a financier from Philadelphia, a friend of the Astors, who came from a family that was influential in banking circles.

3. Stephen Girard, another resident of Philadelphia, and one of the richest men in the United States, who was a major stockholder in the First Bank. When the Congress failed to renew its charter, Girard bought the building of the First Bank and set up his own bank (see chapter 2).

4. Jacob Barker, a prominent Quaker from New York who had influence with the Madison administration.

5. John C. Calhoun, a member of the House of Representatives from South Carolina, who just began his political career as a nationalist and ardent supporter of the Second Bank.

6. Alexander Dallas, born in Jamaica of British parents, educated in England, who came to reside in Philadelphia. He was a lawyer and a founder of the Democratic-Republican Party in Pennsylvania. He was a close friend of Gallatin, and he would eventually become secretary of the treasury shortly before the political struggle to charter the Second Bank.[37]

These men supported the creation of the Second Bank for various reasons. Astor, Parish, and Girard owned large amounts of government stock, and they would stand to profit if its market value increased by the formation of a national bank. All of them, including Barker wanted to make commissions by floating future government-stock issues, as well as the stock of the bank itself. At the same time, as businessmen and patriots, they wanted the return of a stable currency that would restore confidence in the government, and enable it to prosecute the War of 1812.[38]

The movement toward another national bank began with a meeting at Dallas's home on April 6, 1813, with Gallatin, Parish, Astor, Girard, and Dallas in attendance. Gallatin desperately needed funds to continue the war, and he turned to the financiers for help. Astor, Girard, and Parish agreed to form a syndicate and take over $9 million in government stock at $88 a share, thus closing a $16 million loan. A year later, Barker contracted with the government to take $5 million of a $25 million loan, which George W. Campbell, secretary of the treasury, tried to place.[39] (Gallatin had left the treasury in May 1813 to go to Europe as an American peace envoy. William Jones, secretary of the navy, became acting secretary of the treasury until February 1814, when Campbell took over.)

By early 1814, it became apparent to Astor, Parish, Girard, Barker, Dallas, and Calhoun that the only means by which the treasury could be provided with sufficient funds to prosecute the war and maintain a stable currency was to create another national bank. Barker, in particular, gave the movement new life, as he had trouble finding others to join him in taking the $5 million in stock which he had contracted. In a Washington publication, the *National Intelligencer*, he declared that a national bank was crucial to the nation's survival.[40]

In the Congress, Calhoun fought for the passage of tax and loan bills to help provide the necessary funds for the treasury, and then he became the champion for a national bank. Dallas, who appreciated Calhoun's struggles, called him "the Young Hercules who carried the war on his shoulders."[41] When petitions for new bank bills were presented to the Congress by groups of businessmen from New York and Philadelphia in January 1814, Calhoun presented his own plan. He called for a national bank to operate only in the District of Columbia, with the states allowed to buy its stock according to their representation in the House of Representatives. Astor, Parish, and Girard all appreciated Calhoun's efforts, but they were against the plan—they wanted the bank in Philadelphia, the site of the First Bank and the financial capital of the United States at the time.[42]

The Madison administration was not supportive of a new national bank. Madison had been an ardent opponent of the First Bank in 1791, but favored its rechartering in 1811 on the grounds of "expediency and necessity."[43] After the demise of the First Bank, Madison thought that the government could do without such an institution. However, by April 1814, both the president and Treasury Secretary Campbell came to the realization that the government could not fill the $25 million loan, and they reluctantly supported a new national bank.[44] On April 2, 1814, Felix Grundy, a supporter of the administration from Tennessee, offered a resolution in the House of Representatives that a committee be appointed "to inquire into the expediency of establishing a National Bank." Though the opponents of the measure attempted to delay it indefinitely, the Grundy motion was passed seventy-six to sixty-nine.[45]

That same month, Parish asked his good friend Dallas to help him find support for the bank. Dallas, very much involved in politics, wrote numerous letters on behalf of the Second Bank of the United States. He wrote Navy Secretary William Jones, Senator Jonathan Roberts, and Congressman William Findley, all from Pennsylvania. He assured these men that arguments against a national bank, based on the constitutional question, were no longer an issue in 1814, while admitting that it might have been in 1791. He emphasized the importance of a national bank to the financial operations and credit of the government.[46]

A week after Grundy had made his motion on the national bank, the Madison administration withdrew its support. As mentioned above, Madison only wanted the bank if it was a necessity to continue funding the war. However, rumors were now running rampant that Great Britain wanted to make peace. On April 8, 1814, Grundy moved that the bank committee be dissolved; this motion was quickly passed so everybody could hurry home.[47]

The government's financial situation worsened by the end of the summer. Campbell only had been able to acquire from Barker and other businessmen $11,750,000 of the $25 million he needed. Subscribers were not willing to depart with their money and provided no more than $80 a share. At the same time in August 1814, specie suspension occurred, as commercial houses closed their doors and businesses throughout the nation came to a halt.[48]

Just before the capture of Washington by the British, Barker had rushed there to see his friends in the Congress and the White House. He told them that only a national bank could provide the funds necessary to save the nation, and they promised him that they would support a national bank at the next session of the Congress.[49] Leaving nothing to chance, Barker went to the financial section of New York City to solicit signatures for a petition to the Congress in support of the bank, while both Parish and Astor began organizing business leaders for a march on Washington, when the Congress reconvened late in September 1814.[50]

While Barker, Astor, and Parish were busy drumming up support for a national bank, Astor had developed his own bank plan, which he sent along with a letter to Dallas, requesting that both be sent to Dallas's friends in the Madison cabinet. Dallas copied both the letter and the plan and forwarded them to Secretary of State James Monroe. In a covering letter, Dallas said, "My principal inducement in troubling you with it arises from the suggestion that it is a result of a deliberate concert among the capitalists; and perhaps, the Secretary of the Treasury may draw some useful hints from the plan, as well as from Mr. Astor's letter."[51]

Certainly one of the useful hints that Dallas was talking about in the Astor Plan pertained to how the bank's capital would be provided. Astor and his friends were well aware that the country was suffering from a shortage of specie, and so he suggested to Dallas that instead of using specie as capital, real estate should be considered. This was similar to the old land bank idea which Hamilton had opposed many years before.[52]

When the Congress reconvened in September 1814, Campbell estimated that the government's budget deficit would be almost $14 million by the end of the year. He declared that the administration needed at least $5 million more in revenue if the war were to be continued through 1815, but made no suggestions on how to do it. The frustrated and incompetent Campbell resigned as treasury secretary on September 26th.[53]

Madison, realizing the desperate financial condition of the government, turned to his friend and confidant Dallas to take over the treasury department. Actually, he had asked Dallas to run the treasury as early as February 1814, but he had respectfully declined due to the great financial sacrifice he would have to endure.[54] This time Dallas, realizing that his country needed him, and encouraged by Astor, Parish, and his associates and friends in the business community, accepted the appointment. On October 5, 1814, Madison submitted his name to the Congress, and the very next day, it approved the nomination.[55]

Dallas's appointment was celebrated by Astor and his friends, for they realized that they had an ally in the treasury secretary who had the respect and attention of Madison. Dallas believed that a national bank was crucial to the welfare of the country. He had told Jones in September 1814 in a letter that "the state of public credit admits of no palliative remedy. There must be established an efficient, productive system of taxation. There must be established a National Bank to anticipate, collect and distribute the Revenue."[56] There was no question now that there would be a Second Bank of the United States, but only how long it would take to establish it.

NOTES

1. Ralph C. H. Catterall, *The Second Bank of the United States* (Chicago: University of Chicago Press, 1902), p. 1.

2. E. James Ferguson, ed., *Selected Writings of Albert Gallatin* (Indianapolis, IN: The Bobbs-Merrill Company, 1967), pp. 276-277.

3. Ibid.

4. Bray Hammond, *Banks and Politics in America from the Revolution to the Civil War* (Princeton, NJ: Princeton University Press, 1985), p. 229.

5. Davis R. Dewey, *The Financial History of the United States* (New York: Augustus M. Kelley Publishers, 1968), p. 144.

6. John F. Chown, *A History of Money from AD 800* (London: Routledge, 1996), p. 162.

7. Henry Adams, ed., *The Writings of Albert Gallatin*, vol. 3 (Philadelphia, PA: J. B. Lippincott and Company, 1879), p. 285.

8. Ibid., pp. 386-387.

9. Dewey, *The Financial History of the United States*, p. 145.

10. Margaret G. Myers, *A Financial History of the United States* (New York: Columbia University Press, 1970), p. 81.

11. Catterall, *The Second Bank of the United States*, p. 1.

12. Myers, *A Financial History of the United States*, p. 75.

13. Henry Adams, *The Life of Albert Gallatin* (New York: Peter Smith, 1943), pp. 450-451.

14. Ibid.

15. Ibid., p. 452.

16. Ibid.

17. Dewey, *The Financial History of the United States*, pp. 138-139.

18. Myers, *A Financial History of the United States*, p. 78.

19. Adams, *The Life of Albert Gallatin*, p. 454.

20. Ibid., pp. 473-474.

21. Ibid., p. 474.

22. Dewey, *The Financial History of the United States*, p. 132; Myers, *A Financial History of the United States*, p. 76.

23. Myers, *A Financial History of the United States*, p. 76.

24. Dewey, *The Financial History of the United States*, pp. 133-134.

25. Hammond, *Banks and Politics in America*, p. 229.

26. Ibid.

27. John Jay Knox, *United States Notes* (New York: Charles Scribner's Sons, 1899), p. 22; Myers, *A Financial History of the United States*, p. 77; Richard H. Timberlake, *Monetary Policy in the United States: An Intellectual and Institutional History* (Chicago: University of Chicago Press, 1993), p. 14.

28. Timberlake, *Monetary Policy in the United States*, p. 14.

29. Catterall, *The Second Bank of the United States*, p. 3.

30. Timberlake, *Monetary Policy in the United States*, p. 15.

31. Hammond, *Banks and Politics in America*, p. 227.

32. Chown, *A History of Money from AD 800*, p. 164; Catterall, *The Second Bank of the United States*, p. 4.

33. Hammond, *Banks and Politics in America*, p. 228.

34. Ibid.; Catterall, *The Second Bank of the United States*, p. 6.

35. Catterall, *The Second Bank of the United States*, pp. 4-5.

36. Chown, *A History of Money from AD 800*, p. 164.

37. Raymond Walters, Jr., "The Origins of the Second Bank of the United States," *Journal of Political Economy* 53 (1945): 115-116.

38. Ibid., p. 116.

39. Ibid., p. 117.

40. Ibid., p. 118; *National Intelligencer*, March 16, 1814.

41. Walters, "The Origins of the Second Bank of the United States," p. 117.

42. *Annals of Congress*, 13th Cong., 1st and 2d Sess., 1813-1814, pp. 595, 598, 740, 844, 873, 1058, 1235, 1578-1585.

43. Hammond, *Banks and Politics in America*, p. 210.

44. Walters, "The Origins of the Second Bank of the United States," p. 119.

45. *Annals of Congress*, 13th Cong., 2d Sess., 1814, pp. 1941-1945, 1954-1956.

46. Walters, "The Origins of the Second Bank of the United States," pp. 119-120.

47. Ibid., p. 120.

48. Ibid.

49. Ibid.

50. Ibid., pp. 120-121.

51. Ibid., p. 121.

52. Ibid., p. 120.

53. Ibid., p. 122.

54. Ibid., pp. 121-122.

55. Ibid.

56. Ibid.

4

The Creation of the Second Bank of the United States

ALEXANDER DALLAS AND THE SECOND BANK OF THE UNITED STATES

Shortly after Dallas's appointment as secretary of the treasury in October 1814, he developed a plan for a national bank similar to the First Bank, but with significant differences:

1. The new bank would be chartered for thirty years instead of twenty.
2. Its headquarters would once again be situated in Philadelphia, but like the old bank, it could open offices of discount and deposit in other cities.
3. Its capital was set at $50 million, $20 million of which was to be subscribed to by the government. Of the remaining $30 million, subscribed to by corporations and individuals, ninety percent could be paid for in government stock and treasury notes that were issued during the War of 1812; the other $3 million had to be in specie.
4. The government could appoint five of the fifteen directors, including the bank president, and the stockholders were to choose the others.
5. The bank was to make "reasonable loans to the United States if required by an Act of Congress."
6. William Jones, secretary of the navy and at one time acting secretary of the treasury, would be the bank's first president.[1]

However, before Dallas submitted his plan to the Congress, he met with President Madison, Secretary Jones, and other members of the cabinet. As a result of these meetings, he changed his plan in four important ways:

1. It called for a charter of twenty years.
2. The specie required for payment of the bank's capital was increased from $3 million to $6 million.
3. The president of the United States could authorize the bank to suspend specie payments at any time. This was not stated in the original proposal.

4. The bank was required to make a loan to the government of $30 million when it began operations, but it was prohibited from selling any of its government stock to do so.[2]

Dallas made a concerted effort to get his banking bill passed by the Congress. In October, he met with members of the House Ways and Means Committee and urged them to support his bank plan. He then appeared before a special Senate committee led by Senator Rufus King of New York, a good friend of the late Alexander Hamilton. King had been a supporter and a director of the Federalist-sponsored First Bank of the United States, but was now opposed to this Democratic-Republican Second Bank of the United States. It did not take Dallas long to understand that King's support had little to do with the importance of the bank itself, but rather which party sponsored it.[3] Though not opposed to the bank on principle, many Federalists opposed the Dallas plan only because they thought that it would give a political advantage to the Democratic-Republican party and would grant the Madison administration excessive economic power.[4]

There was even strong opposition to the bank within the Democratic-Republican House where John W. Eppes of Virginia, son-in-law of Thomas Jefferson, led the antibank forces. Like his famous father-in-law, he was a strict constructionist, and he believed that if the Constitution did not say you can have a bank, then you are prohibited from creating one. Eppes believed that most supporters of the bank thought it was important to maintain a stable circulating medium to foster economic growth. He stated that the bank was unnecessary if the government issued interest-bearing treasury notes in small denominations as a circulating medium.[5]

The most difficult opponent of the Dallas plan proved to be a friend of the bank— none other than John C. Calhoun, a congressman from South Carolina. Dallas had shown Calhoun his banking bill just before he submitted it to the Congress, and the congressman then gave it his full support. However, after the plan was submitted to the Congress and opposition began to grow, Calhoun decided to offer his own bank plan as an alternative. His objective was to unite both the supporters and opponents of the Dallas plan.[6] The Calhoun plan called for the creation of a national bank with a capital base of $50 million, one-tenth of which was to be paid in specie and the remainder in new treasury notes. This was done to satisfy Eppes and his followers. To satisfy the Calhoun supporters, the bank would have to pay in specie at all times, and would not be required to make loans to the government. To gain the support of the Federalists, the government was prohibited from participating in the direction of the bank, and there was to be no provision that subscriptions be made only in stock that was issued during the war.[7]

The supporters of the Dallas bank plan were shocked when Calhoun presented his own plan. Astor told business associates that it would "ruin the country," and he wrote Calhoun that his plan would not attract the necessary subscribers to put the plan into operation.[8] On November 27, 1814, Dallas wrote to William J. Lowndes, a member of a select congressional banking committee which was considering the Calhoun plan. Actually, it was Lowndes who solicited Dallas's opinion on having the capital of the bank composed of treasury notes. Dallas told Lowndes that the Calhoun banking plan was dangerous and impracticable, and he ridiculed the idea that a bank that was privately controlled would be able to circulate treasury notes effectively. He also contended that it was unfair to the present creditors of the government to place them in an equal or inferior position with the new creditors, if the bank became a private institution. The secretary of the treasury made it very clear to Lowndes that any bank created had to help the government, whose finances were already in an alarming state. The government would have $5,526,000 due in treasury notes on January 1, 1815, and had only $3,772,000 on hand to meet the debt. Simply put, the Calhoun plan would be unable to restore the nation's credit and provide the necessary liquidity for the business community. Dallas's description of the finances of the government sobered the Congress. The Lowndes select committee returned the Calhoun bill to the House, stating that no compromise could be reached. When the speaker made a motion to read the bill for a third time, it was defeated by a vote of 104 to forty-nine.[9]

On December 2nd, less than a week after Dallas wrote to Lowndes, Senator King reported a national banking bill favorable to Dallas, and a week later the Senate passed the bill by a vote of seventeen to fourteen. It was interesting to note that no amendments were allowed and that the Federalist opposition proved ineffective.[10] However, the bill ran into trouble again when it reached the House in late December 1814. Here the principal opposition was led by Daniel Webster of New Hampshire, the undisputed leader of the Federalist minority and perhaps the greatest orator in the Congress. Webster was not opposed to a bank on constitutional grounds, but refused to vote for any legislation that helped the government wage the war. He said, in January 1815, that "to look to a Bank as a source capable not only of affording a circulating medium to the country but also of supplying the ways and means of carrying on the war—especially at a time when the country is without commerce—is to expect much more than ever will be obtained."[11]

Webster also opposed the bank because it threatened the financial institutions in his own district, primarily the state banks, and because the national bank would issue paper money, which Webster disliked. He was a firm believer in the sanctity of hard money. He said that the Dallas banking bill would create "a system of rank speculation, and enormous mischief, one that would found a bank on the insolvency of the government and create a paper department of government.[12]

The Dallas bill was finally put to a vote on January 2, 1815, with Lowndes voting for and Calhoun and Webster against. The vote was eighty-one in favor of the bill and eighty against it. Speaker of the House Langdon Cheves, who had not voted yet, stated that "the bill proposed a dangerous, unexampled, and, he might almost say, a desperate resort;" he finally cast his vote against the bill, causing its defeat.[13]

Several days after the Dallas bill was defeated, Webster proposed his own banking bill which was modified by Calhoun and Lowndes. It called for a bank with capitalization of $30 million, composed of one-sixth in specie, one-third in war stock, and one-half in treasury notes. The bank was to be privately controlled, but it allowed the government to subscribe an additional $5 million. The bill prohibited the bank from suspending specie payment, and from lending any of its capital to the government, both of which made the Calhoun and Webster supporters happy.[14] The measure passed the House on January 7, 1815, by a vote of 128 to thirty-eight. Two weeks later, it was accepted by the Senate.[15]

Dallas opposed the new national banking bill primarily because it did not help the government in financing the war. The new bank would be a commercial bank that would go into operation after the war.[16] The secretary of the treasury urged Madison to veto the banking bill and the president did so. In his veto message on January 30th, Madison echoed Dallas when he stated that the Calhoun-Webster-Lowndes bank bill would give the government and nation little help. He asserted that the bill would do nothing to help the public credit nor would it provide an elastic money supply, "furnish loans, or anticipations of the public revenue . . . during the war."[17]

Several days after Madison's veto, leaders of the Democratic-Republican party met with the president to hear his suggestions for a banking bill. Calhoun and his supporters were also invited to attend. However, the South Carolina congressman refused to go along with what was decided at the meeting. Calhoun felt that the compromise bill was too close to the Dallas plan, and he would not support it.[18] On February 6, 1815, Senator James Barbour of Virginia introduced the new banking bill, and five days later, on February 11th, the Senate voted eighteen to sixteen to accept it.[19]

Two days after the Senate vote, the bill was sent to the House, but before a vote could be taken, news of the signing of the peace treaty at Ghent had reached Washington. The treaty had been signed in December 1814, but it took about six weeks for the news to travel in those days. In any event, some congressmen, including Calhoun, wanted a vote taken in the House, but Lowndes, who still wanted a national bank, declared that chartering one at this time would delay the resumption of specie payments by the state banks; other congressmen saw no need for a national bank now that the war was over. On February 17th, the House, by a vote of seventy-four to seventy-three, postponed the Barbour bank bill indefinitely.[20]

With the end of the war, the different perceptions between Calhoun and Dallas on the nature of the bank became irrelevant, as it was no longer necessary to have a national bank to secure loans for the government. However, peace failed to make the need for a bank any less important. Though there was a general improvement in the national economic situation, outside the New England area state banks continued to refuse to make payments in specie. If the state banks had done otherwise, a Second Bank of the United States might not have come into existence.[21] Another problem facing Dallas was the lack of a national circulating medium. The secretary of the treasury had made three attempts to provide the country with a circulating medium through a voluntary association of banks, but it failed as he was unable to convince enough of them to join.[22]

In December 1815, Dallas stated in his annual report that a national bank was crucial for the economic welfare of the country. He contended that it was the best way for the government to recover its control over the currency and place it on a uniform national basis.[23] On December 5th, Madison gave his endorsement to a national bank in his annual message to the Congress. He said, "If the operation of the State banks cannot produce this result [the establishment of a medium of exchange], the probable operation of a National Bank will merit consideration."[24] Though Madison gave his support of a national bank to resolve the money problem, it was lukewarm backing, for he still believed that the government's financial problems could be corrected with the issuance of treasury notes.[25]

The push for a national bank would have ended if not for the alliance of Dallas and Calhoun. The South Carolina congressman was gratified that Dallas was now supporting a bank as a means to expedite the resumption of specie, rather than a way of securing loans for the government.[26] When Congress convened, Speaker of the House Henry Clay of Kentucky appointed Calhoun to the chairmanship of a special committee to consider the feasibility of a national currency. Calhoun asked Dallas for the treasury's opinions on the matter, and on December 24, 1815, the secretary of the treasury gave the congressman his bank plan. The plan was very similar to the First Bank of the United States, which made it difficult for the Federalists, supporters of the First Bank, to oppose it.[27] The plan called for a twenty-year charter, with capitalization of $35 million which could later be increased to $50 million. The government would subscribe one-fifth of the stock and the public the remainder. Subscriptions would be paid one-fourth in specie and three-fourths in government stock and treasury notes. The bank would have twenty-five directors, five appointed by the government and the remainder by the shareholders. The bank's president was to be appointed by the president of the United States. The bank would not be obligated to lend money to the government, and it was prohibited from suspending specie payments unless authorized by the Congress.[28]

Both Calhoun and Dallas equally contributed to the above bank plan. Dallas favored government involvement in the financing and direction of the bank, and Calhoun demanded that the bank pay in specie at all times.[29]

On January 8, 1816, Calhoun officially reported a bill to create a national bank, and on February 28th, he opened the discussion in the Congress. He argued that resumption was necessary for the financial stability of the country, but it was impossible to obtain without a national bank. He said that a national bank "paying specie in itself would have a tendency to make specie payments general, as well by its influence as by its example. . . . The restoration of specie payments would remove the embarrassments on the industry of the country, and the stains from its public and private faith."[30] He declared that the economy could not be entrusted with the state banks, because those banks found it profitable to have unsettled conditions. He said, "Those who believe that the present state of things would ever cure itself must believe what is impossible; banks must change their nature, before they will aid in doing what it is not their interest to do."[31]

Opposition to the banking bill mounted as the bill was vigorously debated in March 1816. Congressman Webster and Senator King led the Federalists against the bill, and they were joined by Democratic-Republican John Randolph of Virginia. The Federalists concentrated on two issues: the size of the capital (they wanted it reduced to $20 million) and the closeness of the government with the bank.[32] Randolph, on the other hand, protested the provision that would make it possible to suspend specie payments with permission of the Congress. Many of his supporters, Virginia strict constructionists, also feared the new bank would exert a restraining influence on many local banks in their states, and that it would become a powerful force working against the interests of the country. They also opposed giving the president of the United States the right to appoint the president of the bank.[33]

Calhoun, now the bank's champion, responded to the bank's critics. He asserted that it was necessary to have a capital "large enough to prevent undue profit, yet small enough to prevent a loss to the stockholders" and a capital of $35 million met those conditions. He also defended the bank's close connection to the government because the bank had to be closely associated with the country's finances, keep public deposits, transfer public funds, and pay pensions.[34]

In February 1816, the Dallas-Calhoun bill was modified to make it more palatable to some of its critics. For example, the bank had to pay in specie at all times, taking away the power of the Congress to suspend specie payments. The bank's president was now chosen by the shareholders and not the president of the United States. The bank's capital would not be reduced below $35 million, but it was not permitted to rise to $50 million as was written in the original bill. Finally, treasury notes would not be accepted in payment for bank stock.[35]

On March 14, 1816, the House passed the Dallas-Calhoun national bank bill by a vote of eighty to seventy-one, and on April 3rd, the Senate gave its approval by a wider margin of twenty-two to twelve. One week later, on April 10th, Madison signed the bill that created the Second Bank of the United States.[36]

Just as in 1791, when the Congress passed the bill creating the First Bank, the vote on the Second Bank was divided geographically. In 1791, the Federalists were in power: The North supported the bank and the South was against it. In 1816, the Republicans were now in power, and it was the South and West that voted to reestablish the bank, and the North that opposed it. Clay had joined forces with Calhoun to push for the bank, and Webster and the Federalists voted against it.[37] In looking at the vote by states in the House, the New England states, New York, New Jersey, Pennsylvania, and Delaware voted forty-five to thirty-five against the bank, and the nine southern and western states voted forty-five to twenty-six for it. In the Senate, more than half of the twenty-two votes for the bank came from the South and West.[38] If we combine the votes of both houses, New England and the four middle states gave forty-four votes for the bank and fifty-three against it; the southern and western states gave fifty-eight for it and thirty against. Virginia was the only southern state delegation to give more votes against the bank than for it, and that vote was eleven against and ten in favor.[39]

It was ironic that the party of Thomas Jefferson should have reestablished the bank that Hamilton had created. There was no doubt that changes had occurred within the Democratic-Republican party during the war years. The interests of agrarian strict-constructionists of the South became less significant than the commercial, nationalistically minded Democratic-Republicans of the northern and middle states.[40] Years later, when Calhoun reflected upon his career, he told the Senate that "the bank owes as much to me as to any other individual in the country; and I might even add that, had it not been for my efforts, it would not have been chartered."[41]

The charter of the Second Bank of the United States would not have been passed in Congress if the state banks had not received assurances that there would be no sudden resumption of specie payment forced on them. The Second Bank was gentle with the state banks at the beginning of its operation. The treasury promised to withdraw their public balances slowly from the state banks, and the Second Bank would come to the aid of any state bank which found itself in difficulty. The date of transfer of government funds from the state banks to the Second Bank was July 1, 1817. The banks along the Atlantic Coast would transfer their funds at this time, but the banks in the interior of the country were given until August 1st, though they had to pay the Second Bank interest from July to August.[42]

THE ORGANIZATION OF THE SECOND BANK

The First and Second Banks of the United States had similar charters. The old Bank was capitalized at $10 million and the new one at $35 million. The old shares had a par of $400 and the new a par of only $100. Hopefully, the lower par for the Second Bank's stock would encourage wider ownership. In the old Bank, the government had owned temporarily $2 million, or one-fifth of the stock, and in the new Bank it still owned one-fifth or $7 million in stock. However, in the Second Bank, the government received an additional $1.5 million payable in three installments during the first few years of operation. Both banks had charters that ran for twenty years, with their head offices in Philadelphia, and both had the right to create branches as the directors saw fit. Like the old Bank, the new one was the principal depository of the United States Treasury and subject to government inspection. The liabilities, in the charters of both banks, were restricted to the amount of capital held, and the ratio of specie capital to the gross capital was the same one-fifth. Both banks had twenty-five directors, but in the Second Bank, five of the directors were to be appointed by the president of the United States, with the approval of the Senate.[43]

The subscriptions to the capital stock began on the first Monday of July 1816 and lasted for three weeks. To make it easy on the population, as travel was difficult in those days, with few good roads, the bank took orders for subscriptions in twenty different cities. Every state was represented among the thirty-one thousand persons who put down their names. However, at the end of the subscription period, $3 million in unsold securities remained, and that was purchased by Stephen Girard, one of the five government directors appointed by the president.[44]

The charter of the Second Bank called upon subscribers of the stock to pay one-fourth in specie and three-fourths in specie or government securities. At the time, a premium of eight percent existed on specie, which meant that it took $108 worth of Bank credit to get $100 in coin. Therefore, the subscribers of the Bank's capital had to pay on one-fourth of their subscription $108 for each $100 subscribed. At the same time, the credit of the government improved, which caused its stock to sell at a premium, and this made it difficult for the shareholder who now had trouble paying for his subscriptions. The result was that the Second Bank had to come to the rescue of its subscribers by accepting their promissory notes as payment, which was backed by the Bank's own stock valued at a premium of twenty-five percent.[45] Legally the Second Bank was prohibited from doing this, and it was compelled to lend its own notes which were accepted as specie. This was based on the principle that the notes of any bank that redeemed its obligations in specie were the equivalent of specie. It was very similar to Hamilton's principle in 1790 that the notes of any specie-paying banks were the same as specie. However, Hamilton's rationalization for this was to allow debtors to make payments to the government. The situation in 1816 was entirely different—it avoided having to place silver and gold in the Second Bank's vaults. As it turned out, the Second Bank received neither the specie nor the government stock it was owed, for if the stock could be paid for using specie notes as specie, it was much simpler to use them to pay the entire subscription rather than the scarce specie or government stock.[46]

What the Second Bank did was to put itself at a disadvantage before it began to operate. The shareholders were supposed to provide $7 million in coin and $21 million in government securities; however, after resorting to the above scheme, the Bank received $2 million in specie, $14 million in government securities, and $12 million in personal notes. To acquire the $7 million in specie to legally operate, it sent John Sergeant, a Philadelphia attorney, to Europe in December 1816 to negotiate for the necessary specie.[47] Shortly after his arrival, Sergeant received a contract with Baring Brothers and Reid, Irving, and Company for $3,195,000 in silver to be paid for within twenty months. From the summer of 1817 to the end of 1818, the Second Bank imported $7,300,000, $675,000 of which was gold from Lisbon and London, and the rest was silver from France and Jamaica.[48] It should be noted that the requirement that the capital be paid in specie did not mean that the Bank had to retain it, and at no one time did the Second Bank have $7 million in specie in one place.[49]

Officially, the main office in Philadelphia opened in January 1817. The First Bank's charter left branch creation to the discretion of the directors; the charter of the Second Bank included their establishment.[50] By the end of 1817, the Second Bank had established eighteen branches. From 1826 to 1830, an additional seven branches were created, as two were discontinued. The maximum number of branches at any one time was twenty-five in 1830. The branch offices, including the main branch, were established as follows:

1.   1817   Philadelphia, Pennsylvania
2.   1817   Augusta, Georgia (discontinued in 1817)
3.   1817   Baltimore, Maryland
4.   1817   Boston, Massachusetts
5.   1817   Charleston, South Carolina
6.   1817   Chillicothe, Ohio (discontinued in 1825)
7.   1817   Cincinnati, Ohio (discontinued in 1820 and reestablished in 1825)
8.   1817   Fayetteville, North Carolina
9.   1817   Hartford, Connecticut (opened in Middletown but moved to Hartford in 1824)
10. 1817   Lexington, Kentucky
11. 1817   Louisville, Kentucky
12. 1817   New Orleans, Louisiana
13. 1817   New York City
14. 1817   Norfolk, Virginia
15. 1817   Pittsburgh, Pennsylvania
16. 1817   Portsmouth, New Hampshire
17. 1817   Providence, Rhode Island
18. 1817   Richmond, Virginia
19. 1817   Savannah, Georgia
20. 1817   Washington, DC
21. 1826   Mobile, Alabama
22. 1827   Nashville, Tennessee
23. 1828   Portland, Maine
24. 1829   Buffalo, New York
25. 1829   St. Louis, Missouri
26. 1830   Burlington, Vermont
27. 1830   Utica, New York
28. 1830   Natchez, Mississippi[51]

Many of these branches were hard to control and had no limit on what they could lend in the first two years of operation. In fact, it could be said that the branches behaved as whole institutions, making loans before the main office received information or made their feelings known. There was little question that they were poorly supervised from Philadelphia.[52]

The reason the Second Bank had such a poor start in its first two years had to do with its leadership. Madison wanted to make the national bank a Republican bank, and he named all five government directors from his own party. The shareholders, being less partisan, chose ten Federalists and ten Democratic-Republicans to serve as directors. The majority of these directors were committed to naming William Jones, former secretary of navy and treasury, as the bank's first president, and this decision was fully supported by Madison.[53] This proved to be a poor choice and would cost the bank dearly in its first two years.

Girard, a government director, a purchaser of $3 million of bank stock, and influential in the chartering of the bank, opposed the appointment of Jones. He blamed the majority of public directors for Jones's appointment, stating, in October 1816, that "intrigue and corruption had formed a ticket of twenty directors of the Bank of the United States who I am sorry to say appear to have been selected for the purpose of securing the presidency for Mr. Jones."[54] In January 1817, the day the bank opened for business, Girard declared, "If I live twelve months more I intend to use all my activity, means, and influence to change and replace the majority of directors with honest and independent men. . . ."[55]

Unfortunately, Girard failed to oust the corrupt directors and Jones, and refused to serve another term. Bank historian Bray Hammond contended that as powerful and prominent as Girard was (he was a promoter of the Second Bank, a large stockholder, wealthy, and a government director of the bank), he proved helpless against the new breed of businessmen that were now emerging. Girard belonged to the eighteenth century, and his conservatism was out of style with the new entrepreneurs of the nineteenth century who had "contempt for established codes and old-fashioned honesty."[56]

Girard knew what he was doing in trying to keep Jones from the bank presidency. Jones did not keep his ideas on a national bank a secret. Both he and James McCulloch, the cashier of the Baltimore office, were critical that the First Bank made so few loans. In February 1817, McCulloch gave Secretary of the Treasury William Crawford his impressions of the First Bank. He said, "Instead of extending its operations so as to embrace every real demand of commerce; instead of expanding its views as the country and its trade grew, it pursued a timid and faltering course."[57]

Jones demonstrated what kind of leader he would be when he described the First Bank's role to Crawford. He wrote Crawford in July 1817 that he was "not at all disposed to take the late Bank of the United States as an exemplar in practice; because I think its operations were circumscribed by a policy less enlarged, liberal, and useful than its powers and resources would have justified."[58] Jones believed that the Second Bank should be operated for the benefit of its shareholders, and that it should set an example by paying specie on demand for its notes. He also stated that the Second Bank would have to make concessions to the state banks to prevent ill feeling on their part. For example, he would indulge the state banks by expanding credit to them. Under his watch, the Second Bank would acquire the notes of the state banks on government account, agreeing not to demand specie from them, and then pay out its own notes which were redeemable in specie. This resulted in serious economic problems for both the national bank and the economy. The Second Bank suffered a serious specie shortage, and the state banks, given excessive freedom, were making too many loans, which led to the Panic of 1819. At no time during the first two years of its operation did the Second Bank's specie holdings reach $3 million. By April 1817, it held only $1.8 million in specie, and the following July, after payment on the third installment to its capital, its specie increased only to $2 million.[59]

THE SECOND BANK UNDER JONES

The directors in Philadelphia were Jones's associates in ignorance. They were either blind to the problems facing the bank or ignored them. For example, the capital for the branches was not fixed, and the officers at the branches were not forced to settle their accounts. The branches did not have to furnish funds by using bills of exchange nor transfer specie when they drew for funds by issuing banknotes or selling drafts. The officers and boards at the southern and western branches were either incompetent or disobedient, as they paid more attention to local interests and concerns than to the directors in Philadelphia.[60] These branches were as irresponsible as state banks, and continued to make numerous loans, as there was no fixed capital restraint on them. For example, the Cincinnati branch loaned over $1.8 million in June 1818; the branch in Lexington, Kentucky, loaned $1.6 million in the same month and $1.7 million in November 1818. It was interesting to note that the loans made at the Boston and New York branches were not much larger than the loans made in the much smaller western towns. To make matters worse, most of these loans made in the west were redeemed in the eastern offices where the majority of business took place. This caused specie to flow from east to west, and as a result, there was a severe specie shortage in the eastern branch offices.[61]

At the same time that the western and southern branches were making more loans, the Second Bank was permitting the state banks to lend more of their notes. The national bank should have returned the state banknotes for payment in specie which it dearly needed, but it lacked the courage to do so. The Second Bank was apparently fearful of irritating the many influential shareholders who sat on the boards of the state banks.[62]

The Second Bank found itself in a difficult situation when it confronted the state banks in 1818. The national bank had a shortage of specie, yet had to pay in specie for its notes. If it failed to pay the state banks a certain amount in specie, it had to pay a twelve percent penalty on that amount, but even worse, one of the reasons for creating the Second Bank was to show the state banks that the government's bank was a responsible specie-paying bank. To fail to do so was to lose the reason for its very existence.[63]

In July 1818, demand liabilities outstanding were over $22 million, and specie on hand stood at only $2.3 million. In October of the same year, the treasury needed $2 million in specie to pay off the government's obligations, resulting from the purchase of the Louisiana territory. Because the $2 million was all the specie in the Second Bank, the government had to import specie from London.[64]

The Panic of 1818 forced the directors in Philadelphia to recognize the crisis within the banking system. They began to reduce credit and curtail the import of specie which was already in short supply. However, in taking this action to restore confidence in the banking system, they ended up reducing the money supply, which made the economy worse. Unfortunately, the Second Bank allowed expansion from 1816 to 1818 when the economy was strong and now had to contract when it should have expanded.[65]

THE SECOND BANK AND SPECIE RESUMPTION

As early as March 1816, the government had been urging the state banks to resume payment in specie. On April 30, 1816, Webster, believing the banks had plenty of specie in their vaults, pushed a joint resolution through Congress, requiring that after February 20, 1817, all payment to the government should be made either in gold and silver "or in Treasury notes, or in the notes of the Bank of the United States, or in the notes of banks payable and paid on demand in specie."[66] On July 22nd, Treasury Secretary Dallas released a circular asking that the state banks, "beginning with October, should resume to the extent of paying specie for all their notes of a smaller denomination than $5." The state banks were willing to resume specie payments, but not until July 1, 1817.[67] Crawford succeeded Dallas as treasury secretary in October 1816, and on December 20th, he urged the state banks to meet the congressional resolution deadline of February 20th. Once again the state banks, which held over $11 million in public deposits, refused to meet the February 20th deadline, and Crawford contended that the government could not force the issue.[68]

Both the government and the Second Bank found itself in a delicate situation. Professor Ralph Catterall described this dilemma in the following manner: "The situation was extremely critical for both the government and the bank. Without the consent of the state banks the government could not possibly collect its revenues after February 20, because it could not evade the joint resolution; and yet that resolution would be of no effect in securing specie or specie-paying paper." The Second Bank was also in jeopardy of losing its own specie to the state banks if it redeemed its notes and they did not redeem theirs.[69]

On February 1, 1817, a month after the Second Bank opened for business, it asked the representatives of the associated banks of Philadelphia, New York, Baltimore, and Richmond to attend a convention to discuss specie resumption and to avoid a possible financial disaster that might occur after February 20th. An agreement was worked out where the state bank representatives agreed to recommend to their directors to resume specie payment by February 20 in return for the following considerations by the Second Bank:

1. The Second Bank allowed debtor banks credit for checks on other banks that were parties to the agreement. For example, a bank in New York, which owed the national bank for checks and notes received by the treasury and deposited in the Second Bank, could pay their debt by drawing on banks in Richmond or Philadelphia, places where the New York bank had funds.
2. The Second Bank would take responsibility for all government deposits held by the

state banks; however, the actual transfer of those funds, almost $9 million, would not take place until July 1, 1817, at which time the state banks would pay them with interest.

3. The Second Bank agreed to delay payment of other funds owed by the state banks until the national bank lent $2 million in New York, $2 million in Philadelphia, $1.5 million in Baltimore, and a mere $500,000 in Virginia, "assuming there was demand for credit to such amounts." This provision would allow funds for the local money markets to aid them in meeting their financial obligations. However, as Catterall points out, it put a strain on the Second Bank by forcing it to make large loans and preventing it from acquiring specie from the state banks, while giving those banks the right to draw specie from it.

4. The Second Bank and the state banks would mutually support each other in any emergency.[70]

The Second Bank proved successful in getting an agreement with the state banks to resume specie payments by February 20, 1817. Hammond gave most of the credit for the agreement to Secretary of the Treasury Crawford who supplied the brains. He worked with the Second Bank's president, Jones, but central banking policy at the time was more intelligently conducted in the treasury than in the national bank. Crawford was able to bring the right personnel of the Second Bank and the state banks together. He assured the Pennsylvania, Delaware, and Maryland banks in a letter dated January 28, 1817, that they could trust the new national bank. He said, "The deep interest which that institution must feel for the credit of the paper system and its intimate connexion with the government are considered sufficient guarantees for the intelligent and disinterested manner in which this operation will be effected, independent of the power of the Treasury Department to control its proceeding at any moment by changing the deposits to the state banks." Crawford then urged the national bank to be conciliatory toward the state banks. In a letter to Jones dated February 7, 1817, he said, "If the state banks can be brought, by a concession of this nature to move harmoniously with each other and with the Bank of the United States, the beneficial consequences resulting from it will be cheaply attained by such a concession."[71]

SPECULATION AND FRAUD IN THE SECOND BANK

At the time the Second Bank was founded, the country was in the midst of inflation and bank stock speculation. The best example of gambling in bank stocks were in the cities of Philadelphia and Baltimore. In Baltimore, 40,000 shares were bought in the names of 15,628 people, and in Philadelphia twice the amount was subscribed for 3,566 people. The majority of the shares were purchased by a few individuals who then put them in the names of others. This enabled a few people to increase the number of votes (no shareholder was allowed more than thirty votes) and control the bank. For example, in Baltimore, George

Williams, a director of the Second Bank, owned 1,172 shares, but registered them under 1,172 different names, as he acted as attorney for all. Williams had thirty-nine times the maximum number of votes the charter permitted to any one share-holder. It was interesting to note that about fifteen people in the Baltimore office held about seventy-five percent of the stock there. This permitted a few people in Baltimore and Philadelphia to control the affairs of the national bank, and to use their position to manipulate the price of the Second Bank's stock on the market.[72]

Many of these speculators were directors of the Second Bank, such as Williams, James Buchanan, and Dennis Smith of Baltimore. They could not have successfully manipulated the price of the stock without the help of the cashiers at the Philadelphia and Baltimore branches and the incompetency of Jones. Though Jones himself was not directly involved in the speculation, he lacked the courage to prevent it, and he simply ignored its existence. What made matters worse was that he accepted a gift of $18,000 in profits that resulted from stock speculation. Jones had also bought and sold 1,575 shares from October 1817 to August 1818 from prices ranging from $139 to $153 per share.[73]

Buchanan headed the branch in Baltimore and James McCulloch was the cashier. Together with Williams, they formed a company to manage the bank's stock. The major goal was to manipulate the stock's price in order to enrich them-selves. They received cooperation from the Philadelphia office where Williams and Buchanan were directors. In the first two years, both Buchanan and McCulloch had made extensive stock purchases. By March 1819, they held about forty-seven thousand shares with a market value of $6 million.[74]

These men crossed the thin line between greed and fraud when they found themselves with insufficient funds to purchase their stock. They then decided to borrow from the Second Bank which agreed to accept the bank stock at twenty-five percent above par as security for the loans. They used the borrowed money to purchase more stock, pledging the stock they already owned. According to Catterall, they borrowed about $1,957,700 from the Philadelphia office and an additional $1,629,436 from the Baltimore branch. However, as the bank historian points out, the loans in Baltimore lacked security. He said, "though the loans were presumably secured by stock, there were actually only 2,558 shares in the office to cover the entire debt. At an advance of twenty-five percent. these shares secured only $329,750 out of a total of over $1.6 million. The conspirators loaned themselves the remainder without giving any security whatever."[75]

Buchanan, Williams, and McCulloch were able to cover their scheme only because the latter, as cashier, was the keeper of the pledged stock, and the direc-tors didn't have a clue that there wasn't any stock submitted. The speculators could acquire any sum necessary, without security and without having to worry about being detected by the Board of Directors. If the Baltimore Board ever inquired as to what was going on, Buchanan and McCulloch would declare that they were engaged in executive business, and that they had authority from the main office in Philadelphia to make loans. Thus, the Baltimore directors paid little attention to what these men were doing.[76] It was interesting to note that all loans had to be entered on the books of the bank, and it was the directors' duty to examine these books, but they failed to do so. Catterall suggested that the directors failed to do their duty because they thought they lacked the authority to make inquiries into the loaning of stock.[77]

The conspirators were discovered during the Panic of 1818 when the central board in Philadelphia demanded lists of the stock loans at all the branches. McCulloch had promised to forward the information, but realized that to do so would unmask his scheme. In November, he wrote the board in Philadelphia that he was gathering the list, but it was taking time because he had to examine all the loans to make certain that they were on stock rather than bills on personal security. McCulloch was able to delay the discovery of his fraud, and to protect himself and his associates, by transferring the sum of $852,683 from loans on stocks to loans on personal security. This allowed McCulloch and Buchanan to send a list that revealed enough stock to secure a $645,400 loan, which was exactly the amount they owed.[78]

After Jones's resignation in January 1819, the board in Philadelphia discovered the fraud perpetrated by the Baltimore conspirators, after it began a major movement toward bank reform. On January 22, 1819, it prohibited loans or loan renewals on the security of stock without its approval. On February 19th, it demanded the board in Baltimore to reveal the exact amount of the loans made there on stock security. The following month, McCulloch and his associates admitted involvement, and that they were unable to pay their debts which amounted to $1,401,685.[79]

INVESTIGATION INTO THE SECOND BANK AND THE RESIGNATION OF JONES

In November 1818, John C. Spencer, a member of the House of Representatives from New York, introduced a resolution to investigate the Second Bank. A committee, chaired by Spencer, was charged to conduct the investigation and reported its findings on January 16, 1819. It criticized the managers of the national bank for mismanagement, speculation, and violations of the charter. The violations consisted of the following: buying $2 million of the public stock for the government; assisting the stockholders to evade the requirement of specie down payments for the second installment; paying dividends to the stockholders who had not paid up their subscriptions; and allowing the stockholders to cast more than thirty votes in the first and second elections for the directors.[80]

The congressional report failed to recommend any action because "the Secretary of the Treasury has full powers to apply a prompt and adequate remedy." Speculation was that the remedy was the removal of all government funds from the Second Bank.[81] However, some members of the House asked for a motion to repeal the Bank's charter, but it was rejected by large majorities. Instead, the House passed an act which declared that in the future, stockholders could not cast more votes than they were entitled.[82]

In January 1820, the Senate defeated resolutions to compel the Bank to obtain the approval of the states for the creation of branches and to reveal its accounts with private individuals.[83] There was little question that the Congress believed that the national bank was worth keeping if it was able to restore public confidence. Unfortunately, the corrupt administration of the Second Bank under Jones caused its reputation to decline rapidly, and it was never really able to recover. William Gouge, an antibank Jacksonian, wrote that "the Bank was saved and the people were ruined."[84]

Soon to be president of the United States, John Quincy Adams declared that government seemed the only party interested in saving the Bank in 1820, and in his opinion, the shareholders should abolish their charter. By January 1819, things could not have looked worse for the future of the Second Bank as its stock fell below par and Jones resigned the presidency only two weeks after his re-election. James C. Fisher became the acting president on January 25th until the appointment of Langdon Cheves who officially took over as the second president of the Second Bank in March 1819.[85]

NOTES

1. Raymond Walters, Jr., "The Origins of the Second Bank of the United States," *Journal of Political Economy* 53 (1945): 122-123.

2. Ibid., p. 123.

3. Ibid.; Bray Hammond, *Banks and Politics in America from the Revolution to the Civil War* (Princeton, NJ: Princeton University Press, 1985), p. 239.

4. Walters, "The Origins of the Second Bank of the United States," p. 124.

5. Ibid., p. 124.

6. Ibid., p. 125.

7. Ibid.

8. Ibid.

9. *Annals of Congress*, 13th Cong., 3d Sess., 1814-1815, pp. 652-654, 686.

10. Ibid., pp. 119-120, 123-127; Ralph C. H. Catterall, *The Second Bank of the United States* (Chicago: University of Chicago Press, 1902), p. 14.

11. Hammond, *Banks and Politics in America*, p. 238.

12. Walters, "The Origins of the Second Bank of the United States," p. 126.

13. *Annals of Congress*, 13th Cong., 3d Sess., 1814-1815, pp. 1025-1026; Catterall, *The Second Bank of the United States*, p. 15.

14. Walters, "The Origins of the Second Bank of the United States," p. 126.

15. *Annals of Congress*, 13th Cong., 3d Sess., 1814-1815, pp. 173-174, 975-991, 994-1032, 1039-1045; Catterall, *The Second Bank of the United States*, pp. 15-16; Walters, "The Origins of the Second Bank of the United States," p. 126.

16. Walters, "The Origins of the Second Bank of the United States," p. 126.

17. Ibid., p. 127; Catterall, *The Second Bank of the United States*, p. 16.

18. Catterall, *The Second Bank of the United States*, pp. 16-17.

19. *Annals of Congress*, 13th Cong., 3d Sess., 1814-1815, pp. 230-232.

20. Ibid., pp. 1149-1153, 1167-1168; Walters, "The Origins of the Second Bank of the United States," p. 127.

21. Catterall, *The Second Bank of the United States*, p. 17.

22. Walters, "The Origins of the Second Bank of the United States," p. 127.

23. Ibid., p. 128.

24. Catterall, *The Second Bank of the United States*, p. 17.

25. Walters, "The Origins of the Second Bank of the United States," p. 128.

26. Ibid.

27. Catterall, *The Second Bank of the United States*, p. 18.

28. Walters, "The Origins of the Second Bank of the United States," p. 128.

29. Ibid., p. 129.

30. *Annals of Congress*, 14th Cong., 1st Sess., 1815-186, pp. 1064-1065.

31. Catterall, *The Second Bank of the United States*, p. 18.

32. Ibid., pp. 18-19.

33. Ibid., p. 19; Walters, "The Origins of the Second Bank of the United States," p.129.

34. Catterall, *The Second Bank of the United States*, p. 19.

35. Walters, "The Origins of the Second Bank of the United States," p. 129.

36. For the March debates and the text of the bill, see *Annals of Congress*, 14th Cong., 1st Sess., 1815-1816, pp. 235-281, 494-514, 1060-1067, 1070-1089, 1091-1114, 1118-1122, 1136-1137, 1139-1149, 1151-1155, 1157, 1189-1195, 1200-1219, 1812-1825.

37. Walters, "The Origins of the Second Bank of the United States," p. 129.

38. Hammond, *Banks and Politics in America*, p. 240.

39. Ibid.

40. Walters, "The Origins of the Second Bank of the United States," p. 130.

41. Ibid.

42. Catterall, *The Second Bank of the United States*, p. 26.

43. Hammond, *Banks and Politics in America*, p. 244.

44. Catterall, *The Second Bank of the United States*, p. 22; Margaret G. Myers, *A Financial History of the United States* (New York: Columbia University Press, 1970), pp. 83-84.

45. Hammond, *Banks and Politics in America*, pp. 253-254.

46. Ibid., p. 254.

47. Ibid., p. 255.

48. Ibid.

49. Ibid.

50. Ibid., p. 256.

51. Ibid.

52. Ibid.

53. Catterall, *The Second Bank of the United States*, p. 22.

54. Hammond, *Banks and Politics in America*, p. 252.

55. Ibid.

56. Ibid., pp. 252-253.

57. Ibid., p. 253; Myers, *A Financial History of the United States*, p. 85.

58. Hammond, *Banks and Politics in America*, p. 253.

59. Richard H. Timberlake, *Monetary Policy in the United States: An Intellectual and Institutional History* (Chicago: University of Chicago Press, 1993), p. 23; Catterall, *The Second Bank of the United States*, p. 29.

60. Catterall, *The Second Bank of the United States*, p. 30.

61. Ibid., p. 34.

62. Ibid., pp. 35-36.

63. Ibid., pp. 37-38.

64. Hammond, *Banks and Politics in America*, p. 258.

65. Ibid.

66. Catterall, *The Second Bank of the United States*, p. 23.

67. Ibid.

68. Ibid., p. 24.

69. Ibid.; Hammond, *Banks and Politics in America*, p. 247.

70. Hammond, *Banks and Politics in America*, pp. 247-248; Catterall, *The Second Bank of the United States*, pp. 25-26.

71. Hammond, *Banks and Politics in America*, p. 249.

72. Catterall, *The Second Bank of the United States*, pp. 39-40; Hammond, *Banks and Politics in America*, p. 257.

73. Catterall, *The Second Bank of the United States*, pp. 40-41.

74. Ibid., pp. 43-44.

75. Ibid., p. 44.

76. Ibid., pp. 44-45.

77. Ibid., p. 46.

78. Ibid., p. 48.

79. Ibid., pp. 48-50.

80. Hammond, *Banks and Politics in America*, p. 258; Myers, *A Financial History of the United States*, p. 85.

81. Ibid., p. 259.

82. *Annals of Congress*, 15th Cong., 2nd Sess., 1819, p. 2522.

83. Ibid., 16th Cong., 1st Sess., 1820, pp. 58-68.

84. Hammond, *Banks and Politics in America*, p. 259.

85. Ibid., p. 259.

5

The Second Bank and the Panic of 1819

THE PANIC OF 1819

In 1819, 3 million people or one-third of the population were directly affected by the Panic of 1819. Samuel Hopkins, the president of the Genesee Agricultural Society, declared at its annual meeting in October 1820 that "my first wish would be to speak in a tone that should rouse the tenants of every log-house in these counties, and make them stand aghast at the prospect of families naked—children freezing in the winter's storm—and the fathers without coats or shoes to enable them to perform the necessary labours of the inclement season."[1]

The harshness of the depression affected both urban and rural areas. In Philadelphia, an investigating committee was formed in August 1819 to study the effects of the panic in thirty industries and found that employment had decreased in those industries from 9,672 in 1816 to 2,137 in 1819, a seventy-eight percent decline. Propertied classes also suffered as real estate values declined rapidly along with earnings capacity. In Baltimore, rents had fallen from forty to fifty percent, and a third of the property was held by the banks. In Richmond, real estate values declined by seventy-five percent and half of it was mortgaged to the banks.[2]

The Second Bank also experienced losses in capital due to the Panic. The Baltimore office lost about $1.6 million, and the branches located in Norfolk, Charleston, Washington, and Savannah also took heavy hits. The estimated capital loss in the South was $2,234,000.[3] Though the bank also suffered losses in western states such as Ohio and Kentucky, it proved less severe due to the western real estate which the bank took in liquidation of its debts in 1819. The Second Bank acquired this land when real estate values had plummeted to their lowest levels. But after the Panic, the land values would dramatically increase in the west mostly due to the growth in Cincinnati. It was interesting to note that the Second Bank would own a large part of that city, including hotels, warehouses, stores, and stables. In addition, the bank acquired approximately fifty thousand acres of good farm land in Ohio and Kentucky from debtors who failed to meet their obligations. Needless to say, this did not make the Second Bank many friends in the western states. Thirteen years later, in 1832, Senator Thomas Hart Benton of Missouri declared that "all the flourishing cities of the West are mortgaged to this money power. They may be devoured by it at any moment. They are in the jaws of the monster! A lump of butter in the mouth of a dog! One gulp, one swallow, and all is gone!"[4]

The causes of the Panic of 1819 were due to a sizable unfavorable balance of trade, and inflationary credit policies which led to land speculation, among other things. Before the War of 1812, the United States was mostly an agricultural producing country, exporting large amounts of cotton, wheat, and tobacco. Many cities were located near water, making transportation easy, and urban living made up only seven percent of the country's population. With the outbreak of war in 1812, foreign trade became nonexistent, and this led to the tremendous growth of domestic manufactures, the beginning of the cotton and woolen textiles industry. In 1807, only four textile factories were established, though seven years later, in 1814, forty-three were created. What stimulated the growth of the manufacturing industry was the idle capital held by merchants in foreign trade, who now invested it in textiles.[5]

When the war ended, Americans were anxious to purchase British textiles that they could not obtain during the conflict, and the British were only too willing to dump them on the American markets. Total imports rose from $5.3 million in 1811 to $113 million in 1815 and to $147 million in 1816. The increase in the supply of imported goods lowered their prices in the United States and stimulated American demand. For example, imported commodity prices at Philadelphia in 1816, in one month's time, declined from an index of 231 to 178 and by 1817, it fell to 125.[6] The surplus of imports put a serious strain on the new American textile industry that grew up during the war. This infant industry suffered great losses in the immediate postwar years and did not recover until 1823. The index of prices of industrial commodities in Philadelphia such as dyes, chemicals, metals, textiles, sugar, soap, and glass had increased from 141 to 214 during the war, but fell to 177 in March 1815 and continued to fall reaching 127 in March 1817.[7] Though exports expanded in the postwar years, the United States ran a trade deficit of $60 million in 1815 and $65 million in 1816. American merchants who had invested capital in the manufacturing enterprises began to demand protection, and Congress passed the Tariff Act of 1816, which for the first time gave American manufacturers relief against the lower costs and greater efficiency of European industry.[8]

As mentioned in the last chapter, there was no national bank during the war, and the government had to rely on note-issuing state banks that kept little specie as capital and, outside of New England, had suspended specie payment. Many of these banks had printed notes in denominations as low as six cents, which contributed to the vast note expansion. During the war, prices of domestic goods rose as a consequence of the rapid expansion of the money supply, and the prices of imported goods, which were scarce due to the British blockade, also increased. Domestic commodity prices increased by about twenty to thirty percent during the war years. Cotton, the most important export staple, doubled in price, and imported commodity prices rose by about seventy percent.[9]

When the Second Bank came into existence, there was approximately $68 million in state banknotes in circulation. One of the goals of the new national bank was to resolve the specie problem by redeeming its notes in specie and to get the state banks to resume specie payments, which they did by February 20, 1817. Unfortunately, branches of the Second Bank followed the example of the state banks and also made too many loans in paper currency, especially in the south and west. The boom continued into 1818 as the national bank expanded its notes rather than trying to slow down the economy. This expansion was due to the decision of the Second Bank and the treasury to allow the notes of the state banks to be treated as specie, and the national bank accumulated these notes, refusing to return them to the state banks for payment.[10]

The overextension of credit resulted in inflation and indebtedness caused by loans to farmers with no security except mortgages on real estate. Many of these loans that were spent on permanent improvements could not be repaid on demand. After all, borrowers never thought they would have to repay when the notes came due, as the custom was to renew the notes over and over again. The Committee of the Pennsylvania legislature issued the following report in 1820: "The plenty of money, as it was called, was so profuse, that the managers of the Banks were fearful that they could not find a demand for all they could fabricate, and it was no infrequent occurrence to hear solicitations urged to individuals to become borrowers, under promises of indulgences the most tempting."[11]

The state banks made large investments in real estate, turnpikes, and farm improvement projects, and the national government encouraged large-scale speculation, on easy credit terms, by opening up tracts of land in both the north-west and southwest to land speculators. Public land sales of $4 million per year in 1816, fueled by excessive bank credit, had risen to $13.6 million in 1818.[12]

The Second Bank was incapable of stopping the current bank inflation in 1817 and 1818, and to make matters worse, speculation in its own stock only fueled the inflation. Finally, in August 1818, the Second Bank, realizing the dangers of note expansion, decided to change course and implement a policy of note contraction. This precipitated the Panic of 1819 as branches of the national bank now called on the state banks to redeem heavy balances and notes held by the Second Bank.[13] The requirement that each branch redeem the notes of every other branch was rescinded, ending the liability of the more conservative eastern branches of the Second Bank to redeem the paper of the expansionist western and southern branches. This put pressure on specie, causing suspension of payment by banks in many areas. The contraction, which began under Jones and was continued by Cheves, remained in force until gold and silver became a greater proportion of the money supply. For example, in 1818 and 1819, the specie reserve of the Second Bank was $2.5 million, and as loans were recalled it rose to $3.4 million in January 1820 and to $8 million in the spring of 1821. At the same time, total demand liabilities of the Second Bank declined from $22 million in the fall of 1818 to $12 million in January 1819 and to $10 million in January 1820.[14]

The contraction of the money supply placed numerous state banks in debt to the Second Bank. For example, the state banks in South Carolina had to recall their loans to make payments to the national bank. In 1819, they owed the Second Bank approximately $500,000, and when the national bank tried to collect $130,000 from the banks in Charleston, they threatened to get their state legislature to pass laws that would prevent the national bank from collecting.[15] In North Carolina, conditions were similar. There the state banks offered to make payments in the notes of other banks or in the notes of other offices of the Second Bank. When the Second Bank refused the offer and demanded specie payment, the state banks declared the new national bank was destroying the people and the economic foundation of the state by drawing away specie from North Carolina.[16]

The monetary contraction lasted through 1820 and led to a plethora of bankruptcies throughout the country. The value of banknotes in circulation was $68 million in 1816, and this was reduced to $45 million in January 1820.[17] This led to a rapid drop in prices including real estate, rents, and export staples such as cotton and tobacco. In August 1818, the Index of Export Staples was 169 and that dropped to 77 in June 1819. As American income dropped rapidly, the demand for imports fell to all-time lows. Total imports dropped from $122 million in 1818 to $74.5 million in 1820. The drastic reduction in imports ended the specie drain.[18]

The rapid decline in the money supply and credit contraction caused public land sales to fall from $13.6 million in 1818 to $1.3 million in 1821. As cash became scarce, interest rates rose rapidly as investment spending dropped. Farmers saw their incomes fall and their debts to the banks rise. Land speculators who made money during the boom were now confronted with heavy debt burdens. As prices continued to decline, merchants in large cities and small towns went bankrupt. William Greene, secretary to Governor Ethan Allen Brown of Ohio, described the situation of the debtors in the west in April 1820 in a memo to his boss. He wrote, "One thing seems to be universally conceded, that the greater part of our mercantile citizens are in a state of bankruptcy—that those of them who have the largest possessions of real and personal estate . . . find it almost impossible to raise sufficient funds to supply themselves with the necessities of life—that the citizens of every class are uniformly delinquent in discharging even the most trifling of debts."[19]

Though Panic of 1819 slowly came to an end in 1821, many state banks and businesses blamed the Second Bank's contractionary policy for their ruination. State legislatures began to impose taxes and other barriers against the national bank in 1817. The state of Maryland laid a tax of $15,000 per year on the Second Bank's office in Baltimore in February 1818. In November of the same year, Tennessee imposed a tax of $50,000 on any bank that was not chartered by the state legislature. The first constitution of Illinois created in August 1818 only permitted state banks to exist. In January 1819, the Kentucky legislature imposed the largest tax of all—a $60,000 tax annually on each of the branches of the Second Bank. If the Supreme Court did not intervene, the Second Bank would have been taxed out of existence.[20]

THE SECOND BANK AND THE
SUPREME COURT

Though there were a number of cases involving the Supreme Court and the national bank, *McCulloch vs. Maryland* established the legal precedent that protected the bank against state taxation. In February 1818, the Maryland Assembly passed a law that imposed a tax of $15,000 a year on all banks or branches in the state of Maryland that were not chartered by the state legislature. The state believed that they had every right to tax, corporations, businesses, and individuals within their jurisdiction. In fact, the Supreme Court case, the *Bank of the United States vs. Deveaux*, in 1809 supported the state's position (see chapter 2). However, the Maryland branch refused to pay just like the First Bank's branch in Georgia did in the *Deveaux* case. The state of Maryland then sued the Baltimore branch in the name of McCulloch, its cashier. This was only several months before McCulloch's speculation in his bank's stock was noted. The Second Bank lost in the state courts, and the case was appealed to the Supreme Court of the United States.[21]

As mentioned above, the case was crucial to the survival of the Second Bank. Other states, such as Tennessee, Georgia, North Carolina, Kentucky, and Ohio, were also taxing the branches of the Second Bank. To make matters worse, the Bank was suing to protect its legal status at a time when both its reputation and financial condition were questionable. Jones had resigned from the Bank's presidency and Cheves had not yet taken over.[22]

The lawyers on both sides had excellent reputations. Luther Martin, the attorney general of the state of Maryland, acted as the state's chief counsel, and the lawyers for the Second Bank were William Wirt, the attorney general of the United States, William Pinkney, and Daniel Webster. Before the hearings began on February 22, 1819, Chief Justice John Marshall of Virginia had sold seventeen shares of the Second Bank's stock, and never purchased any again. The case before the court lasted nine days with Pinkney doing the majority of speaking for the Bank.[23]

Pinkney's defense of the Second Bank was based on Hamilton's justification of the Bank in a letter to President Washington in 1791 (see chapter 2). Pinkney declared that the federal government had to possess certain powers to govern effectively. He said, "it is being asked, once again, whether a government invested with such immense powers has authority to erect a corporation within the sphere of its general objects and in order to accomplish some of these objects."[24] Pinkney portrayed the state of Maryland's tax on the Bank as a destructive force. He declared, "There is a manifest repugnancy between the power of Maryland to tax, and the power of Congress to preserve, this institution. A power to build up what another may pull down at pleasure is a power which may provoke a smile but can do nothing else."[25]

The court's unanimous decision was delivered by Marshall on March 7, 1819, the day after Cheves took office as the Second Bank's president. It was interesting to note that this decision went beyond the issue of the bank, as it enhanced the power of the national government over the states. Again, Marshall, like Pinkney, depended a great deal on Hamilton's defense of the constitutionality of the Bank in 1791. The chief justice began be denying the state of Maryland's tax imposed on the Baltimore branch. He said,

If we apply the principle for which the state of Maryland contends to the constitution, generally, we shall find it capable of changing totally the character of that instrument. We shall find it capable of arresting all measures of the government, and of prostrating it at the foot of the states. The American people have declared their constitution and the laws made in pursuance thereof to be supreme; but this principle would transfer the supremacy, in fact, to the states. If the states may tax one instrument, employed by the government in the execution of its powers, they may tax any and every other instrument. They may tax the mail; they may tax the mint; they may tax patent-rights; they may tax the papers of the customs-house; they may tax judicial process; they may tax all the means employed by the government, to an excess which would defeat all the ends of the government. This was not intended by the American people. They did not design to make their government dependent on the states. . . . We are unanimously of opinion that the law passed by the legislature of Maryland imposing a tax on the Bank of the United States, is unconstitutional and void.[26]

This decision made the supporters of the national government and the Second Bank very happy, and it angered the proponents of states rights who believed the court would rule in their favor based on the *Deveaux* case in 1809. But the court made it clear in *McCulloch vs. Maryland* that the issue was based on constitutional grounds and not on jurisdiction, as was the earlier example. It was not a question of what the Bank did or how it was done, but a question of the Bank's legality to operate. The decision was also important because it did question state sovereignty, and declared that national law superseded state law whenever the two conflicted.[27]

The *McCulloch* case was important because it established the precedent that determined the case *Osborn vs. Bank of the United States* and put an end to all state taxation on branches of the Second Bank. In February 1819 the Ohio legislature placed a $50,000 tax on each branch of the bank in the state—one in Chillicothe and one in Cincinnati. When the decision in the *McCulloch* case became known, Ohio officials delayed the collection of the taxes until pressure was put on them by the public and the state legislature. The state auditor Ralph Osborn took action in September 1819 by entering the Chillicothe office of the Second Bank and taking possession of its vault. The Bank's officials were outraged and obtained an order from the Federal Circuit Court requiring the state treasurer to return the money. When he refused, he was incarcerated and federal officers took the keys of the state treasurer and reacquired the bank's money. The government of Ohio appealed to the Supreme Court, contending that federal intrusion within the state, the taking of the keys, and the arrest of the state treasurer violated the sovereignty of the state. In fact, the Ohio assembly voted to "recognize and approve" the Virginia and Kentucky Resolutions of 1798 and 1799, which were written mostly as a response to Hamilton's contention that the Bank of the United States was constitutional in 1791. In 1824, the Supreme Court again reaffirmed *McCulloch* by upholding the sovereignty of the national government over the state of Ohio. The enemies of the Second Bank would now have to fight it in the legislature because the judiciary offered it no redress.[28]

THE PRESIDENCY OF LANGDON CHEVES

When Langdon Cheves, former speaker of the House, from South Carolina, became president of the Second Bank in March 1819, he found it in a poor financial state and on the verge of suspending specie payment. The specie drain from the eastern offices had burdened the bank, and it sent officers abroad to find specie in Europe, all to no avail. In the meantime, the government stock held by the Bank had been sold, and it appeared that the Bank was only days away from closing its doors. The usually optimistic treasury secretary, William Crawford firmly believed the Second Bank was doomed. He said, "The stoppage of specie payments by the bank and by the state institutions is inevitable."[29]

It would have been easy for Cheves to allow the bank to falter and blame its failure on the policies of his predecessor. However, Cheves would have none of that. He remained decisive and firm in resolve in attacking the central problem. He blamed the bank's predicament on the policies of the southern and western branches. He immediately ordered these offices to suspend issuing their notes, "while the bank itself ceased to purchase and collect exchange on the south and west."[30] However, he was determined to collect the balances due from the state banks, and he was able to secure a loan in Europe which was payable in three years. While this was done, the Second Bank was given time by the government to transfer public funds "from the places where they were collected to the places where they were to be disbursed."[31] Cheves's hard work saved the national bank in the short run as suspension was avoided, currency improved, and the Bank's capital was localized. He accomplished this task within seventy days of taking over the Second Bank. He breathed new life into the Bank, provided it with a state of safety, a degree of power, and restored its reputation and capital. Though he incurred the wrath of some of the shareholders, he refused to pay out dividends until the original capital was replaced.[32]

During the four years under Cheves, the Second Bank had contracted the money supply. The new president's thinking was that the Bank should be small and decentralized, and that each branch should be independent and responsible in specie for its own notes. Cheves refused to allow the Second Bank to become a central bank—a regulator of the money supply, much like the Federal Reserve system of today. With the resumption of specie payments, Cheves had reaffirmed the importance of the specie standard, and it was that standard that regulated the money supply and not the Second Bank.[33]

One of the most important things Cheves did was the assignment of capital to the various branches. He recognized that the southern and western branches of the Second Bank had caused a drain of specie from the northern and eastern offices. To remedy the situation, he transferred funds from the southern and western branches to the northern and eastern branches. When this was done, the branches in the south and west had to pay for everything in specie, and when they could not, they lost considerable business. However, this corrected the uneven distribution capital which had occurred during the Jones presidency.[34]

Cheves also succeeded in holding the state banks to accountability. He demanded that these banks reduce their bank debts, settle all future balances at specified intervals, and forced the state banks to pay specie upon the presentation of their notes.[35] A good example of Cheves's commitment to sound banking took place in Kentucky and Ohio where he took mortgage and collateral security, and accepted real estate on terms easy to the debtors. For example, by August 30, 1822, he acquired, in both the above states, $950,000 from a debt due, when Cheves became the new bank president, of over $6 million.[36]

Cheves implemented internal reforms at the Second Bank, not all of which were popular. He reduced the salaries and expenses of the employees, and fired incompetent officers, including those who committed fraud. McCulloch was forced out of the Baltimore branch and Buchanan resigned (see chapter 4). Lawsuits were started against them for conspiracy to defraud the bank. Though the lower court acquitted the defendants, the Court of Appeals called for a new trial. However, on retrial in 1823, the defendants were acquitted for a second time.[37]

Though Cheves worked to implement reforms, he was more a politician than a banker. He had erred in allowing the branch offices to overdraw their accounts, and in making loans on the security of the Second Bank's stock. He exercised little control over the branches. He had problems with the state banks, as their currencies fluctuated widely. For example, in April 1819, bank paper at New York ranged from par for New England notes to seventy-five percent discount for other state banknotes.[38] At Baltimore, in August 1819, New England notes were depreciated from one percent to six percent and the notes of New York from par to eight percent. To make matters worse, all the banks in North Carolina suspended specie payments on May 31, 1819, and the banks in South Carolina refused to pay in specie until 1823.[39]

The Second Bank was determined to make the state banks redeem their notes in specie and decided to make its stand in the state of Georgia. The banks of Savannah, the Planters Bank, and the State Bank of Georgia had a habit of not paying their debts owed the Second Bank in specie. When Jones was the president, these obligations were ignored. However, when Cheves took over, he insisted that all debts owed the national bank be paid in specie. This would prove a considerable hardship for the Savannah banks, as they would have to reduce their business.[40] The directors of the Second Bank and Cheves, the consummate politician, not wanting to irritate the state banks in Savannah and the Georgia state legislature, proposed a compromise solution. They allowed the banks in Savannah a permanent credit of $100,000, held in the Second Bank's Savannah branch in state banknotes. In other words, the national bank did not return $100,000 of state banknotes to the Savannah banks for payment in specie. To sweeten the agreement, the Second Bank made it an interest-free credit. However, the Savannah banks were responsible for payment of debts beyond the $100,000 in specie. In 1820, the total indebtedness of the Savannah banks was over $500,000, and they paid no interest. Though the Savannah banks refused the deal in January 1821, they agreed to a compromise where the Georgia banks would pay their debts in weekly rather than daily installments at six percent on the balance due it in excess of $100,000.[41]

The compromise lasted only until June 1821 because the Georgia banks were unable to make enough loans to satisfy the appetite of their customers. When Cheves declared that the Planters Bank and the State Bank of Georgia had suspended specie payments, the legislature of the state of Georgia, in December 1821, prevented the Second Bank from recovering specie in the state. It said that the state banknotes held by the Second Bank "shall not be redeemable in specie."[42] The directors of the Second Bank refused to back down, fearful that it would set a bad example in the other states. They quickly brought a lawsuit against the Georgia banks to force them to pay all their obligations in specie. The case, *Bank of the United States vs. Planters Bank*, was resolved in 1824 in favor of the national bank.[43]

In July 1822, Cheves informed the stockholders that he would resign by the end of the year. He said, "It was my desire to have done so very soon after I entered upon the duties of the office."[44] Cheves knew that a number of stockholders were unhappy with his performance as president, especially when he suspended dividends and then reduced them to reinvigorate the bank. He was a smart enough politician to know when to leave.

In October 1822, Albert Gallatin, former treasury secretary and a favorite of the stockholders, turned down the job to succeed Cheves. Late in November, delegates, representing the stockholders in several seaboard states, convened a meeting to select a candidate and finally settled on Nicholas Biddle. On January 6, 1823, he was officially elected the third and last president of the Second Bank of the United States.[45]

NOTES

1. Samuel Rezneck, "The Depression of 1819-1822, A Social History," *American Historical Review* 39 (October 1933): 30.

2. Ibid., pp. 31-32.

3. Ralph C. H. Catterall, *The Second Bank of the United States* (Chicago: University of Chicago Press, 1902), pp. 66-67.

4. Bray Hammond, *Banks and Politics in America from the Revolution to the Civil War* (Princeton, NJ: Princeton University Press, 1985), p. 259.

5. Murray N. Rothbard, *The Panic of 1819: Reactions and Policies* (New York: Columbia University Press, 1962), pp. 1-2.

6. Ibid., pp. 4-5.

7. Ibid., p. 5.

8. Ibid., p. 6.

9. Ibid., p. 4.

10. Ibid., pp. 7-8.

11. Rezneck, "The Depression of 1819-1822," p. 28.

12. Rothbard, *The Panic of 1819*, p. 9.

13. Ibid., pp. 11-12.

14. Ibid., p. 12; Richard H. Timberlake, *Monetary Policy in the United States: An Intellectual and Institutional History* (Chicago: University of Chicago Press, 1993), p. 25.

15. Catterall, *The Second Bank of the United States*, p. 63.

16. Ibid., p. 64.

17. Rothbard, *The Panic of 1819*, p. 13.

18. Ibid.

19. Ibid., pp. 14-15.

20. Catterall, *The Second Bank of the United States*, pp. 64-65.

21. Hammond, *Banks and Politics in America*, p. 263.

22. Ibid., p. 264.

23. Ibid.

24. Ibid., p. 265.

25. Ibid.

26. Stanley I. Kutler, ed., *The Supreme Court and the Constitution: Readings in American Constitutional History* (New York: W. W. Norton and Company, 1977), pp. 59-60.

27. Hammond, *Banks and Politics in America*, p. 266.

28. Ibid., pp. 266-268.

29. Catterall, *The Second Bank of the United States*, pp. 68-70.

30. Ibid., p. 70.

31. Ibid., p. 71.

32. Ibid., pp. 71-72.

33. Timberlake, *Monetary Policy in the United States*, p. 29.

34. Catterall, *The Second Bank of the United States*, p. 73.

35. Ibid., p. 77.

36. Ibid., p. 78.

37. Ibid., pp. 78-79.

38. Ibid., pp. 82-83.

39. Ibid., p. 83.
40. Ibid., p. 84.
41. Hammond, *Banks and Politics in America*, pp. 272-273.
42. Catterall, *The Second Bank of the United States*, pp. 85-88.
43. Ibid., p. 89.
44. Hammond, *Banks and Politics in America*, pp. 276-277.
45. Ibid., p. 277.

6

Nicholas Biddle and the Second Bank

THE ELECTION OF NICHOLAS BIDDLE

Nicholas Biddle was not the overwhelming choice to succeed Langdon Cheves as president of the Second Bank. In fact, Cheves did not want him as his successor, as he preferred Thomas Ellicott of Baltimore. However, Ellicott, a Quaker, remained unpopular with the shareholders and had little chance of succeeding Cheves. John White, a cashier at the Baltimore branch, was a favorite of many shareholders, but he was considered too young and unknown. Albert Gallatin did not want the job, and the old reliable Thomas Willing, the president of the First Bank, had died in October 1822.[1]

When R. L. Colt, a close friend and shareholder, asked Biddle whom he thought the next Bank's president would be, Biddle refused to name a person, but instead listed the qualifications necessary to be a successful president. He declared that it was not enough for a good president to be a gentleman, but he must have a talent for business, be able to work with the government, and be a resident of Philadelphia. He was very careful to distinguish between having a talent for business and being a businessman. Just being a businessman does not make an individual an effective administrator, and many problems of the western branches were caused by men of business. He said, "The fact is that the misfortunes of the Bank which grew principally out of the injudicious extension of the Western Branches were actually occasioned by the men of business & their errors were precisely the faults into which the men of business were most likely to fall."[2] He also elaborated on what he meant by being able to work with the government. This did not mean that the Bank president had to be a good politician who was involved in the party system but, more importantly, a man who could work with the public sector. He made it clear that the government should not have a direct or indirect influence over the Bank but, because the government was a stockholding customer of the Bank, cooperation was necessary. He said, "It would be not unwise to consult to a certain extent the feelings of the government where the great interests of the Bank may depend so much on its countenance & protection."[3] As to being a resident of Philadelphia, Biddle declared that though it was not essential, it was desirable. He feared that a nonresident president would have a hard time getting the cooperation of the board of directors. He said, "Now I fear that a stranger would not easily obtain the aid of such a Board as ought to be collected. If yet such is the importance of that circumstance that I am not sure whether the wisest plan would not be first to make a list of 20 Directors & and best names of the City & then see under which President 15 or 16 of them would consent to serve—and name him accordingly."[4]

It so happened that the qualities that Biddle wanted in the next Bank president were those that he himself possessed. In fact, Colt replied that he would welcome Biddle's candidacy. He said, "I could secure you a strong support from this quarter and particularly so as I am sure we could have in your favor all the influence of government. . . . I do not ask you to run, but I do ask you not to make up your mind positively against it."[5] Biddle's response to Colt made him an active candidate for the Bank presidency. He said, "I should neither seek nor shun, that I would engage in no intrigue and mingle in no parties but if a respectable majority of the stockholders wished me to be placed at the head of the institution, I would serve if elected."[6]

Biddle would eventually be elected thanks to Cheves, but not before some maneuvering by Colt and some of Biddle's supporters on the board of directors. As early as November 1822, Cheves backed William Meredith, the president of a Philadelphia bank, for the next presidency of the Second Bank. However, Meredith did not have enough support to get elected, and Cheves was concerned that his longtime foe Elihu Chauncey of Philadelphia would succeed him. Under no circumstances did Cheves want Chauncey to be his successor. However, Cheves did not think highly of Biddle, whom he blamed for hastening his own departure. If Biddle, as a member of the board of directors, had supported Cheves, then he might have attempted to continue on as Bank president. Though their relationship remained strained, and they did not publicly speak of their differences during or after Biddle's presidency, Cheves, in November 1822, decided to back Biddle, especially after both President Monroe and Treasury Secretary William Crawford highly recommended Biddle for the job.[7]

BIDDLE—THE INTELLECTUAL BANKER

Biddle, who was born on January 8, 1786, came from an old and distinguished Philadelphia family. His father, Charles Biddle, was a wealthy merchant who served in the American Revolution. At the age of thirteen, he finished his course of study at the University of Pennsylvania, but failed to receive his degree due to his youth. He attended Princeton College, where he studied law and graduated at the top of his class. Though he was admitted to the bar, he did not practice law. Instead, he gave his time to literature and language, becoming a contributor to Joseph Dennie's *Port Folio*, a prestigious magazine published in Philadelphia.[8] In 1804, at the age of eighteen, he traveled abroad to become secretary to John Armstrong, the American minister to France. Two years later, he became secretary to James Monroe, the American minister in London. This appointment turned out to be advantageous to Biddle, as Monroe held him in high regard and would support him in his future banking career. In 1807, Biddle returned to Philadelphia to become editor of the *Port Folio* and Lewis and Clarke's *Journal*.[9]

In 1810, Biddle entered politics as a Democratic-Republican and was elected to the lower house of the Pennsylvania legislature. At the same time his father was elected as a Federalist to the state senate. In 1814, Biddle himself became a member of the state senate, holding his seat until 1817 when he left to manage his estate, which he inherited through marriage to the daughter of John Craig, one of Philadelphia's wealthiest men.[10]

In January 1819, President Monroe nominated Biddle as one of the five government directors of the Second Bank. He wrote the president that even though he had little experience in banking matters, he was eagerly willing to accept the position. He said, "The Bank is of vital importance to the finances of the government and an object of great interest to the community." He admitted that the Bank had been corrupted under Jones and hoped to play an important role in its revitalization. Exactly four years later at the age of thirty-seven, he became the third president of the Second Bank of the United States.[11]

Though Biddle had no administrative experience, never learned to share re-sponsibilities with others, was an idealist, who was strong-willed and impatient with stupidity, and had a bad temper, he still possessed many virtues for the job at hand. He was charming, intelligent, influential, sincere, and, above all, he had faith in reason and truth. Even his political enemies liked him personally. For example, Martin Van Buren, an ardent opponent of the Second Bank, knew Biddle well. He said that although Biddle's "official conduct as president of the Bank has been and always will continue to be with me the subject of unqualified condemna-tion . . . his private and personal character has never to my knowledge been successfully impeached."[12]

However, John Jacob Astor, the New York financier, and an ardent supporter of the Second Bank, held a different view of Biddle. In his opinion, the Bank's new president did not have the personality for the job. He asked how someone who loved "elegant literature and general politics" could be tough enough to run the country's national bank profitably. Astor saw Biddle as too much of a statesman and not enough of a businessman, who would fail to make the Bank a profitable organization for its shareholders.[13]

Though Biddle had little banking experience, he loved and studied the subject of political economy. During the four years that he was on the board of directors of the Second Bank, he became an avid reader of the classical economists such as Adam Smith, David Ricardo, and Robert Malthus. After reading their theories on the economy, he rejected their deterministic doctrines. To Biddle, it made little sense that economic activity was governed by natural laws that one should not interfere with. During and after the War of 1812, Biddle saw firsthand how the expansion and contraction of the money supply affected business activity. He became an ardent proponent of the tariff to protect infant industry in the United States, and he favored Henry Clay's program of internal improvements, calling for more roads and canals.[14]

BIDDLE'S CENTRAL BANK

The Bank that Biddle had taken over in January 1823 was located in Philadelphia on Chestnut Street, where it remained until 1824. That year a new structure was built in white marble, patterned after the Greek Parthenon, on the south side of Chestnut between fourth and fifth streets, just east of Independence Hall.[15]

The beautiful and imposing building was only matched by the excellent financial condition of the Bank that Biddle inherited. Thirteen million dollars of the Bank's funds were safely invested in government loans, and more than $3.5 million of the Bank's stock was held in its treasury. These securities could be sold in the United States or Europe, allowing the Second Bank to increase its liquidity by more than $16 million if it ever needed cash.[16]

Biddle, more than any of the other Bank presidents, believed that the Second Bank should be both a national and central bank. As a national bank, it would continue to act as an agent of the treasury, hold government deposits, and pay the national debt. As a central bank, Biddle believed it should restore the currency by issuing its own notes, and receive from the population the notes of other banks.[17] He wanted the Second Bank to control the specie held at individual branches, limiting their autonomy, and centralizing the nation's specie reserve, especially that part used in the making of international payments.[18]

Biddle's view of the central bank activities of the national bank was noted as early as 1819, during a banking investigation by Representative John C. Spencer of New York. Biddle responded to Spencer on January 27, 1819, only days before Monroe appointed him a government director. He said,

I think that experience has demonstrated the vital importance of such an institution to the fiscal concerns of this country and that the government, which is so jealous of the exclusive privilege of stamping its eagles on a few dollars, should be much more tenacious of its rights over the more universal currency, and never again abandon its finances to the mercy of four or five hundred banks, independent, irresponsible, and precarious.[19]

Shortly after Biddle became president, he made a decision to increase the money supply of the Second Bank, a policy that his predecessor Cheves had opposed. The former Bank president believed that any increase in the notes of the Bank would only make the situation more difficult for it. He felt that because the notes were legally receivable in payments to the government, they could be returned to the Second Bank for redemption in specie. Cheves was concerned that the national bank would be put in an embarrassing situation if it did not have enough specie to meet its payments. As far as he was concerned, an increase in the Bank's circulation was simply an enlargement of the Bank's indebtedness.[20]

However, Biddle refused to accept the simplistic reasoning of Cheves, and asserted that the debts of a bank are not the same as the obligations of ordinary debtors, because they play a monetary role. He claimed that they were not necessarily paid by conversion into specie. For example, if people received banknotes in payment of goods sold, they used them to purchase other goods. Biddle saw the notes used primarily as a medium of exchange, and contended that they would be converted into specie only if their value fell. Biddle had hoped that the Second Bank, by increasing its circulation, would become the sole bank of issue and that this would eventually lead to a national currency.[21]

Biddle's concentration on making the Second Bank a central bank proved successful. It regulated the money supply, restrained the expansion of bank credit, supervised the exchanges, protected the investment market, and continued to serve the Treasury Department. However, many of the Bank's shareholders remained unhappy with Biddle's priorities. They felt that he should pay more attention to the Bank's prosperity and dividend policy. As early as May 1825, Biddle had defended himself against the shareholders in a letter to Robert Lenox, a conservative merchant, confidential advisor, and good friend from New York. He said,

The truth is simply this. The Bank is doing very well. During my connection of six years with it, I have never seen its affairs in so satisfactory a state, as at the present moment. It will have certainly have earned during the last six months more than three percent. But then I am clearly of opinion that we should never advance our rate of dividend, till we are perfectly satisfied that we will never have occasion to diminish it. In Jany. 1823, we began without one dollar in our pockets—and we have been trying ever since to accumulate a fund in reserve, so as to equalize our dividends. You may be very sure of two things: in the first place that no determination with regard to the next Dividend has been generally formed, & in the second place that whatever that Dividend may be the succeeding dividend will be at least as much.[22]

Nonetheless, the shareholders were unhappy with Biddle's position on the dividends of the Bank stock. Dividends were at six percent from 1826 to 1828 and then at seven percent but never any higher. In June 1828, a stockholder in Baltimore complained of Biddle's penchant for central banking at the expense of his profits, and in a letter to the Second Bank president, he said,

You are doubtless aware of the opposition to your administration of the affairs of the Bank over which you preside, which has recently manifested itself in your City, New York and elsewhere. The Stockholders are under the impression that your object is to keep in check the State Banks, and to regulate the Currency of the Country *at their cost*. This they say may not be inconvenient to you, while you receive the salary of President of the Bank, but it does not suit them. The most effectual method for you to put down the Opposition, is to give a dividend equal to what is usually given by the State banks in your City and elsewhere.[23]

BIDDLE'S BANKING POLICIES

Shortly after Biddle became president of the Second Bank, Lenox suggested that he appoint confidential advisors to the various branches; the advisors were expected to keep him informed of all the affairs in the offices. Biddle liked the idea so much that he asked Lenox if he would be his confidential advisor in New York. This spy system worked to perfection, as Biddle was always able to know what was going on at every branch of the Second Bank.[24]

In the first years of Biddle's presidency he acted in a conservative fashion, demonstrating restraint when it came to the expansion of the branches in the unprofitable western and southern regions. He saw the cities, especially New York, as areas where the Bank could make money. In a letter to Lenox, he wrote,

The view which I have of the true policy of the Bank is this. We have had enough & more than enough of banking in the interior. We have been crippled & almost destroyed by it. It is time to concenter our business—to bank where there is some use & profit in it, and therefore (while anxious to do business in the interior the moment there is clear prospect of doing it usefully & and safely) to make at present the large commercial Cities the principal scene of our operations. With this impression my object is to give to the Office at New York the command of the business of N. York—to make it the first banking institution there. To this it is entitled from its Capital its resources, and the character of its Direction.[25]

Though Biddle wanted to make the New York branch the center of his system, he worried that it catered too much to the state banks by issuing their notes, and that this would weaken the branch's operations. He said, "It never can have the power which it ought to possess, if it suffers itself to be crowded out of its proper sphere by the State Banks & to be constantly preyed upon by them." He demanded that the New York branch cease issuing state banknotes and only use its own currency.[26] At the same time, he ordered the New York branch to reduce the balances of the city banks, and forced them to settle their obligations in specie at least once a week and sometimes daily.[27] The representatives of the Second Bank and the state bank officials often met to interchange notes received the preceding day. Biddle described the process in his own words:

The balances are struck accordingly. But no bank ever calculates on its balances remaining for any length of time and whenever it grows a little too large, no bank ever hesitates to send for ten or fifteen or twenty thousand dollars from its debtor. . . . Thus it goes around no one complains and everyone is satisfied. In truth, it is only when these balances accumulate and remain for any time that they become oppressive to both parties and excite mutual ill will.[28]

This process kept the state banks under constant restraint. As soon as the state banks issued too many notes, they were forced to settle with the Second Bank, which often meant that they would have reduce their lending activity. Biddle's policy changed the relationship of the national bank to the state banks. During the Cheves presidency, a great deal of hostility existed between the Second Bank and the state banks. Under Biddle, they worked together to provide credit for a growing economy, as local banks provided community needs, and the Second Bank supplied "the means for the internal exchanges of the products of the labor of citizens" throughout the country.[29]

Biddle was successful in increasing the total note circulation of the Second Bank during his term in office. When he took over in January 1823, note circulation was a mere $4.4 million, which increased to $6.7 million in June 1825 and to $9.6 million a year later.[30] Since 1822, the Bank's resources had risen by $21 million, and past losses of the Bank had been turned into profit. For the year ending on July 1, 1828, its profits were more than $800,000 greater than in the years 1821-1822 and almost one million more than the average for the three years preceding July 1, 1822. Private deposits had increased between $2 million and $3 million by September 1825, and the discounts on notes and domestic bills had risen by the same amount; the European debt of $1.3 million had been paid.[31]

Biddle wanted to increase the Second Bank's notes while reducing the issues of the state banks. As noted above, he began this policy at the New York branch and eventually put it into effect at the Philadelphia, Richmond, Savannah, and Charleston offices. The purpose of this policy was to provide the country with sound currency, and it could only be accomplished by forcing the state banks to redeem their notes in specie on demand. This could only be done by making the Second Bank a creditor institution.[32]

Biddle had differed from Cheves in the type of loans the Second Bank should make. Cheves had favored loans on the security of stock, but these loans tended to become long term or permanent and tied up the funds of the Bank. When this happened, it prevented the Bank from regulating the money supply.[33] Biddle demanded that all loans by the national bank should be short term and on good commercial paper. He refused to make loans longer than sixty to ninety days, and maybe for a special customer 120 days. However, when a branch president sought permission from Biddle to extend the time of a loan for a special customer because he was certain that it would profit the Bank, Biddle refused to sanction it. He said, "Let us not by hope of doing better or getting more business risk the prosperity and safety of the institution."[34] On April 22, 1825, during an economic crisis, Biddle wrote to Isaac Lawrence, the president of the New York branch, and told him to keep his loans within reasonable limits to protect the Second Bank and keep it strong. Biddle warned Lawrence that he always had to be prepared for a demand for specie on the Bank. He said, "Since the 18th of March when I wrote to you on the subject of your ability to do business paper falling due on or about the 1st of July, your discounts have increased $700,000, a fair addition to your business which would be attended with no inconvenience did not an extraordinary demand for Specie which has arisen render the extension more hazardous by exposing you to calls for Specie against which every consideration of prudence requires you to guard." He went on to tell Lawrence that as difficult and painful it was to decline good business, he should not make any more loans.[35]

Biddle had refused to make any loans on stock or real estate, claiming that these assets were not good enough security for the Bank. In regard to real estate, he said that "it is entirely inconsistent with its design and its safety that a bank should lend its funds on the security of real estate, should lend on permanent accommodation to the parties not in business."[36] He showed he was a man of conviction by denying a long-term loan to a senator from Louisiana in 1826, and refusing another long-term loan on real estate to an old and intimate friend in 1827.[37] Biddle had also declined to create special committees to make a certain class of loans when he was asked to do so by some of the directors, and he refused to keep directors who were "large or habitual borrowers."[38]

Another difference between Cheves and Biddle was their policies toward the branch offices. Cheves had restricted branch business, especially in the regions of the west and south. Biddle, on the other hand, believed that the branch offices should be able to increase their business, providing that they were more strictly controlled. He accomplished this by demanding some say over the choice of the branch presidents. For example, when there was an election of a new branch president, the central board in Philadelphia, controlled by Biddle, would choose someone by placing his name at the head of the list of directors and would forward it to the branch office. Though the directors of the branch had the primary responsible to choose its president, it would seldom ignore the advice of the central board.[39]

In 1825, Biddle further strengthened the central boards' control of the branches by declaring that those directors of the central board who lived in cities with branches could sit at the local boards. Though they could not vote, they had the right discuss all matters pertaining to the local board policy.[40]

Biddle also changed the way cashiers were chosen at the Second Bank branches. He believed that the cashier of any branch should show loyalty to the central board. He said, "My own theory of the administration of the Bank and my uniform practice, is to consider the Cashier of an Office, as a confidential officer of this Board, to rely on him and to hold him responsible for the execution of their orders." As far as Biddle was concerned, the cashier had to obey, first and above all, the orders from Philadelphia, even if it meant going against his local board.[41] The Second Bank president was able to acquire more competent cashiers by choosing them from among those trained at the Philadelphia branch. Most of these cashiers learned how the Bank operated by doing training in Philadelphia, and they proved less prone to bribery and making loans to friends and relatives, because they were placed in localities where they did not have personal ties. The cashiers, and all those who worked for them, were also forbidden to borrow from the branches where they worked.[42]

Biddle worried about having enough cash on hand to meet the Bank's obligations. As soon as he took over the national bank, he put forward a plan to accumulate a surplus. Keep in mind that Cheves had concentrated only on restoring the Bank's capital and was unconcerned about running a surplus. In January 1823, Biddle's first month in office, the Bank did not have "a dollar of reserved profits." The new president worked hard to amass a surplus that would strengthen the Bank's financial position. By July 1825, the surplus exceeded $550,000, and it continued to increase dramatically until at the expiration of the charter in 1836, it was more than $6 million.[43]

In 1825-1826, Biddle's fear of not having enough cash on hand to meet the obligations of the Bank almost became a reality when the government was scheduled to pay or refinance two loans that were made during the War of 1812 and also a payment to Spain.[44] Biddle was ready for the worst scenario—the loss of money that would interfere with the functioning of the Bank and would deprive farmers and businessmen of bank credit. Biddle's nightmare was the possibility that the Bank would have to pay an excessive amount of money on a specific day, and that would force it to accumulate the necessary funds. To accomplish this, Biddle would have to make less loans and stop its purchases of foreign exchange. The Bank would then lose its control to regulate the money supply, which could lead to an economic panic.[45] Biddle, not wanting to put the Bank in this precarious position, developed a plan of action. Just prior to the first payment, which was due January 1, 1825, he asked the fund holders to refrain from waiting for the last moment to find an object of investment and instead to make a bank loan on the security of their government stock in advance of the payment day. This would avert the rush to invest if they all waited until the last moment. Fortunately for the Bank, enough of the government's creditors took advantage of this offer, and payments were made over a period of four months instead of all on a specific day.[46]

Biddle had another reason for wanting to keep additional cash on hand to protect the integrity of the Bank. In the latter half of 1824, the Second Bank had increased its loans, which in turn increased the number of its banknotes in circulation. This situation caused the branches of the national bank to become a debtor of the state banks in their respective area at settlement time. If additional cash had not been found, the national bank would have had to either pay out its precious specie or reduce its normal loans and purchases of exchange.[47] Biddle showed his acumen in administration by anticipating this problem. He requested the treasury secretary to recommend to the Congress that in making the two loans necessary to raise the funds for paying the debt, it should allow the Bank to participate in the bidding. After Congress had agreed, both loans of $10 million were sold to the national bank, which was now added to the $16 million of government loans, given to him by Cheves, and together, with the foreign exchange, helped the Second Bank to meet all its financial obligations, without having to increase its debt to the state banks.[48]

Though the Bank was successfully maintaining its liquidity, it was being attacked in the House of Representatives. On December 13, 1827, P. P. Barbour, of Virginia, introduced a resolution in the House of Representatives calling for the sale of all Second Bank stock owned by the government. Barbour, a major opponent of the Bank, was hoping that this would "lead to permanent distrust in the stability of the institution." Though the price of the stock temporarily fell, it recovered quickly when the resolution was decisively defeated by a vote of 174 to nine.[49] Representative John Sargeant, Biddle's friend from Pennsylvania, wrote to the Bank president that, in his opinion, this was the beginning of a political attack on the Bank. He said that though the resolution would not succeed, "it will do some mischief, and, if considered as the beginning of an attack, lead to permanent distrust in the stability of the institution which will somewhat enfeeble it. The motion will have the effect, too, of putting the Bank among the topics to be handled by those who are seeking popularity. I am sorry for it."[50]

One of Biddle's friends, Joseph Gales, Jr., coeditor of the *National Intelligencer*, wrote him that the defeat of the Barbour resolution was a portent that the Bank's charter would be renewed in the future, but he feared that its stock would rise too rapidly. He said,

I consider this vote as definitively settling, in advance of its agitation, the question of the renewal of the charter, as well as the subordinate question to which it [is] more immediately related. All my fear, now is that the Stock will again, as once it has before, mount too rapidly, a consequence of the late decision which I trust, if it appears probable, the Mother Bank will occasionally check by throwing into market portions of the Stock which it holds itself or can control.[51]

Biddle experienced another banking crisis in the winter of 1827-1828. The government experienced a large increase in the imports of manufactured goods while exports declined significantly. The United States now became a debtor to Europe, having little money to meet its payments.[52] Biddle tried to come to the rescue of the government by expanding the note issue of the Bank, knowing that it was inappropriate at the time. Manufacturers in Great Britain and France were taking advantage of the United States by flooding its market with imports, while the cotton, tobacco, and rice exports, which were needed to raise the income to pay for the imports, were not being provided by the farmers, who, discouraged by low prices, were hoarding their crops. The consequences brought about a rapid rise in the exchange rates, and Biddle worried that this would initiate the export of specie, which, in turn, would cause a severe drop in loans. The end result would be a lower money supply in the United States, falling prices, and the onset of a severe recession, which would lead to bankruptcies and bank failures.[53]

Biddle tried to prevent this disaster by telling the eastern offices to make no more loans to the merchants and brokers who were involved in the export of specie. He also sold government stock in the New York market to reduce the money held by the stockholders, who would then have less money to buy imported goods. He used the money from the stock sales to replenish the Bank's specie.[54] It is interesting to note that Biddle's Bank was acting very similar to today's Federal Reserve when he sold government stock to shareholders to reduce their money holdings to slow down the economy. Today, the Federal Reserve Board of Governors uses open market operations to slow the economy down. They sell bonds to the banks to reduce their money supply so they will make fewer loans. Here, Biddle was acting as a central banker, trying to reduce the money supply;

however, he failed, as the importation of foreign goods continued, southern crops remained in the warehouses, exchange rates stayed high, and specie exports were greater then ever.[55]

Biddle refused to give up hope that he could turn things around. He demanded that the Second Bank's branches hold loans at their existing levels to permit the accumulation of government deposits and to bring the state banks into their debt. Whenever demands were made for specie, the branches turned to their debtor banks by presenting notes for redemption.[56] This policy was put into effect in March 1828, and several months later in May, the state banks began to significantly reduce their loans. Disaster was prevented as only a few merchants went bankrupt, imports slowed considerably, and specie remained in the United States.[57]

In slowing the money supply, Biddle did not want to control the domestic industry or foreign trade of the United States. He was simply making the money supply elastic by expanding and contracting it, so that it would conform to the changes in business and economic activity to safeguard the economy. Though trade activity eventually corrected itself, as prices changed from country to country, the Second Bank facilitated the process by causing financial readjustments. In the interest of time, as merchants often acted on credit, the Bank proved useful. For example, if a merchant were called upon to pay the whole portion of his debts, he would have defaulted, had not Biddle provided the time for individuals to make their own adjustments.[58]

In November 1828, Biddle's contributions to the economy were recognized by Richard Rush, secretary of the treasury. He commended the Second Bank for stabilizing the currency of the country and abolishing the debt during the last four years. Rush asked Biddle if he could add additional information on the Bank's role in the economy to put in his annual report.[59] Biddle responded within a week, detailing how the Bank played an important role in the collection of funds in and around the country and transferring them to points where the public debt was payable, without charging the government. Biddle wanted Rush to put in his report that in Great Britain the government payed more than $1 million for the management of the debt by the Bank of England.[60]

As Biddle used the Second Bank to restrict the growth of credit and money, certain speculators, whose profits were threatened, disliked his policies. Alexander Brown of Alexander Brown and Sons in Baltimore had profited from the wide fluctuations in the exchange rates whereas the Bank had attempted to keep the rates lower and more uniform.[61] Here we have a conflict between the desire to make a profit by a private entrepreneur and Biddle's Second Bank which wanted to do what was best for the economy. Brown did not understand why Biddle opposed his policies, because they did not directly harm the Bank. However, Biddle's position was that the export of silver caused a drain to the country's specie reserves, which threatened the welfare of the national economy. He had ordered the branches to deny loans to the Browns as long as they continued to ship coin abroad. What eventually happened was that the Browns and other exporters of specie halted their operations and, as exchange rates fell, it was no longer profitable to export silver.[62]

The Second Bank, under Biddle, played a major role in the foreign exchange market. It was able to protect the national economy from problems that began abroad. Whenever there was a negative balance of trade, the rates on the British and European exchange markets would rise. It was now cheaper to ship coin to Europe than to purchase bills. When this occurred, American citizens, owing debts in Europe, would withdraw their silver from the banks, causing a reduction in the money supply and limiting the amount of business banks could conduct.[63] It was the Second Bank's role to maintain a stable money supply to keep prices, income, and employment from fluctuating. The Bank accomplished this by becoming the largest purchaser and seller of foreign exchange in the country, and could draw on Baring Brothers in London and other Continental bankers for help. In periods when European exchange was in short supply in the United States, when imports exceeded exports, the Bank intervened to prevent the rate from remaining long beyond the point when large shipments of specie were needed. If it proved impossible to prevent the shipments of specie abroad, the Bank worked to slow down its outflow to make deflation as painless as possible.[64]

By 1825, Biddle had made the Second Bank a creditor of the state banks. In New York, the center of speculation, Biddle had substituted paper for specie and had instructed the New York branch to increase its short-term loans.[65] His working relationship with both the James Monroe and John Quincy Adams administrations was excellent, as both presidents valued the services of the national bank. In fact, in 1827, the Bank was given a government loan at par, notwithstanding the fact that the private banks offered a premium for it. Treasury gave its preference to Biddle primarily because the government owned twenty percent of the Bank's capital, and stood to gain on any profit the Bank would make.[66]

By 1828, the Second Bank had proven its value as a central bank, and had become a profitable and well-managed institution under Biddle. He had begun a policy of contraction in 1828, which lasted from February 12th to May 1st. By doing so, he was able to prevent inflation, which would have resulted from too many loans being made by the state banks.[67] Biddle's overall policy in management from the years 1823 to 1828 proved successful. In looking at the January 1st figures of the Second Bank in 1823 and 1828, progress was evident. Total investments rose from $41.75 million to $51.3 million; circulation of the money supply more than doubled from $4.4 million to $9.8 million; deposits of individuals rose from $3.4 million to $6 million; and specie holdings increased from $4.4 million to just over $6 million.[68] By July 1828, the annual income of the Bank jumped by $823,312 over its income in 1822, the amount representing profits on $21 million. This increase had been secured under Biddle's watch and was due to the sale of the Bank's stock, profitable loans, and the buying and selling of foreign exchange.[69] The Second Bank felt so secure about its financial situation in 1828 that it informed the government that it was making good on the loss of $20,000 of pension funds that had been recently embezzled in Albany, and that in paying the pensions, it was providing the services of its many branches, without charge to the government.[70]

It was interesting to note that the Second Bank made extensive profits in the foreign exchange market beginning in 1826. Before that year, it was not an important part of the Bank's earnings, but as a result of the increasing cotton trade in the south, the Bank became a large buyer of foreign bills in that region, which they sold in the north, making enormous profits. In the first six months of 1826, the profits from foreign exchange operations were $60,000. By 1827, the national bank had a monopoly in the foreign exchange market, and in the process of driving out its competitors, it created future enemies.[71]

Due to the shortage of banknotes, Biddle implemented what became known as branch drafts. The charter of the Bank declared that all banknotes had to be signed by the president and countersigned by the branch cashiers. Unfortunately, it was impossible to sign enough small notes to supply the branches with the needed currency to carry out their daily transactions. Biddle had asked the Congress to remedy this situation by allowing other officers of the Bank to become signers. However, due to politics, the Congress refused to amend the Bank charter for this purpose. Thus, Biddle created the branch drafts as a remedy to the shortage of banknotes. The Second Bank president did this only after he consulted with Henry Clay on the legality of the drafts. Clay assured him that because the issue of checks upon the Bank by its branches was ordinary banking operations, he saw no problem with the drafts.[72]

Biddle authorized the issue by his branches of five and ten dollar drafts signed by the branch presidents and cashiers, "drawn on the principal cashier at Philadelphia and payable to some officer of the branch, or his order." When the officer endorsed the drafts "payable to the bearer," he turned them into a circulating medium.[73] All the drafts, similar in appearance to banknotes (legally they were checks or bills of exchange, and the five dollar drafts were redeemed at all the branches) were prepared in blank at the main office in Philadelphia and then sent to the various branches. The first issue came out in June 1827 in five and ten dollar denominations, and in 1831, twenty dollar drafts were printed. Though the branch drafts were accepted by the government for payment of taxes, they were criticized in the Congress, and in 1832, when that body renewed the Bank's charter, they inserted a clause that prohibited their use after 1836.[74]

THE CONSEQUENCES OF BIDDLE'S SYSTEM

It was necessary for Biddle, in 1828, to demonstrate to the public how indispensable the Second Bank had become to the national economy. Already the Bank was a central bank, regulating state bank loans, ending depreciated state bank currencies, issuing more of its own notes and branch drafts, and controlling the business of the country. Certainly this would prove that it deserved to be rechartered when the time came to do so.[75]

When Biddle took over the Bank in 1823, he was determined to reduce banking operations in the southern and western regions of the country, due to the risky financial position of the Bank in those areas.[76] However, as the years passed, Biddle had changed his mind and decided to expand the Bank's operations in the south and west. He realized that the regular payment of the public debt had caused the termination of the Bank's holdings of the public stock, and now it had to find other areas to invest its money. By the summer of 1831, the government was ready to liquidate its stock note for $7 million—a note that it had used to pay, in 1817, for its shares of the Bank's stock. By November 1831, the Second Bank did not have any government funded debt. Thus, one of the ways Biddle tried to make up for this situation was to invest in the stocks of the states, and this meant that he had to increase the volume of banking in the south and west.[77]

Another reason for Biddle's decision to increase the Bank's investment in the south and west was that those areas were experiencing an economic boom in the late 1820s and the early 1830s. Trade, industry, and internal improvements all grew very rapidly in the years 1831-1832. The Erie Canal was finished in 1825, whereas the Baltimore and Ohio Railroad was just started in 1828. The steamboats were king of the rivers and lakes, as they were found everywhere from the Hudson to the Mississippi. As technology increased in the field of transportation, its cost declined rapidly. Even the cost of the goods transported by steamboat had fallen to all-time lows, and this especially affected cotton which, at the time, was America's fastest growing industry.[78]

As demand for cotton in Europe brought its revenue to new highs, speculation in the cotton industry increased, and businessmen borrowed money to buy land, hoping to become instant millionaires. The Second Bank, along with the state banks, took advantage of the economic boom, causing an expansion of bank loans. The Second Bank increased its loans from $54.8 million in May 1828 to $70.4 million in May 1832, and circulation rose from $2.7 million to $10.5 million over the same period.[79] However, specie holdings hardly kept pace with the expansion. In May 1828, it was at $6.3 million and in May 1832 at $7.9 million. This put the Bank in a very precarious position, as its demand liabilities had risen approximately thirteen times as fast as its ability to meet them.[80]

The loans in the south and west were the fastest growing loans. They increased from over one-third to one-half in the 1828 to 1832 period. In May 1828, these loans stood at $13.7 million of the total of $39.4 million; in May 1832, they were $36.4 million of $70.4 million. Most of these loans were made at the following five branches: New Orleans, the busiest port for commerce in all the south; Nashville; Louisville; Mobile; and Natchez.[81]

By October 1831, the excessive loan problem was compounded by rapid outflow of specie to Europe and inflation. The Bank's directors attempted to halt the export of specie by the selling of foreign exchange, but they failed, as the Bank did not have enough funds on which to draw the bills of exchange. To make matters worse, the government decided to take its deposits from the Bank to make a payment on the public debt.[82] Stephen Girard, a Philadelphia banker, was very worried about the excessive loan expansion. He said in a letter to a friend:

I confess I am alarmed at the picture. Their loans have been increased in the year from forty-five to sixty-six millions, while their specie has decreased from twelve to seven millions. The bank has now outstanding that vast amount of loans—(which it will be difficult to reduce or call in) its specie low—no funds in Europe to draw for; on the contrary, in debt a million and a half—exchange at eleven percent premium—specie shipping by every packet—more than twenty millions of their notes in circulation, which the pressure of the times will bring back upon them rapidly—and their private deposites liable to be withdrawn. They have acted like madmen, and deserve to have conservators appointed over them.[83]

By the end of October 1831, Biddle was compelled to contract the money supply. He demanded that the branches make fewer loans and purchase bills of exchange, hoping to transfer the Bank's funds to the east. However, it took time for the contraction to take hold, and expansion continued as loans rose from $60 million in October 1831 to $70.4 million in May 1832. It was only after May 1832 that the economy experienced a contraction in the money supply.[84]

The Second Bank, under Biddle's leadership, in the years 1823 to 1828, prospered, proved innovative, and was run conservatively. Biddle demonstrated his ability in making the Bank a "balance wheel of the banking system."[85] It performed central banking activities such as regulating the money supply and the expansion of credit. It dominated the exchanges, protected the investment market, worked closely with the treasury department, and gave the nation a better currency. It was only after 1828 that the Bank encountered problems, for which it had mostly itself to blame. It became involved in the speculation mania of the early 1830s, as its loans increased much more rapidly than its specie holdings, which was discussed above. However, Biddle and the Second Bank would face a far greater challenge to its existence with the election of Andrew Jackson to the presidency in 1828.

NOTES

1. Thomas P. Govan, *Nicholas Biddle: Nationalist and Public Banker, 1786-1844* (Chicago: University of Chicago Press, 1959), p. 75.

2. Reginald C. McGrane, ed., *The Correspondence of Nicholas Biddle Dealing with National Affairs, 1807-1844* (Boston: Houghton Mifflin Company, 1919), pp. 26-27.

3. Ibid., p. 28.

4. Ibid.

5. Govan, *Nicholas Biddle*, p. 76.

6. Ibid.

7. Ibid., pp. 76-77; Bray Hammond, *Banks and Politics in America from the Revolution to the Civil War* (Princeton, NJ: Princeton University Press, 1985), pp. 277-278.

8. Hammond, *Banks and Politics in America*, pp. 287-289.

9. Ibid., p. 288.

10. Ibid., p. 290.

11. McGrane, *The Correspondence of Nicholas Biddle*, p. 12.

12. Hammond, *Banks and Politics in America*, pp. 295-296.

13. Govan, *Nicholas Biddle*, p. 81.

14. Ibid., pp. 70-71.

15. Hammond, *Banks and Politics in America*, pp. 298-299.

16. Govan, *Nicholas Biddle*, p. 84.

17. Hammond, *Banks and Politics in America*, p. 307.

18. Ibid., p. 308.

19. Hammond, *Banks and Politics in America*, p. 301.

20. Ibid., p. 303.

21. Ibid.

22. McGrane, *The Correspondence of Nicholas Biddle*, pp. 36-37.

23. Ibid., pp. 51-52; Hammond, *Banks and Politics in America*, p. 304.

24. Ralph C. H. Catterall, *The Second Bank of the United States* (Chicago: University of Chicago Press, 1902), pp. 93-94.

25. McGrane, *The Correspondence of Nicholas Biddle*, pp. 31-32.

26. Ibid.

27. Catterall, *The Second Bank of the United States*, pp. 95-96.

28. Govan, *Nicholas Biddle*, pp. 85-86.

29. Ibid., p. 86.

30. Catterall, *The Second Bank of the United States*, p. 98.

31. Govan, *Nicholas Biddle*, p. 99; Catterall, *The Second Bank of the United States*, p. 99.

32. Catterall, *The Second Bank of the United States*, p. 99.

33. Govan, *Nicholas Biddle*, p. 85.

34. Catterall, *The Second Bank of the United States*, pp. 99-100.

35. McGrane, *The Correspondence of Nicholas Biddle*, pp. 34-35.

36. Govan, *Nicholas Biddle*, p. 88.

37. Catterall, *The Second Bank of the United States*, p. 100.

38. Ibid., p. 101.

39. Ibid., p. 102.

40. Ibid.

41. Ibid., p. 103.

42. Ibid., pp. 103-104.

43. Ibid., p. 105.

44. Govan, *Nicholas Biddle*, p. 90.

45. Ibid.

46. Ibid., p. 91.

47. Ibid.

48. Ibid.

49. Catterall, *The Second Bank of the United States*, p. 169.

50. McGrane, *The Correspondence of Nicholas Biddle*, p. 43.

51. Ibid., pp. 46-47.
52. Govan, *Nicholas Biddle,* p. 95.
53. Ibid., p. 96.
54. Ibid.
55. Ibid.
56. Ibid.
57. Ibid., pp. 96-97.
58. Ibid., p. 97.
59. McGrane, *The Correspondence of Nicholas Biddle*, p. 55.
60. Ibid., pp. 56-58.
61. Govan, *Nicholas Biddle*, pp. 97-98.
62. Ibid., p. 98.
63. Ibid., p. 87.
64. Ibid.
65. Catterall, *The Second Bank of the United States*, p. 108.
66. Hammond, *Banks and Politics in America*, p. 311.
67. Catterall, *The Second Bank of the United States*, p. 110.
68. Ibid., pp. 110-111.
69. Ibid., p. 111.
70. Hammond, *Banks and Politics in America*, p. 311.
71. Catterall, *The Second Bank of the United States*, pp. 111-112.
72. Ibid., pp. 115-118.
73. Ibid., p. 119.
74. Ibid.
75. Ibid., pp. 122-123.
76. McGrane, *The Correspondence of Nicholas Biddle*, pp. 31-32.
77. Catterall, *The Second Bank of the United States*, pp. 134-135.
78. Ibid., pp. 135-136.
79. Ibid., p. 136.
80. Ibid., pp. 136-137.
81. Ibid., p. 143.
82. Ibid., p. 146.
83. Ibid., p. 145.
84. Ibid., pp. 147-148.
85. Hammond, *Banks and Politics in America*, p. 323.

7

The Jacksonians and the Second Bank

The conflict between President Andrew Jackson and the Second Bank of the United States can be viewed in three phases. The first began right after the election of 1828 and ended in January 1832 with Biddle asking the Congress to recharter the Bank. During that period, relations between Biddle and Jackson remained cordial as the Bank and the government worked together in a businesslike manner. Though Biddle attempted to convince Jackson to favor the rechartering of the Bank, many of the new president's supporters, known as Jacksonians, were making speeches against it. The second period lasted from January 1832, when the rechartering bill went to Congress, until 1834. It was the height of the Bank war, which included the passage of the rechartering bill, its subsequent veto by Jackson, the election of 1832, and the removal of the government's funds from the Bank. The third period began in the middle of 1834 and lasted to March 1836. During this time, the Bank found itself on the defensive, acquiring a charter from the state of Pennsylvania, and trying to weather the difficulties of a financial crisis. This chapter concentrates on the first phase, and subsequent chapters cover the second and third phases of what has become known in American history as the Bank war.

THE ELECTION OF 1828

The Second Bank was not an issue in the election of 1828. The candidates, President John Quincy Adams and his opponent General Andrew Jackson, fought a long and bitter campaign based on personalities. It began in 1825, after Jackson had resigned his seat in the Senate to begin preparations for the next election. He was convinced that Adams and Henry Clay had stolen the election from him in 1824.[1]

Looking at presidential and vice presidential candidates in 1828, three of the four were ardent supporters of the Bank. Both Adams and his vice presidential choice, Richard Rush, former secretary of the treasury, praised the role of the Bank in maintaining a stable economy. Jackson said nothing negative about the Bank during the campaign, and many of his supporters were friends of the Bank. William Lewis, John Overton, and George Washington Campbell, three of Jackson's Tennessee friends who persuaded him to run, did not agree with the general's opposition to the establishment of the Nashville branch in 1827, and his vice president, John C. Calhoun, was responsible for passage of the bill chartering the Bank in 1816. According to historian Thomas P. Govan, Biddle, who had voted for Jackson, was not being politically naïve when he thought that his election in 1828 would not threaten the Bank.[2] In fact, about six weeks after the election, Biddle wrote his friend George Hoffman, a director of the Baltimore and Ohio Railroad, that he did not worry about the change in the administration. He claimed that Rush's treasury report extolling the virtues of the Bank would be enough to keep it in business. He said, "I should think that no administration would venture to set the monied concerns of the country afloat as they were. When we see who is to be our new Secy of the Treasy, we can consider seriously the application for a renewal [of the charter]."[3]

As confident as Biddle was about the survival of his Bank, he should have paid more attention to the events that occurred right after the election. For example, in late December 1829, a few Jacksonians had claimed that some of the Bank's branch officers had supported Adams' reelection, which Biddle vehemently denied. The Bank president had written Senator Samuel Smith of Maryland, a friend and ally of the future secretary of state, and then governor of New York, Martin Van Buren, that every officer of the Bank must abstain from politics. Biddle said:

The course of the Bank is very clear and straight on that point. We believe that the prosperity of the Bank & its usefulness to the country depend on its being entirely free from the control of the Officers of the Govt, a control fatal to every Bank, which it ever influenced. In order to preserve that independence it must never connect itself with any administration—& never become a partizan of any set of politicians. In this respect I believe all the officers of the institution have been exemplary. The truth is that with us, it is considered that we have no concern in politics. Dean Swift, said you know, that money is neither, whig nor tory, and we say with equal truth, that the Bank is neither Jackson man nor Adams man, it is only a Bank.[4]

Jackson was also concerned about the involvement of the Bank in the election, and told his friend Amos Kendall that the Louisville and Lexington branches had donated $250 to the Adams campaign and that their officers had actively supported Adams's reelection by refusing loans to members of his Democratic party.[5] In January 1829, Senator Richard Johnson of Kentucky, an opponent of the Bank, wrote to Postmaster General John McLean, a Jacksonian, soon to be appointed to the Supreme Court, and asked him to speak to Biddle about investigating these charges. At the same time, McLean gave Biddle names of Democrats who could be appointed as directors in the Kentucky branches.[6]

Biddle's investigation proved superficial, as he asked for the formation of a committee of men from those very branches that were under suspicion to undertake the investigation. They wasted no time in exonerating themselves of being politically partial. Biddle believed that the investigation was a waste of time as the charges were unfounded and politically motivated. He responded to McLean on January 11, 1829, declaring that the Bank should abstain from all political connections and controversy and every officer part of the institution was made aware of that. He said, "I have never heard of any suspicion even, that any officer of the Bank has intermeddled with politics, except on one occasion, and that suspicion, I am satisfied after inquiry, was without foundation."[7] Biddle also told McLean that the names of people that the Jacksonians wanted as directors of the Kentucky branches were unfit to serve. He contended that he had already placed loyal members of Jackson's party on both the Lexington and Louisville boards, and that there was no impartiality in the granting of loans.[8]

Biddle believed that Jackson was not behind the attempt by Kentucky congressmen to control the branches in their state, and he believed that he could eventually persuade Jackson to support the rechartering of the Bank when the time came. However, his failure to satisfy the Jacksonians in Kentucky was a mistake, for in June 1829, mismanagement and political interference charges were made against Jeremiah Mason, president of the Portsmouth, New Hampshire, branch by Senator Levi Woodbury, a Jacksonian. He told Biddle that Mason had discriminated in awarding loans, refusing loan applications to Jackson's friends, as well as interfering in the election of Democrats.[9] Mason had been put in charge because the branch had already been mismanaged under a previous director. However, it did not help Mason that he was a good friend of Daniel Webster, the senator from Massachusetts, who vigorously campaigned against Jackson in 1828. Biddle dismissed the charges in a letter to his good friend Robert Lenox in July 1829. He explained that Mason was put in charge to remedy the problem of bad loans. He said that "this operation you know, is not a pleasant one—& has raised against Mr. Mason a number of enemies who complain loudly. Such complaints are generally ill founded, & we are disposed to receive them with great distrust."[10]

However, this time Biddle traveled to New Hampshire to personally investigate these accusations, and it was not due to the fact that he believed them, but because he had little choice in the matter. Woodbury had sent a letter to Samuel Ingham of Pennsylvania, soon to be treasury secretary, and a good friend of Calhoun, who was a strong supporter of the Bank. Ingham had sent Woodbury's letter to Biddle and had asked him to look into the matter, and Biddle could not afford to dismiss his request.[11]

Just as Biddle was on his way to New Hampshire, Isaac Hill admitted that he and not Woodbury was behind the charges against Mason. Hill was the former editor of the New Hampshire *Patriot*, and soon to be U.S. senator from New Hampshire. Later he became a prominent member of Jackson's unofficial Kitchen Cabinet. He had sent two petitions to Philadelphia asking for modifications of the branch at Portsmouth. One signed by the merchants and the other by Jackson members of the legislature. The petitions stated that Mason had lent money to his brother-in-law in Boston, but had refused to make loans to Jacksonian business-men and merchants. Hill said, "The friends of General Jackson in New Hamp-shire have had but too much reason to complain of the branch at Portsmouth. All they now ask is, that this institution in that State may not continue to be an engine of political oppression."[12]

After spending several days interviewing the directors of the New Hampshire branch, Biddle had concluded that Mason was innocent of all charges. On August 28th, he wrote General Thomas Cadwalader, an important Bank director and good friend, praising Mason and rebuking his critics. He wrote, "I can now say with the upmost confidence that the whole is a paltry intrigue got up by a combination of small bankrupts & smaller Demagogues—that if the choice were to be made again, we ought to choose Mr. Mason—and that to have him out or not to support him fully would be to suffer ourselves to be tramped down by the merest rabble."[13] These words by Biddle only increased the Jacksonian hostility toward the Bank, especially after the directors had reelected Mason for another term.[14]

On September 15th, Biddle wrote Ingham that the charges against Mason were groundless and that Mason had been reelected. Ingham showed Jackson Biddle's letter, and he told Ingham to inform Biddle that the president "reserves his constitutional powers to be exercised through Congress, to redress all grie-vances complained of by the people of the interference by the Branches with the local elections of the states, and all their interference with party politicks, in every section of our country, where those complaints have reached the Executive."[15]

The next day, on September 16th, Biddle wrote his good friend Asbury Dickens that he was annoyed with all the politics involving the Bank. He said, "I will not give way an inch in what concerns the independence of the Bank to please all the administrations, past, present, or future. The bigots of the last reproached me with not being for them, the bigots of the present will be annoyed that the Bank will not support them. Be it so, I care nothing for either class of partisans and mean to disregard both."[16] The Portsmouth affair was the first shot fired in the Bank war.

ANDREW JACKSON AND THE BANKS

Andrew Jackson was a lawyer, legislator, jurist, merchant, land speculator, individualist, and self-made man. He was both an aristocrat and a slave owner, who was always ready to duel if his honor was impugned. He enjoyed such activities as cockfighting, horse racing, and gambling. As a young man in North Carolina he studied the law. In 1788, at the age of twenty-one, he moved to Nashville, Tennessee, where he practiced the law and purchased a modest plantation overlooking the Cumberland River. By the time Tennessee became a state in 1796, Jackson was a successful landowner and socially a part of the aristocracy.[17]

Jackson's basic views were agrarian oriented or Jeffersonian, though he held a low opinion of Jefferson. He despised individuals who failed to pay their debts and always paid his own obligations on time. He was against the western relief measures, such as those passed by the Kentucky legislature during the Panic of 1819. The Relief party made up of small farmers, debtors, and lawyers had won control of the legislature and passed laws to prevent foreclosures and imprisonment for debt. It even chartered the Bank of the Commonwealth to issue $3 million in paper currency. Jackson was opposed to the whole agenda of the Relief party, and he was a friend of creditors, which included, interesting enough, the Second Bank.[18]

Jackson had opposed all banks and the entire mercantile and credit system since the 1790s. In a letter to his good friend William Lewis in 1820, he wrote, "You know my opinion as to the banks, that is, that the Constitution of our state, as well as the Constitution of the United States, prohibited the establishment of banks in any state. Sir, the tenth section of the first article of the federal Constitution is positive and explicit, and when you read the debates in the convention you will find it was introduced to prevent a state legislature from passing such bill."[19] In 1833, in a letter to James K. Polk, he said that "Everyone that knows me, does know that I have been always opposed to the United States Bank, nay all banks."[20]

What soured Jackson on the banking and credit system can be traced back to 1795 when he traveled to Philadelphia to sell fifty thousand acres of land which he owned with his associate John Overton. He was also authorized to sell another eighteen thousand acres for a man named Joel Rice. He eventually sold the land to David Allison, a Philadelphia merchant and speculator, for twenty cents an acre. Allison had given Jackson promissory notes covering the entire amount of the sale. When Jackson returned to Tennessee, he used his share from the sale to open a trading post, buying supplies from Meeker, Cochran and Company, and paying them with Allison's notes. There were no problems until Allison went bankrupt in the fall of 1797, and Meeker and Cochran told Jackson that he was responsible for the notes. Jackson now had to find a seller for his trading post, which he did for thirty-three thousand acres of land. He then sold the land for twenty-five cents an acre, accepting a draft instead of cash from William Blount, a good friend and political ally. Jackson now hurried to Philadelphia with his draft only to discover that Blount was also involved with Allison, and caught in the same financial situation as Jackson. Eventually, Jackson took Allison's paper for the $20,000 owed him and Allison became indebted to Jackson. However, Jackson took heavy losses because the land he had originally sold (fifty thousand acres at twenty cents an acre in 1795) was worth over $200,000 in 1798. Poor Allison had expired in debtor's prison, but prior to his death, he had mortgaged eighty-five thousand acres of good Tennessee land to Norman Pryor. Later, both Pryor and Jackson had sued Allison's heirs to obtain title to the land, five thousand acres of which were put aside for Jackson in payment of the $20,000 debt. As soon as Jackson won the lawsuit, he quickly sold the five thousand acres that he was given.[21]

In 1810, George W. Campbell, a friend of Jackson, told him that his victorious lawsuit against Allison's heirs was invalid because the Federal Court lacked jurisdiction in those types of cases. This angered Jackson, who was now liable to a lawsuit for selling the five thousand acres. What made matters worse was that his liability was not for the original price of the land, but for its much higher current value. Jackson now faced financial ruin all because of promissory notes and paper currency. He was able to extricate himself from this mess by obtaining the cooperation of the Allison heirs, who signed over all the land they owned in Tennessee belonging to David Allison. He now had the deed which allowed him to give clear and uncontested title to those who purchased the five thousand acres. In return, Jackson released the Allison heirs from the $20,000 debt.[22]

This experience, in 1795, had been responsible for Jackson's harsh opinions concerning debts, paper, and speculation. Jackson had dabbled in land speculation, but after 1795, it was, for him, an evil practice, as paper currency became the tools of the swindler and cheat. Jackson saw only specie as the true money component, and because all banks speculated in land and issuing paper notes, he came to distrust them.[23]

In the late 1820s, Jackson had opposed a creation of a branch of the Second Bank in his state of Tennessee, and he fought the merchants who supported it. He declared that the branch would fail to benefit business in the state, and, in fact, it would only help those economic interests outside Tennessee, because specie would flow from Tennessee to other areas. He said that "the intention was to introduce a branch of the united states [sic] Bank which would drain the state of its specie to the amount of its profits for the support and prosperity of other places, and the Lords, Dukes and Ladies of foreign countries who held the greater part of its stock."[24]

The Tennessee state legislature had passed a law that levied a $50,000 tax on any bank chartered outside the state, with Jackson's support. By 1827, the tax was repealed and a branch was opened in Nashville. However, Biddle, recognizing the importance of gaining Jackson's approval, sent his good friend Cadwalader to Nashville to speak with Jackson. The general continued to oppose the branch, declaring, "I have been opposed always to the Bank of the u.s. [sic] as well as all state Banks of paper issues, upon constitutional grounds believing as I do, that the congress has no constitutional power to grant a charter and the states are prohibited from granting charters of paper issues."[25]

Seventeen years later, in 1837, Jackson held the same position. In a letter to Senator Thomas Hart Benton of Missouri, he wrote, "My opinion now is and has ever been since I have been able to form an opinion on this subject that Congress has no power to charter a Bank and that the states are prohibited from issuing bills of credit or granting a charter by which such bills can be issued by any corporation or order."[26]

It should also be noted that Jackson had a political motive for attacking the Bank, which was based on his state right's views, and it pushed him to challenge the constitutionality of the Bank. He believed that the Bank was a threat to the liberty of the American people, due to its concentration of enormous power in the hands of private citizens, and it used this power to influence elections, control legislators, and to get its way with the government. Jackson emphasized that the Bank was an example of monopoly power, with special privileges granted by the government.[27]

Yet when all was said and done, Jackson still remained an enigma to the historians when it came to his position on banks. Bray Hammond, the bank historian, asserted that "General Jackson's prejudices were stronger than his convictions, and that he was himself among the least consistent and stable of the Jacksonians."[28] Though he berated the banks for issuing paper currency, Jackson himself did more than any presidents prior to him to increase the issue of those very notes, as we shall see later. He also used the services of banks and had the friendship and support of bankers. He never ceased to transact personal or family business with the Nashville branch of the Bank, even though he opposed its creation.[29]

THE JACKSONIANS

The Republican party in 1828 was divided between the National Republicans led by John Qunicy Adams and the Democratic Republicans of Andrew Jackson. Many of the National Republicans would form a new political party in the 1830s, called the Whig Party. They were supporters of Henry Clay's American System that called for more internal improvements, a national bank, and a high protective tariff. Whig was used to denote their opposition to Jackson, referring to him as King Andrew, just as the whigs of England in the eighteenth century did with King George III. Jackson's Democratic Republicans would call themselves Democrats, and those most loyal to the general would be referred to as Jacksonians. Most of the Jacksonians tended to favor low tariffs and opposed the national bank though they split on government aid for internal improvements and hard money versus paper issue.[30] For example, many westerners who supported Jackson and opposed the Bank were debtors. They did not appreciate the Bank, in 1819, recalling specie and checking the note issues of the state banks. They desired the printing of paper money, better known as cheap money. The sin against the Bank in Kentucky was that it did not circulate enough paper to satisfy the demands of the debtor classes. The champion of the debtor classes in Kentucky was Richard M. Johnson, a Jacksonian, and Bank opponent, who sat on the House Committee which investigated the Bank in 1832.[31]

Other Jacksonians, including Jackson himself, were vehemently opposed to paper issue. The chief proponent of hard money was Senator Thomas Hart Benton from Missouri. Like Johnson, he was a Jacksonian and a westerner who opposed the Bank, but his views on money were radically different. Benton had witnessed the Panic of 1819 and the collapse of the paper system, and from then on became the leading champion of hard money in the Senate. On February 2, 1831, he gave a stirring speech in the Senate on the value of hard money. He said, "Gold and Silver is the best currency for a republic; it suits the men of middle property and the working people best; and if I was going to establish a working man's party, it should be on the basis of hard money; a hard money party against a paper party."[32]

Though Benton praised the value of hard money, he remained critical of the Bank in the same February 2nd speech. He declared,

First: Mr. President, I object to the renewal of the charter . . . because I look upon the bank as an institution too great and powerful to be tolerated in a Government of free and equal laws. Secondly, I object . . . because its tendencies are dangerous and pernicious to the Government and the people. . . . It tends to aggravate the inequality of fortunes; to make the rich richer, and the poor poorer; to multiply nabobs and paupers. . . . Thirdly, I object . . . on account of the exclusive privileges, and the anti-republican monopoly, which it gives to the stockholders.[33]

When Jackson ran for the presidency in 1828, he had to be careful not to declare his views on paper issue and internal improvements when campaigning in the western states. Aside from opposing paper issue as mentioned above, Jackson, a states' rights supporter, opposed any federal money for internal improvements. He understood that his position was not popular in the west, and his friends there, such as Amos Kendall, editor of the *Argus of Western America*, had to assure their readers that Jackson was not against federal support for the building of roads and highways. The general was able to hide his views and win the election in 1828. However, in 1830, he was opposed by many of his western Jacksonian supporters, such as Johnson, Lewis, and Eaton, when he vetoed a bill that would have authorized the government to provide funds for a turnpike from Maysville to Lexington.[34]

Though the Jacksonians were not united on all the key issues of the time, they did agree on the destruction of the Second Bank in its present form. They brought together five elements on their attack against the Bank.

1. There was Wall Street's desire to become the money-banking center of the United States, and that meant the termination of the Second Bank located on Chestnut Street in Philadelphia.
2. Merchants and businessmen disliked the Bank for restraining the use of bank credit by prohibiting the state banks from making excessive loans.
3. The politicians in the west and south had resented the Bank's interference with states' rights.
4. There was popular dislike for the Bank because it appeared that it associated with the aristocracy of business.
5. The farmers, mostly debtors, saw the state banks as friendly, where easy money could be obtained, but had no such feelings toward the Second Bank, which restricted credit frequently.[35]

Certain Jacksonians played an important role in the demise of the Second

Bank. Some of them were Jackson's closest advisors and members of his cabinet; others were part of his unofficial cabinet, better known as the Kitchen Cabinet.

Duff Green was a westerner who was born in Kentucky but moved to Missouri as a young man. He became a land speculator and a wealthy merchant in St. Louis. In fact, he was responsible for establishing the first line of stages west of the Mississippi. He purchased the paper, the *United States Telegraph*, and after moving to Washington in 1825, became an ardent supporter of Jackson's presidency. His paper praised Jackson and denounced Biddle and the Second Bank. After Jackson's victory, he became a member of the Kitchen Cabinet, but because he was a good friend of Calhoun, he soon found himself out of favor with the other Jacksonians.[36]

Samuel Ingham became Jackson's first secretary of the treasury. He started out as a Pennsylvania farmer and became a businessman and politician. Ingham, coming from Pennsylvania, was sympathetic toward the Bank and had a good relationship with Biddle. In fact, Ingham praised Biddle for the way the Bank paid off a large amount of the government debt in July 1829. When Jackson wanted to announce his hostility toward the Bank in his inaugural address, Ingham was one of the advisors to dissuade him from doing so. According to Govan, Ingham was hoping that Jackson would see the value of the Bank and would support its recharter. However, the truth was that he opened the assault on the Bank as secretary of treasury and remained a Jackson loyalist.[37]

Ingham's assistant in the treasury was Isaac Hill of New Hampshire, another member of the Kitchen Cabinet. For the tolerance Ingham showed toward the Bank, Hill wanted to destroy it. He saw the Second Bank as an institution of the aristocracy, a tyranny against the common people, and himself as an organizer of the "honest yeomanry." He was a publisher, bank director, bank president, and a businessman, and, above all, he pointed out that he was self-made. He did not inherit wealth, nor was he born with a silver spoon like Nicholas Biddle and others of his class, "those sons of fortune who have been from their very cradle nursed in the lap of luxury, who have never known what it is to grapple with adversity, who have found every wish anticipated and every want supplied almost before it was experienced."[38]

Martin Van Buren was one of the most brilliant politicians of his time and a leader among the Jacksonians. He was elected governor of New York the same year that Jackson won the presidency. Jackson asked him to be his first secretary of state, during which time he turned Jackson against Calhoun, the vice president. During Jackson's second administration, Van Buren was himself vice president and became Jackson's successor to the presidency in 1836. Van Buren was a supporter of the constitutional principles of Thomas Jefferson; he opposed a strong national government that consolidated power. It was Van Buren who helped unify banking in New York, by urging the state legislature to pass the Safety Funds Act, which tied the state banks into a single system.[39] Van Buren and his Wall Street friends supported the economic interests of New York, and they refused to accept the existence of the Second Bank in Philadelphia. Rush had warned Biddle of the

New York threat to the Bank in December 1828. He said, "You have probably as much or more to fear for the Bank, from New York, as from Virginia, and with even less excuse. In Virginia, there are still constitutional scruples. In New York, none."[40]

Francis P. Blair became one of the chief spokesmen of the Jacksonians. He established his journal the *Globe*, which relentlessly attacked Biddle and the Bank. In May 1831, he wrote, "I have always been opposed to the Bank of the United States. It is now doing what for many years what I predicted it would do, set up to make presidents for the people. It will lend all its influence and spend a million by the way of loans to induce the people to crush Old Hickory."[41] Blair had been the president of the Commonwealth Bank in Kentucky and coeditor with Amos Kendall of the *Argus of Western America*. He was a major borrower from the Second Bank, owing around $20,000. When he could not make his obligations, a deal was struck where he would pay ten cents on the dollar.[42]

Amos Kendall, a native New Englander, was educated at Dartmouth. In 1814, he moved to Kentucky to become a tutor for Henry Clay's children and later the editor of the *Argus of Western America*. Kendall was the leader of the Kitchen Cabinet—the inconspicuous thinker, planner, and doer of the Jacksonians. In 1835, he became postmaster general of the United States, making major reforms in the postal system. Kendall had turned against the Bank in 1819 because of its restrictive monetary policies. He declared that the Bank was the major cause of the Panic of 1819, resulting in the suffering of the people.[43] He considered the Bank an artificial monopoly, and later on, when he spoke of the major achievements of the Jackson administration, he declared that "chief of these was its severance from the banking power organized and exercised under the charter of the Bank of the United States."[44]

Churchill C. Cambreleng was a member of the Congress from New York and a close associate of Van Buren. He was called New York's "commercial representative," a self-made man and friend of John Jacob Astor. He had supported the Bank prior to Jackson's election. In 1829, Biddle had hired Cambreleng, who understood the operations of the Bank fully, to find a location for an additional branch of the Bank in western New York. He hoped to use Cambreleng to prove to Van Buren that the Bank was politically neutral. As a promoter of New York's economic interests, Cambreleng turned against the Bank in Congress during the 1830s.[45]

Roger B. Taney, Jackson's second attorney general, fourth secretary of the treasury, and later appointed chief justice of the Supreme Court by the general, hated the Bank passionately. He had been a Federalist, but left the party in 1812 to later become an ardent Jacksonian. He was a Baltimore attorney and a member of the landed aristocracy from southern Maryland. Taney was a director of two banks and an attorney to the Union Bank in Baltimore—a bank that benefitted when Jackson ordered all government funds removed from the Second Bank. Taney thought Biddle acted too high and mighty, and that his Bank had become a monopoly. He said, "It is the power concentrated in the hands of a few individuals, exercised in secret and unseen although constantly felt—irresponsible and above the control of the people or the Government for the twenty years of its charter; that is sufficient to awaken any man in the country if the danger is brought distinctly to his view."[46] Taney always believed that the national bank had discriminated against the state banks, and in *McCulloch vs. Maryland*, he opposed Marshall's decision that the states could not tax the Bank. He said,

The stockholders in the state banks, who are generally men of moderate circumstances, are subject to the weight of unlimited war taxation whenever the public exigency may require it—why should the stock in the Bank of the United States, which is generally held by the most opulent monied men, many of them wealthy foreigners, be entirely free from additional taxation which war or any other calamity may bring upon the rest of the community? . . . The money of the citizens employed in the state banks is to be diminished in value by new burthens whenever the wants of the country require it, while the money of the opulent citizen and of the wealthy foreigner . . . is not to be allowed to feel the pressure.[47]

David Henshaw was Jackson's political boss in Massachusetts. He was born into poverty, and through his own efforts became a millionaire. He was a banker, a railway builder, a newspaper publisher, and collector of the Port of Boston. Though he was wealthy, he hated the aristocracy that had snubbed him. Henshaw's *Remarks upon the Bank of the United States*, written in 1831, and his proposal in 1832, calling for a new bank with $50 million in Jacksonian capital, to replace the ogre in Philadelphia, became part of Jackson's veto message against the Bank in 1832.[48]

The only Jacksonian to befriend the Bank was Major William B. Lewis, who held a high regard for both Jackson and Biddle. Lewis was one of Jackson's oldest and closest friends, a planter from Tennessee, who stayed in the White House with the general. Biddle kept up a correspondence with Lewis, hoping that he might be able to convince Jackson on the merits of recharter. Lewis, for the most part, seemed optimistic that Jackson would support recharter. He wrote Henry Toland, Biddle's good friend, on November 11, 1829, and said that Jackson was very happy with the way the Bank had paid off the public debt, and that it might be rewarded accordingly. He stated, "I think we will find the old fellow will do justice to the Bank in his message for the handsome manner in which it assisted the Govt in paying the last instalment [*sic*] of the National debt."[49] Unfortunately for Biddle, Lewis's voice would be muted by the overwhelming number of fellow Jacksonians against recharter.

THE FIRST ASSAULT ON THE BANK

In October 1829, a group of Jacksonians, led by Van Buren, met in Richmond, Virginia, to discuss the destruction of the Second Bank. Van Buren had urged the group that this undertaking should be done with care and caution, as the Bank's charter was not due to expire until 1836, seven years later. Public opinion toward the Bank in 1829 was clearly not as hostile as it had been in 1824, when the last Supreme Court case had protected it against the states. The group agreed that a case had to be made against Biddle's institution. Lewis was the only dissenter among them who saw the value of the Bank to the economy. He urged his fellow Jacksonians to make certain changes in the institution, but to allow it to remain in existence.[50]

Just a week prior to the Richmond meeting, Biddle had assured Lewis that the Bank was not involved in politics. In fact, Biddle had sent him a letter written by Walter Dun, a member of the Lexington board, in which Dun, a Jacksonian, denied any political involvement by the Bank. Lewis responded several days later that Jackson had confidence in Biddle, and that if Biddle said that there was no interference in the elections, then none occurred. Lewis told Biddle that "the President thinks, as you do, that the Bank of the U. States should recognise no party; and that, in all its operations, it should have an eye single to the interest of the Stockholders and the good of the country."[51]

In early November 1829, Biddle went to Washington to meet with Jackson, and the general said almost all the things Biddle wanted to hear. He called the Bank president a man of integrity, and appeared to have exonerated the Bank from interference in the elections.[52] Jackson also thanked him for his plan for paying off the national debt. Biddle had sent him a plan, through Lewis, hoping to show the general what the Bank was capable of doing. He knew that the president wanted to pay the debt off as quickly as possible, and Biddle showed Jackson how to accomplish it. He said that the government should sell its stock in the national bank and then allow the Bank to assume the obligations to pay off the remainder of the debt "in lieu of a bonus for recharter."[53]

If Biddle was hoping that he could convince Jackson at that meeting to recharter the Bank in exchange for his debt payment plan, he was in for a big surprise. The president told Biddle that it was a good plan. He said,

I would have no difficulty in recommending it to Congress, but I think it right to be perfectly frank with you . . . I have read the opinion of John Marshall who I believe was a great and pure mind, and could not agree with him, though if he had said that as it was necessary for the purpose of the national government there ought to be a national bank I should have been disposed to concur; but I do not think that Congress has a right to create a corporation out of the ten mile square.[54]

Jackson played Biddle very well in 1829. He kept him thinking that there was an opportunity that he would support recharter, because he never said explicitly that he wouldn't. The general seldom said anything positive about the Bank, and, in fact, on a number of occasions, he referred to it as a "hydra of corruption," which proved "dangerous to our liberties" due to its political power throughout the land.[55] According to Govan, Jackson did not want to believe that the Bank was not involved in politics. His mind was made up in 1829 that he would destroy it, the only question was when.[56]

As Jackson prepared to give his first annual message to Congress, Colonel

James A. Hamilton, a son of Alexander Hamilton and acting secretary of state for Van Buren (Van Buren had not officially taken office), was asked by Van Buren to help the new president write his speech, especially that part dealing with the Bank. Hamilton met with Jackson on November 28, 1829, for breakfast, when the general showed him a copy of his annual message. As Hamilton perused through it , he saw that the president had gone to great lengths to attack the Bank. Jackson agreed to allow Hamilton to edit his message, which he did that very evening, and the next morning he showed the president the results. Jackson was surprised that Hamilton had removed all the harsh criticism of the Bank, and left only that part which questioned its constitutionality and the soundness of its currency. Jackson was somewhat surprised that this was the extent of the attack on the Bank. He said to his acting secretary of state: "Do you think that is all I ought to say?" Hamilton replied the less said now the better, and Jackson laughed and said, "Oh! My friend, I am pledged against the bank, but if you think that is enough, so let it be."[57]

It was interesting to note that on leaving the White House, Hamilton stopped to tell Van Buren that Jackson agreed to say very little about the Bank. Then he asked Van Buren if he was against the Bank on constitutional grounds. To his surprise, the former governor of New York replied, "Oh! no, I believe with Mr. Madison that the contemporaneous recognition of the constitutional power to establish a bank by all the departments of the government, and with the concurrence of the people, has settled that question in favor of the power."[58] Van Buren only opposed the Bank because he saw it as a threat to the banking system in New York, as mentioned above.

At the same time that James Hamilton was working with Van Buren and Jackson on his speech, his brother, Alexander Hamilton, Jr., was warning Biddle that Jackson would speak against the Bank in his annual message on December 8, 1829. However, Biddle refused to believe Hamilton; after all, he had just spoken to the president who praised Biddle and the fine work the Bank was doing. So when Jackson did question the constitutionality and the soundness of the Bank's currency, declaring that "both the constitutionality and the expediency of the law creating the Bank are well questioned by a large proportion of our fellow citizens; and it must be admitted by all that it has failed in the great end of establishing a uniform and sound currency," Biddle was surprised.[59] According to Biddle, it was all right for the general to hold his opinion on the constitutionality of the Bank, though it was already declared so by Madison and Marshall, but for Jackson to question the soundness of the Second Bank's currency was absurd. Albert Gallatin actually asked the president what he meant by sound currency, but he received no intelligent reply. At the time of Jackson's message, the dollar was sound and very stable.[60]

On December 12, 1829, Biddle wrote Hamilton to apologize for doubting him on Jackson's views of the Bank and to talk about his plans for recharter. He said,

I received this morning you favor of the 10th inst. which I have read with great pleasure.

The views it presents are quite sound & correspond exactly with those entertained here. My impression is that these opinions expressed by the President are entirely & exclusively his own, and that they should be treated as the honest tho' erroneous notions of one who intends well. We have never had any idea of applying to Congress for a renewal of the Charter at the present session—and of course should abstain from doing so now. Our whole system of conduct is one of abstinence and self defence.[61]

By the end of 1829, Biddle should have been convinced that his enemy on the Bank was the president. However, the Bank president remained uncertain of Jackson's hostility toward his institution. He blamed the problems the Bank was having more on Van Buren than Jackson, and he had told several people that he had met that the president's annual message was friendly toward the Bank, and that there was little to worry about.[62]

As for Jackson, he was happy that his message was transmitted to the people, who he claimed would ultimately decide the fate of the Bank. He told James Hamilton on December 19th that "I have brought it before the people and I have confidence that they will do their duty." This statement, according to Jacksonian historian Robert V. Remini, defined the essence of Jacksonian Democracy.[63]

The Congress did not agree with the president when he criticized the Bank on the grounds of questionable constitutionality and not having a sound currency. The House Ways and Means Committee led by George McDuffie of South Carolina, a staunch Calhoun supporter, declared that Jackson's statement on the Bank made no sense. He issued a report claiming that the Bank was indeed constitutional, and that it had provided a currency more stable and uniform than specie itself. McDuffie, a bullionist by conviction, was a realist and recognized that metallic currency had serious limitations as money. He declared that what the country confronted was a choice "between a paper currency of uniform value, and subject to the control of the only power competent to its regulation, and a paper currency of varying and fluctuating value . . . subject to no common or adequate control whatever."[64] It was simply not a choice between paper and bullion.

At the same time, the Senate Finance Committee, chaired by General Samuel Smith of Maryland, concurred with McDuffie, praising the Bank for maintaining a sound economy. It was interesting to note that the congressional reports emphasized that both parties considered the Bank constitutional, and that it should no longer be a question. According to Remini, Biddle actually had written Smith's report, and then submitted it to the Committee through Smith for approval.[65]

The McDuffie committee also attacked Jackson's proposal for the creation of a new national bank, in lieu of Biddle's Bank, "upon the credit of the Government," declaring that it would only lead to political corruption and paper money excesses.[66] The general had decided to recommend the establishment of a government-owned substitute Bank, with branches in various states, years before he became president. However, he only brought it up with Felix Grundy, a Jacksonian candidate for the U.S. Senate from Tennessee in May 1829. When he told Grundy of his plan, shortly after the 1828 election, the Senate candidate praised it, reminding Jackson that Grundy himself had proposed the same idea to the general in 1820, only to have it ridiculed as "wicked, profligate and unconstitutional."[67] However, after initially supporting the idea, Grundy asserted that it was too political. He said that a national bank should be free of direct political influence in order to make financial decisions, and should be subject to public restraint, so that those who controlled the Bank could not use it for private advantage. Jackson wanted all directors of his bank to be appointed annually by the president of the United States, with the consent of the Senate, and this Grundy opposed. He told his old friend the general that the president would be creating a dangerous precedent, by appointing all of the directors, and making them subservient to executive influence. When Jackson asked the advice of Ingham, his treasury secretary, he echoed Grundy's concerns, and asked the president not to mention his substitute bank plan, until further notice. Even his good friend and head of his Kitchen Cabinet, Amos Kendall, had refused to support this substitute bank plan.[68]

Notwithstanding the advice of his advisors and friends, Jackson did include a paragraph on his substitute bank in his annual message to the Congress in December 1829. He told the Congress that if a national bank was necessary, then he had the perfect solution for one. He said,

Under these circumstances, if such an institution is deemed essential to the fiscal operations of the government, I submit to the wisdom of the legislature whether a national one, founded upon the credit of the government and its revenues, might not be devised which would avoid all constitutional difficulties and at the same time secure all the advantages to the government and the country that were expected to result from the present bank.[69]

Biddle had reprinted the McDuffie and Smith reports, using the Bank's money, and disseminated them throughout the country. Biddle, emboldened by the support in Congress, asked his good friend Lewis to try again to change Jackson's mind about the Bank. Lewis did confront Jackson on the Bank issue, and the president told him that he was not interested in confronting the Congress with a veto. He was still hoping that his substitute bank would be approved by the legislature. According to Catterall, Jackson was not opposed to a national bank; however, he was very clear that it had to be organized his way. He remained hostile to the Second Bank, which was a bank "with exclusive privileges in which the whole people could not share."[70]

Notwithstanding the good reports the Bank received in the Congress, the anti-Bank faction in Washington continued to investigate the Second Bank. Other congressional committees continued to keep the Bank on display in a negative way. It still questioned its constitutionality, though portraying it as having a corrupting influence on the political integrity of the country. The rumors continued to claim that the Bank was a monopoly, dominated by Biddle, run by private interests, for the benefit of the wealthy.[71]

Though Jackson said little about the Bank, he was dissatisfied that the Democratic papers were not more active in attacking it. The general was particularly upset with his good friend Duff Green, whose *United States Telegraph* remained mute when it came to criticizing the Bank. The president said, "The truth is that he has professed to me to be heart and soul against the Bank, but his idol [Calhoun] controles him as much as the shewman does his puppits, and we must get another organ to announce the policy, and defend the administration; in his hands, it is more injured than by all the opposition."[72] As mentioned above, this led to the establishment of Blair's *Globe* in December 1830. Jackson loved reading Blair's harsh editorials, which ripped the Bank and criticized Biddle unmercifully.[73]

Though Jackson encouraged criticism of the Second Bank, he continued to give friends of Biddle encouragement that he really did not hate the Bank. On July 20, 1830, Josiah Nichol, president of the Nashville office and a friend of Jackson, wrote to Biddle concerning a conversation he had with the general. Nichol said, "He appears to be well satisfied with the facilities that the Bank have given to the government and individuals in transferring their funds from one point to another and acknowledges that a Bank such as the present only can do so. He appears to be generally pleased with the management of the Bank of the United States and branches—and particularly so with this office." Nichol told Biddle that the general's only concern was that a great part of the stock was held by foreigners, but that would not make him interfere with rechartering the institution. At the same time, Nichol warned Biddle that he was uncertain of the president's intentions, because he always kept his opinions to himself. The concluding paragraph of the Nichol letter dealt with how Jackson held a high opinion of Biddle and that "there is no gentleman that can be found [who] would manage the Bank better or do the Bank & country more justice."[74]

However, Gallatin knew Jackson only too well, and he reminded Biddle that the general could not be trusted. He wrote to Biddle on August 14, 1830, to remind him that though he had the support of the Congress, it would be a difficult battle. He recalled the attempt to renew the First Bank's charter in 1811, when the Bank had a majority of political friends in both Houses and when there were fewer banks in the country, a fight that was lost. Now the former secretary of the treasury believed the situation was worse. He said, "Opposition arising from interested motives pervades the whole country; in this state [New York], for instance, . . . the country banking interest is all-powerful on all questions connected with that subject; with a sect of politicians throughout the union 'state rights' has become a watchword; worst of all, the President has prematurely and gratuitously declared himself and given the signal of attack to his adherents."[75]

In December 1830, Jackson, in his second annual address to the Congress denounced the Bank more harshly than he did the year before. He said that nothing had occurred to diminish "the dangers which many of our citizens apprehend from that institution as at present organized." Again, he recommended his alternative bank to replace the Second Bank, and added that the new bank should be a branch of the treasury, "based on the public and individual deposits, without power to make loans or purchase property," which would remit the funds of the government, and whose expenses would be paid by allowing the bank's officers to sell bills of exchange. Because the bank would not be a corporation, having no stockholders, debtors, or property, there should be no objection to it on constitutional grounds.[76]

Jackson admitted that his bank would also have regulatory function. He said that "the states would be strengthened by having in their hands the means of furnishing the local paper currency through their own banks, while the Bank of the United States [his bank], though issuing no paper, would check the issues of the state banks by taking their notes in deposit and for exchange only so long as they continue to be redeemed with specie." Simply put, Jackson's alternative bank would acquire no liabilities, and would be only a name on a door in the treasury.[77]

Jackson's message appeared to offer Biddle an opportunity to compromise on a rechartering bill. Immediately after the message, Lewis had declared that the rechartering of the Bank, with changes, would be approved by Jackson. Robert Smith, Biddle's friend and associate, wrote to him on December 13, 1830, to discuss his conversation with Lewis. He said, "I gathered from a conversation with Major Lewis, of the President's family, that altho' the President is decidedly in favor of a Bank such as he recommended to Congress, yet if a bill were to pass both houses, renewing the charter of the Bank U. States, with certain modifications, the President would not with hold his approval."[78]

However, Biddle refused to accept Jackson's bank plan as a compromise when it was first presented. He believed that Jackson's plan gave too many concessions to the state governments and their banks. In a letter to Joseph Hemphill, a member of the Congress from Philadelphia, Biddle declared, "The President has himself again thrust it [the Bank issue] before Congress, & seems determined to make it an electioneering topic. By inviting the State Govts. to strengthen themselves by usurping the whole circulating medium of the country, he will probably excite them to instruct their delegations in Congress to oppose the charter, & it is to be presumed that in no event will he sanction a bill for the recharter."[79] According to Remini, Biddle would later make some suggested changes to Jackson that were so irrelevant that the general refused to consider them, rather believing that Biddle was not serious about compromise.[80]

Biddle continued to write numerous articles about the importance of the Bank, while attacking the position of the Jackson administration. He secured letters from former presidents Madison and Monroe, favoring the Second Bank and declaring its constitutionality. Biddle even began paying newspaper editors, with the Bank's funds, to print his propaganda, which only supported Jackson's claim that the Second Bank was using its money to influence politics.[81]

Biddle had realized that the Bank had plenty of votes in both Houses to pass a rechartering bill, but it would not be veto proof. However, in 1831, a cabinet crisis occurred in the Jackson administration that lifted Biddle's spirits. There was contention between Secretary of State Van Buren and Vice President Calhoun. Van Buren viewed Calhoun as an obstacle to his presidential ambitions, and he worked to discredit him in the eyes of Jackson. He had already told Jackson that it was Calhoun's wife who had encouraged the other cabinet wives to snub Peggy Eaton at social functions. Peggy, the daughter of a Washington innkeeper, had been a widow with an unfavorable reputation when Secretary of War John Eaton had married her. Due to her reputation, she was ostracized at social functions. It so happened that Jackson's own late wife, Rachel, had suffered insults during his election campaign for the presidency. Therefore, Jackson sympathized with the Eaton, and when Van Buren told the general who was behind it, his dislike for Calhoun intensified. Van Buren also told Jackson that when Calhoun was in Monroe's cabinet in 1818, he wanted the general censured for his raid into Spanish Florida. These events turned the president against Calhoun and firmly established Van Buren as Jackson's eventual successor to the presidency. In April 1831, Van Buren and Jackson formulated a plan to rid the cabinet of Calhoun's influence. Van Buren would resign as secretary of state, and this would lead to other resignations and the reforming of the cabinet, without Calhoun's supporters. Jackson would then appoint Van Buren as his minister to Great Britain for the remainder of his first term.[82]

Biddle was ecstatic when Jackson elected his new cabinet in 1831. Most of the Jackson's appointees favored the Second Bank. Both the new secretary of state, Edward Livingston of New Orleans, and secretary of the treasury, Louis McLane of Delaware, favored the rechartering of the Bank, which they told Jackson.[83]

Jackson made it known to Biddle that he did not want the rechartering of the Bank to become an issue during the campaign of 1832. Biddle had met with McLane in October 1831, and the treasury secretary said that "the Prest is now perfectly confident of his election—the only question is the greater or the less majority, but he is sure of success & wishes to succeed by a greater vote than at the first election. If therefore while he is confident of reelection this question is put to him as one affecting his reelection, he might on that account be disposed to put his veto on it."[84]

At the same time that McLane sent Biddle this warning, he also (according to Biddle) conveyed to him that the general would recommend the charter's renewal at the appropriate moment. In a memorandum found in his correspondence, Biddle said that "The President is to say that having previously brought the subject [rechartering the Bank] to Congress, he now leaves it with them. The Secretary is to recommend the renewal. This latter point pleases me much."[85]

It appeared that in the fall of 1831 a compromise had been struck between Jackson and Biddle—for the president, a guarantee of postponement until after the election, and for Biddle, an assurance that the Bank would be rechartered. According to Catterall, "Biddle, Livingston, McLane and Jackson now acted under a sort of informal compact: the secretaries to work for re-charter, Jackson to remain quiescent for the present, but to sign a bill in the long run if his wishes were met, and the bank on its part to wait until after the election before presenting its petition for a charter, and to accept the modifications desired by the president."[86]

What were these modifications? They were never clearly stated; however, knowing Jackson's desires, one could make an educated guess. The government would not be able to hold stock in the Bank, and the Bank would use the government stock in helping the government to pay off the national debt. The Bank could hold no more than two offices in any state and must get the permission of the states prior to opening these offices. The Bank's notes could only be issued from the main office, and only two officers were permitted to sign the notes. Finally, the states would be permitted to tax the branches of the Second Bank.[87]

By the beginning of December 1831, everything seemed to be going well for Biddle. He was relieved that he did not submit the banking bill for recharter in 1830. He actually thought about doing just that to keep the Bank from becoming a political issue in the campaign of 1832. However, he decided to wait and try to win over the president, and it now appeared in 1831 that Jackson would support rechartering if the Bank were kept out of the election. In fact, the president had allowed McLane to recommend recharter in his treasury report in 1831.[88]

On December 6, 1831, Jackson delivered his third annual message to the Congress. Though he declared that he had not changed his mind toward the Bank, he told the Congress that he would accept their decision on recharter. The Bank's enemies could not believe how temperate the general's words were on the issue of rechartering, and Taney, now the attorney general, criticized Jackson's speech writer for misleading the public.[89]

However, Biddle was far from satisfied with Jackson's speech, as he expected a presidential endorsement of the rechartering bill. What had happened was that McLane had told Biddle what he believed the president would do. Jackson clarified the situation in a letter to his friend John Randolph on December 22, 1831. He wrote that he had never changed his views on the Bank.

Mr. McLane has on his own authority, in conformity with his sense of a positive duty which he did not feel at liberty to disregard and which it would have been unbecoming in me to controul [sic] ventured the expression that the institution might be so modified as to strip it of the constitutional objections entertained by the Executive. In saying this it was far from his intention or wish to be understood as committing me, in any manner to the friends of the Bank in the support of any schedule for obtaining a new charter.[90]

It was at this point, shortly after Jackson's speech in December 1831, that Biddle decided to listen to Clay, the National Republican presidential candidate in 1832, and make the Second Bank a political issue. Biddle, up to this point, had resisted all of Clay's entreaties to inject a rechartering bill into the campaign of 1832. By refusing to wait until after the election of 1832, Biddle would cause the destruction of the Bank. Senator Willie P. Mangum of North Carolina declared that "by deferring its application to next Session, I have no doubt with but slight modification it would have met with Executive favor.—It is now more than doubtful whether it will.—And the whole may ultimately take the appearance of a trial of strength between Gen Jackson & the Bank. In that case the Bank will go down—For Gen J's popularity is of a sort not to slaken at present."[91]

When Biddle decided to go forward with a rechartering bill prior to the 1832 election, he put himself into a no-win situation. However, he decided to directly confront Jackson because he did not fully trust the president's intentions, even after Jackson appeared ready to compromise on the Bank. Besides, the general's advisors were against any compromise agreement, and Biddle did not believe that Jackson could control his rabidly anti-Bank advisors. It was not so much the regular cabinet that Biddle worried about, but the Kitchen Cabinet where Kendall, its anti-Bank leader, dominated. Biddle said, "What I have already dreaded about this new cabinet was that the kitchen would predominate over the parlor."[92]

Biddle also wondered why the general did not want to make the Bank an issue in the 1832 campaign. Did Jackson really fear that he would lose the state of Pennsylvania, where the Bank was popular? Perhaps, Biddle thought, this might be the best time to resolve the issue, even if it meant confronting the president. He believed that if the president vetoed the bill, congressional candidates up for reelection would have to take a position on the issue, and Biddle thought that most Americans supported the Bank, and that they would elect enough members to the Congress to override the veto.[93]

Biddle was also encouraged in his opinion by John Quincy Adams, Daniel Webster, and especially Henry Clay, Jackson's opponent, who desperately needed an issue against the popular president. Clay wrote to Biddle on December 15, 1831:

Have you come to any decision about an application to Congress at this Session for the renewal of your Charter? The friends of the Bank here, with whom I have conversed, seem to expect the application to be made. The course of the President, in the event of the passage of a bill, seems to be a matter of doubt and speculation. My own belief is that, if now called upon he would not negative the bill, but that if he should be re-elected the event might and probably would be different.[94]

Biddle understood how anxious Clay was to make the Bank an issue in the election, but he also knew that he was wrong when he said that he did not know if the president would exercise his veto. McLane had already told him that Jackson would definitely veto recharter, if tested. Nonetheless, Biddle went ahead and decided to gamble the existence of the Second Bank. On January 6, 1832, a month after Jackson's message, he formally requested that the Bank's application for recharter be submitted to the Congress, four years prior to its expiration.[95]

NOTES

1. For information on the election campaign of 1824 see Raymond H. Robinson, *The Growing of America: 1789-1848* (Boston: Allyn and Bacon, 1973), pp. 68-69.

2. Thomas P. Govan, *Nicholas Biddle: Nationalist and Public Banker, 1786-1844* (Chicago: University of Chicago Press, 1959), pp. 113-114.

3. Reginald C. McGrane, ed., *The Correspondence of Nicholas Biddle Dealing with National Affairs, 1807-1844* (Boston: Houghton Mifflin Company, 1919), p. 62.

4. Ibid., pp. 62-63.

5. Robert V. Remini, *Andrew Jackson and the Bank War: A Study in the Growth of Presidential Power* (New York: W. W. Norton and Company, 1967), pp. 49-50.

6. Ibid., p. 50.

7. McGrane, *The Correspondence of Nicholas Biddle*, pp. 69-71.

8. Govan, *Nicholas Biddle*, pp. 112-113.

9. Remini, *Andrew Jackson and the Bank War*, pp. 51-52.

10. McGrane, *The Correspondence of Nicholas Biddle*, pp. 72-73.

11. Remini, *Andrew Jackson and the Bank War*, pp. 52-53.

12. Ibid.; Govan, *Nicholas Biddle*, p. 116.

13. McGrane, *The Correspondence of Nicholas Biddle*, p. 75.

14. Remini, *Andrew Jackson and the Bank War*, p. 54.

15. Ibid., p. 55.

16. Govan, *Nicholas Biddle*, p. 112.

17. Remini, *Andrew Jackson and the Bank War*, p. 17.

18. Ibid., p. 28.

19. Govan, *Nicholas Biddle*, p. 115; Bray Hammond, *Banks and Politics in America from the Revolution to the Civil War* (Princeton, NJ: Princeton University Press, 1985), p. 349.

20. John Spencer Bassett, ed., *Correspondence of Andrew Jackson*, Vol. 5 (Washington, DC: Carnegie Institution of Washington, 1931), pp. 235-236.

21. Remini, *Andrew Jackson and the Bank War*, pp. 18-19.

22. Ibid., p. 19.

23. Ibid.

24. Ibid., p. 30.

25. Ibid., pp. 30-31.

26. Hammond, *Banks and Politics in America*, pp. 349-350.

27. Remini, *Andrew Jackson and the Bank War*, p. 44.

28. Hammond, *Banks and Politics in America*, p. 348.

29. Ibid., pp. 350, 359.

30. Ibid., pp. 329-330.

31. Arthur M. Schlesinger, Jr., *The Age of Jackson* (Boston: Little, Brown and Company, 1953), pp. 77-80.

32. Ibid., p. 81.

33. Ibid.

34. Ibid., p. 58.

35. Hammond, *Banks and Politics in America*, p. 329.

36. Ibid., p. 330.

37. Ibid.; Govan, *Nicholas Biddle*, p. 115.

38. Hammond, *Banks and Politics in America*, pp. 330-331.

39. Ibid., p. 332.

40. Ibid.; McGrane, *The Correspondence of Nicholas Biddle*, pp. 59-60.

41. Govan, *Nicholas Biddle*, p. 165.

42. Hammond, *Banks and Politics in America*, p. 332.

43. Govan, *Nicholas Biddle*, p. 123.

44. Hammond, *Banks and Politics in America*, p. 334.

45. Ibid., p. 335.

46. Schlesinger, Jr., *The Age of Jackson*, pp. 65, 75.

47. Hammond, *Banks and Politics in America*, pp. 335-336.

48. Ibid., p. 338.

49. McGrane, *The Correspondence of Nicholas Biddle*, p. 85.

50. Hammond, *Banks and Politics in America*, p. 371.

51. McGrane, *The Correspondence of Nicholas Biddle*, pp. 79-80.

52. Govan, *Nicholas Biddle*, p. 119.

53. Ibid., pp. 119-120.

54. Ibid., pp. 120-121.

55. Ibid., p. 119.

56. Ibid., pp. 119-120.

57. Remini, *Andrew Jackson and the Bank War*, pp. 61-62.

58. Ibid., p. 63.

59. John Spencer Bassett, ed., *Correspondence of Andrew Jackson*, Vol. 4 (Washington, DC: Carnegie Institution of Washington, 1929), p. 97.

60. Hammond, *Banks and Politics in America*, pp. 374-375.

61. McGrane, *The Correspondence of Nicholas Biddle*, p. 91.

62. Remini, *Andrew Jackson and the Bank War*, p. 66.

63. Ibid.

64. U.S. Congress, 21st Cong., 1st Sess., 1830, pp. 14, 26, and 27; Govan, *Nicholas Biddle*, p. 128.

65. Remini, *Andrew Jackson and the Bank War*, p. 67.

66. Walter B. Smith, *Economic Aspects of the Second Bank of the United States* (Cambridge, MA: Harvard University Press, 1953), p. 149.

67. Govan, *Nicholas Biddle*, p. 122.

68. Ibid., pp. 122-123.

69. Ibid., p. 124.

70. Ralph C. H. Catterall, *The Second Bank of the United States* (Chicago: University of Chicago Press, 1902), p. 196.

71. Smith, *Economic Aspects of the Second Bank of the United States*, p. 149.

72. Remini, *Andrew Jackson and the Bank War*, p. 68.

73. Ibid.

74. Hammond, *Banks and Politics in America*, p. 380; McGrane, *The Correspondence of Nicholas Biddle*, pp. 106-107.

75. Hammond, *Banks and Politics in America*, pp. 380-381.

76. Ibid., p. 381; Catterall, *The Second Bank of the United States*, p. 203; Remini, *Andrew Jackson and the Bank War*, p. 69.

77. Hammond, *Banks and Politics in America*, p. 381.

78. McGrane, *The Correspondence of Nicholas Biddle*, pp. 117-118.

79. Ibid., pp. 118-120.

80. Remini, *Andrew Jackson and the Bank War*, p. 70.

81. Ibid., p. 71; Catterall, *The Second Bank of the United States*, p. 205.

82. Remini, *Andrew Jackson and the Bank War*, pp. 71-72; Hammond, *Banks and Politics in America*, p. 383.

83. Hammond, *Banks and Politics in America*, pp. 382-383.

84. McGrane, *The Correspondence of Nicholas Biddle*, p. 131.

85. Ibid.

86. Catterall, *The Second Bank of the United States*, p. 210.

87. Ibid., pp. 211-212.

88. Schlesinger, Jr., *The Age of Jackson*, p. 85; Govan, *Nicholas Biddle*, p. 130.

89. Remini, *Andrew Jackson and the Bank War*, pp. 73-74; Hammond, *Banks and Politics in America*, p. 384.

90. Bassett, *Correspondence of Andrew Jackson*, Vol. 4, p. 387.

91. Remini, *Andrew Jackson and the Bank War*, p. 75.

92. Ibid.

93. Ibid., pp. 75-76.

94. McGrane, *The Correspondence of Nicholas Biddle*, p. 142.

95. Remini, *Andrew Jackson and the Bank War*, p. 75; Hammond, *Banks and Politics in America*, p. 386.

8

The Bank War

Nicholas Biddle's call for recharter of the Second Bank, prior to the election of 1832, was strictly his decision. Some historians have erroneously blamed Clay for pressuring Biddle to make the Bank a political issue in the election and for exerting undue influence on him. Though Clay had welcomed Biddle's decision, the Bank president was determined to take action in January 1832. For three long years, the administration had taken an ambiguous stand on recharter, and Biddle firmly believed he could not wait any longer. Simply put, he had come to believe that the Bank would not have been rechartered if left to Jackson's convenience.[1]

Nonetheless, Biddle's decision provided the Bank's enemies, such as Kendall, Blair, Benton, and Taney, with additional ammunition, and Jackson would most certainly veto any recharter bill passed by the Congress. Taney said, "Now as I understand the application at the present time, it means in plain English this—the Bank says to the President, your next election is at hand—if you charter us, well—if not, beware of your power."[2]

Jackson was outraged that Biddle had decided to make the Bank a political issue in the upcoming election. In a conversation with James Hamilton, the president said that he would slay the ogre of Chestnut Street, and that he was not concerned that the Congress might pass the recharter bill, forcing him to veto it. He said, "I will prove to them that I never flinch, that they were mistaken when they expect to act upon me by such considerations."[3]

THE BANK BILL IN CONGRESS

On January 6, 1832 Biddle notified George McDuffie, a Democrat from Pennsylvania and the chairman of the House Ways and Means Committee, and Senator Samuel Smith, chairman of the Senate Finance Committee, that an application for recharter of the Second Bank would be made. Three days later, the memorial was officially submitted to McDuffie, but instead of allowing Smith to handle it in the Senate, it was given to Senator George Dallas, Biddle's friend from Pennsylvania. The Bank's supporters believed that Dallas was more aggressive than Smith in managing the bill in the Senate.[4]

Jackson's choice to lead the anti-Bank forces in the Congress was Senator Thomas Hart Benton of Missouri, a good friend, and an excellent debater and floor manager. Benton's strategy was simple—attack and continue attacking the bank as an evil institution. If successful, he would turn the public against the Bank, and Jackson's inevitable veto would work to his benefit in the election of 1832.[5]

When Biddle began asking the Congress to recharter the Bank, he was told by his friend Charles J. Ingersoll, in February 1832, that Jackson did not really hate the Second Bank any more than the state banks, and that he might still sign the rechartering bill with modifications. This gave hope to Biddle who once again tried to gain the president's support.[6] On February 6, 1832, he instructed Senator Dallas to take a resolution of the Pennsylvania legislature to the president, warning him not to anger the state by vetoing the bank bill, while at the same time agreeing to work with Jackson on a bank bill which they could both agree.[7] Though nothing came of the Dallas venture, Ingersoll did meet Secretary of State Edward Livingston and presented Biddle's agreement to compromise on a bank bill then before the Congress. Ingersoll reported to Biddle on February 9, 1832, exactly what the president wanted. He said that though Jackson did not want the government as stockholders in the Bank, he would continue to appoint directors on the parent board and one director at each of the offices. The Bank would only be permitted to hold a limited amount of real estate, to be determined by need, and the states would be allowed to tax the Bank's property.[8] Two days later, on February 11th, Biddle sent a letter to Ingersoll quickly agreeing to the conditions, while declaring that the Bank was more important to him than who won the election in 1832. He said,

Here am I, who have taken a fancy to this Bank & having built it up with infinite care am striving to keep it from being destroyed to the infinite wrong as I most sincerely & conscientiously believe of the whole country. To me all other considerations are insignificant—I mean to stand by it & defend it with all the small faculties which Providence has assigned to me. I care for no party in politics or religion—have no sympathy with Mr. Jackson or Mr. Clay. . . . I am for the Bank & and the Bank alone.[9]

Just when it looked like a deal had been worked out between Biddle and Jackson on the Second Bank, Benton, in late February, had asked Augustine S. Clayton, an anti-Bank congressman from Georgia, to introduce a resolution in the House, calling for an investigation of the Bank for misconduct and violation of its charter. Benton wanted no part of a Biddle-Jackson compromise. His job was to delay the vote on the Bank until public opinion could be turned against it. The Bank's supporters found themselves in a difficult position. If they had objected to the resolution, it would look like the Bank was trying to hide something, and if they accepted it, the vote on rechartering would be delayed. More important, the

Clayton resolution killed any chance that a compromise between Biddle and Jackson could be worked out on the current Bank bill before the Congress. The president had ceased all negotiations with Biddle until the outcome of the Clayton investigation. In a single stroke, Benton had delayed the Bank bill and put an end to any Jackson-Biddle compromise.[10]

The Clayton resolution, calling for a committee of seven members of the House to investigate the Bank, was adopted on March 14, 1832. The committee consisted of its chairman, Clayton, Richard M. Johnson, Francis Thomas, Churchill Cambreleng, McDuffie, John Quincy Adams, and John Watmough. The first four would always vote as a block against the Bank, and the last three would support it.[11]

During the six weeks that the Clayton Committee worked, it issued three reports in May, a majority against the Bank, and two minority dissents, one by Adams. The majority report condemned the Bank, declaring that it was unconstitutional and antagonistic to the free enterprise system. Adams condemned the majority report which showed an ignorance of banking matters. He praised Biddle whom he claimed was treated unfairly. He said that Biddle's management of the Bank was "marked with all the character of sound judgment, of liberal spirit, of benevolent feeling, and of irreproachable integrity."[12]

In May 1832, Biddle traveled to Washington to make one more attempt to convince the president to revive the deal they had before the Clayton investigation. He met with both Livingston and Secretary of the Treasury Louis McLane, two of the Bank's supporters in the administration. There was nothing they could do, as Jackson was convinced by the Clayton report that the Bank was corrupt, and that the current bill before the Congress should be withdrawn.[13]

Biddle stayed in Washington to lead the battle for his precious bill throughout much of the spring of 1832. He wanted petitions to be sent to the Congress from the states, showing that the great majority were in favor of recharter. While this was being done, many pro-Jacksonian congressmen, who favored the passage of the Bank, continued to urge Biddle to withdraw the bill. They realized that Jackson would veto it, and they did not want to be put in the position of either upholding the veto or supporting the Bank. However, Biddle and his chief lieutenant, Thomas Cadwalader, felt that this was the best time for the bill's passage. Cadwalader declared that "our life depends on this session, and getting the veto now, so that the nation may be roused before the autumnal elections."[14]

The bill first went to the Senate on May 23, 1832, where a number of amendments were made and rejected. For example, no branch could be established without the consent of the states; the states would be able to tax the branches; the president of the United States could appoint all the presidents of the branches and one-half of the directors at the branches and at the main board in Philadelphia; and foreigners would be prohibited from holding stock in the Bank. Finally, on June 11, 1832, the rechartering bill passed the Senate by a vote of twenty-eight to twenty.[15] About three weeks later, on July 3rd, the House voted 107 to eighty-five to approve it. Prior to the vote, Nathan Appleton, a congressman from Massachusetts, suggested that the bill be amended, fearing that Jackson would veto it. Clay asked Appleton to vote for the measure as it stood. He said with the confidence of an experienced legislator that "should Jackson veto it, I shall veto him!"[16]

When we look at the breakdown of the vote in the Congress, the Bank bill had solid support in the New England and the Middle Atlantic states. Opinion was divided in both the northwest and southwest, whereas most of the opposition to the bill came from the south.[17]

Biddle was overjoyed that the first hurdle was overcome. However, he was not ready to celebrate yet, for he expected Jackson to veto the measure, and he had no idea what the final outcome would be. In a letter to Cadwalader dated July 3rd, the very day the bill passed the House, he wrote, "I congratulate our friends most cordially upon their most satisfactory result. Now for the President. My belief is that the President will veto the bill though this is not generally known or believed. This however we shall soon see."[18]

The charter that was passed by the Congress had some new provisions that improved on the original. For example, it was renewed for fifteen years instead of twenty. Under the new provisions, the Bank was permitted to hire two or more officers whose only concern was signing notes of less than $100 denominations; it was to issue no branch bank drafts, or other bank paper not payable at the place where issued under the denomination of $50. It was not permitted to hold real estate for more than five years unless the property was necessary in conducting its business. (This removed the temptation to make loans on mortgages and other real estate security that caused problems for the Bank in 1819.) The Bank could not have more than two offices in any state unless more than that number were already in existence; it had to pay a $200,000 annuity to the United States; the Congress was allowed to prohibit the issue of notes in amounts less than $20; and the cashier of the Bank was to send to the secretary of the treasury each year a list of foreign shareholders, and to the treasurer of the states, if requested, a list of the shareholders residing in their states. These changes in the Bank's charter were made to gain the support of the states and the state banks, but they would not influence Jackson's decision to veto the bill.[19]

JACKSON'S VETO

Jackson vetoed the rechartering bill on July 10th, only one week after its passage. The veto message was prepared by Kendall, who wrote the first draft; Taney who put it in its final form; and the president's secretary, Andrew Donelson, who made some important suggestions. It was one of the most important veto messages in history, based not only on the Constitution, but on political, social, and economic matters. Jackson tried to convince the masses that the Bank was an evil monopoly run by foreigners who cared nothing about the interests of Americans. He portrayed himself as the champion of liberty, and the fighter against the foreign shareholders. He proclaimed that the charter would give a gratuity of many millions to the shareholders, that many were foreigners, and that this gratuity must come directly or indirectly out of the earnings of the American people. He asked, Why should a few foreigners receive financial benefits in the United States? He said, "By this act the American Republic proposes virtually to make them a present of some millions of dollars. If our Government must sell monopolies . . . it is but justice and good policy . . . to confine our favors to our own fellow citizens, and let each in his turn enjoy an opportunity to profit by our bounty."[20]

At the same time, Jackson attacked the Bank as an monopoly granting privileges to the select few. It was opposed to the principles of democracy and proved dangerous to the government of the country. He was the first president to appeal to the poor and middle class against the rich. He said, "It is to be regretted that the rich and powerful too often bend the acts of government to their selfish purposes. Many of our rich men have not been content with equal protection and equal benefits but have besought us to make them richer by acts of Congress."[21] Jackson firmly believed that the charter was an abomination because it favored the rich and stood in the path of a better proposition offered by citizens "whose aggregate wealth is believed to be equal to all the private stock in the existing bank."[22]

Jackson, of course, did not neglect the constitutional question in his veto message. He openly disagreed with *McCulloch vs. Maryland*, claiming that the court was wrong. He stated that the three branches of government,

must each for itself be guided by its own opinion of the Constitution. It is as much the duty of the House of Representatives, of the Senate, and of the President to decide upon the constitutionality of any bill or resolution which may be presented to them for passage or approval as it is of the supreme judges when it may be brought before them for judicial decision. The opinion of the judges has no more authority over Congress than the opinion of Congress has over the judges, and on that point the President is independent of both. The authority of the Supreme Court must not, therefore, be permitted to control the Congress or the Executive when acting in their legislative capacities, but to have only such influence as the force of their reasoning may deserve.[23]

Jackson obviously believed that he could both think and act as an independent member of the government.

Both Webster and Clay attacked Jackson's veto message in Congress. On July 11th, Webster declared that "although Congress may have passed a law, and although the Supreme Court may have pronounced it constitutional, yet it is, nevertheless, no law at all, if he, in his good pleasure, sees fit to deny its effect; in other words, to repeal and annul it."[24] Clay arguments were much the same as Webster's. He said that the "veto is an extraordinary power . . . not expected by the [Constitutional] convention to be used in ordinary cases." He condemned Jackson for using it to interfere with the legislative process and said that his action was "hardly reconcilable with the genius of representative government."[25]

The strength of Jackson's veto was in its appeal to Americans against foreigners, to the poor against the rich, and to democracy against privilege. There was little hope to override it, but the Senate did try in the middle of July and failed by a vote of twenty-two to nineteen.[26] On July 16th, the Congress adjourned and prepared for the upcoming election in November.

Biddle was disappointed that the override proved unsuccessful, but he was hoping that Jackson's veto message would prove that the president was a "deranged demagogue preaching anarchy." He wrote to Clay on August 1st with his impressions of the veto message, and how important Clay's candidacy was to the country:

As to the veto message I am delighted with it. It has all the fury of a chained panther biting the bars of his cage. It is really a manifesto of anarchy—such as Marat or Robespierre might have issued to the mob of the faubourg St. Antoine: and my hope is that it will contribute to relieve the country from the dominion of these miserable people. You are destined to be the instrument of that deliverance, and at no period of your life has the country ever had a deeper stake in you. I wish you success most cordially, because I believe the institutions of the Union are involved in it.[27]

THE ELECTION OF 1832

The National Republican's ticket consisted of Clay as president and John Sargeant, a member of the House of Representatives from Pennsylvania and a good friend of Biddle, as vice president, whereas the Democrats chose Jackson and Van Buren. Both the Democrats and the National Republicans had built an effective party apparatus to do their bidding. For example, they had collected large amounts of funds, founded committees, hired newspapers, and printed circulars to win over voters.[28]

The Bank became the paramount issue in the election, and it was on the side of the National Republicans. Biddle had spent thousands of dollars to defeat Jackson. He paid for the reprinting of Clay's and Webster's speeches, and he distributed thirty thousand copies of Jackson's veto message—all great propaganda for the Bank. Some Democrats were concerned about the large infusions of Republican money into the campaign. Senator William Marcy of New York said, "The U.S. Bank is in the field and I cannot but fear the effect of 50 or 100 thousand dollars expended in conducting the election in such a city as New York."[29]

The Democrats depicted the Bank in a monied alliance with Clay. They blamed it for trying to manipulate the election through bribery of government officials and ordinary citizens. The Jackson newspaper, the *Globe*, declared that the "Golden vaults of the Mammoth Bank" were opened to give electioneers two dollars a day to campaign against the general.[30]

The Democratic editors followed Jackson's example, in his veto message, and played the class card. They referred to the Republicans as the party of the corrupt and wealthy who would take advantage of the poor. On the other hand, the

Republicans referred to Jackson as a despot who understood only three things: "spoils, veto, and dictatorship."[31]

Though the better newspapers in the country had supported Clay and the Bank against Jackson, it made little difference in the outcome of the election, as the general's popularity had assured him a smashing victory. He received 219 electoral votes to Clay's forty-nine; the third party, anti-Mason candidate, William Wirt of Maryland, had seven. Broken down by states, Clay won Massachusetts, Rhode Island, Connecticut, Delaware, Kentucky, and a majority of Maryland. Wirt took Vermont, and Jackson won everywhere else except South Carolina, which gave its eleven electoral votes to John Floyd of Virginia. In the popular vote, Jackson had received 687,502, whereas all his opponents combined for a total of 530,189.[32]

Though Jackson had won almost fifty-five percent of the entire vote, and the number of voters had increased since the last election, the percentage of Jackson's popular majority declined slightly from what he had received in 1828. Some historians believe that the reason for this was that people had disapproved of his Bank policy.[33]

Nonetheless, it was an astounding victory for Jackson and a bitter defeat for Clay and Biddle. The president viewed his triumph as popular approval of his veto, and, more than ever, he felt the righteousness of his cause He now began to plan the demise of the Bank, not willing to wait until its charter expired in 1836.

THE WITHDRAWAL OF GOVERNMENT
FUNDS FROM THE SECOND BANK

The election of 1832 brought an end to the power struggle between Biddle and Jackson over recharter. The president now wanted to go beyond the veto and remove the government's deposits held by the Bank, as his goal was to sever the relationship between the government and the Bank prior to 1836.

In November 1832, Van Buren had written Jackson, suggesting that the government might get along without a bank, but if a bank became necessary, he supported the one that the General had favorer earlier. He wrote, "My choice would be to make another fair effort to get along without a bank, if experience should shew that one is indispensable to the safe conduct of public affairs, then I have not been able to think of a better allowable course than that which you suggested in substance in conversation when I was in Washington in July viz the establishment of a Bank in the District of Columbia."[34] This bank would only have authority within the District of Columbia, and would have no branches unless the states agreed to allow them within their borders.

After the election, Biddle was determined to continue business as usual. He refused to make any reductions in the amount of loans. The only change was "to give gently then gradually the loans of the Bank the direction of domestic bills which being payable at maturity would give the Institution a greater command over its funds." The Bank had no intention of winding down its affairs, as the directors were still hoping that a new charter could be secured prior to 1836.[35] However, in reality it would take a miracle to get a new charter for the Bank, as the anger between the pro and anti-Bank forces increased after the election. The *Globe* made absurd claims that the members of the National Republican party were encouraging their supporters to assassinate the president. It went on to declare that Jackson wanted to take a vacation at his estate the Hermitage, but refused to leave Washington until he put the final dagger into the Bank.[36]

In December 1832, Jackson recommended, in his annual message to the Congress, the sale of the government's stock in the Bank, and an investigation by the Congress into whether it was safe to leave the government's funds in the Bank. Biddle showed no surprise to Jackson's speech, for now he was certain about Jackson's feeling toward the Bank and knew that the president would attempt to discredit the institution in the Congress.[37] However, Biddle was angered and hurt when his friend and former supporter McLane, in his annual treasury report, had sided with Jackson, that the Bank's solvency was questionable and had suggested that the Congress should begin an inquiry into the security of the Bank as a depository of the public funds.[38]

Jackson's message and McLane's report had the desired effect for the anti-Bank forces. They caused concern about the Bank's solvency as its stock declined to new lows. Biddle was so irritated that in January 1833, in a letter to his friend John Watmough, he declared that the general was deserving of impeachment.[39]

The decision to remove the government funds from the Bank was made in January 1833, during a conversation between Blair and Jackson. Blair had told Jackson that Biddle was using public funds "to frustrate the people's will." He said, "He is using the money of the government for the purpose of breaking down the government. If he had not the public money, he could not do it." Jackson replied that "he shan't have the public money! I'll remove the deposits! Blair talk with our friends about this, and let me know what they think of it."[40]

In February, the House of Representatives held hearings on whether the funds were safe in the Bank and on the sale of the government stock. On March 2, 1833, by a vote 109 to forty-six, it repudiated the general by declaring that the public funds were safe and that the government should not sell its stock in the Bank.[41]

Jackson was angered and concerned about what the Congress had done, and he especially blamed Clay and Calhoun who wielded power and influence over the legislature. He wrote to his friend the Rev. Hardy M. Cryer on April 7th concerning this matter:

This combination [of Clay and Calhoun] wields the U. States Bank and with its corrupting influence they calculate to carry every thing, even its recharter by two thirds of Congress, against the veto of the executive, if they can do this, they calculate with certainty to put Clay or Calhoun in the Presidency—and I have no hesitation to say, if they can recharter the bank, with this hydra of corruption they will rule the nation, and its charter will be perpetual, and its corrupting influence destroy the liberty of our country. When I came into the administration it was said and believed, that I had a majority of seventy-five—since then, it is now believed it has bought over by loans, discounts, etc., etc., until at the close of the last session, it was said, there was two thirds for recha[r]tering it.[42]

Though Jackson and Blair were ready to remove the funds from the Bank, many of the president's advisors were opposed to this policy, including the entire cabinet, except for Taney. When Blair informed the general about the opposition in his cabinet, he didn't seem bothered by it. He said, "Oh my mind is made up on that matter. Biddle shan't have the public money to break down the public administration with. It's settled. My mind is made up."[43]

While Jackson prepared to meet with his cabinet to establish his course of action, Biddle still hoped to secure recharter of the Bank. The Bank president was closely following Jackson's political problems with the nullifiers, and he hoped that he would be able to use this to his advantage. Briefly, South Carolina opposed the Tariff Act of 1832, and its state legislature precipitated a political crisis by calling a convention to pass an Ordinance of Nullification. They refused to abide by the Tariff Act by nullifying it, a federal act that applied to all states. Jackson could not allow South Carolina to flaunt federal law. With the aid of Webster, the Force Act was passed by the Congress, giving the general the power to enforce the collection of tariff duties. Eventually, a compromise was worked out that avoided a serious crisis in 1833. During this period, Biddle tried to use Webster, who supported Jackson against the nullifiers, to persuade the president to change his mind on recharter. On April 8, 1833, Biddle had written to Webster asking him for help. He said that "whatever is done in the way of pacification should be done soon—for if the deposits are withdrawn, it will be a declaration of war which cannot be recalled."[44] Two days later, Biddle again wrote to Webster, repeating the urgency of the matter: "I wrote you today that Mr. L. [Livingston, secretary of state] would be in New York. I write to you again to say that I think it would be well to see him. The whole question of peace or war lies in the matter of the deposits." Webster did what he could for Biddle, but his efforts proved futile.[45]

As mentioned above, most of Jackson's cabinet remained opposed to removal of the government funds from the Second Bank. This was especially true of Treasury Secretary McLane. On May 20, 1833, he wrote to Jackson that he opposed the removal of the deposits on both practical and legal grounds. He declared that "no system should be established for the future disposition of the public deposites [sic] nor any change in the places if deposite of the public money sooner than the expiration of the charter of the present bank may render necessary." He went on to explain that the state banks were generally safe, but past experience in the treasury has also proven otherwise. Also the increase in public funds in the state banks would be a great temptation for them to make additional loans, which could prove harmful to the economy. He also pointed out that removal of the deposits would create a rivalry between the state banks and the national bank, which could prove disastrous for the economy.[46]

McLane's opinion was important because the Bank's charter stated that only the secretary of the treasury could remove the government's funds from the Bank. He also was obligated to give an explanation to the Congress on why the action was being taken. Because he clearly opposed removal, Jackson was forced to appoint another treasury secretary to do his bidding. Because the general wanted to keep McLane in the cabinet, he made him the new secretary of state, and Livingston was made minister to France. Meanwhile, William J. Duane became the new secretary of the treasury. He was one of Philadelphia's leading lawyers, the son of William Duane, the editor of the *Aurora*, and who was an ardent opponent of the First Bank.[47]

Jackson had appointed Duane on June 1, 1833, knowing fully that he vehemently opposed the Second Bank. On July 20th, about six weeks after Duane assumed his new duties, the general asked him to appoint Kendall, as a special agent, to locate state banks that would take government deposits on terms beneficial to the administration. Though Kendall had spoken to many bankers, most loyal to the administration, in cities such as New York, Boston, Philadelphia, and Baltimore, he considered his mission a failure. When he returned to Washington, he told the president that, in his opinion, the government's interests would best be served if the public funds were not removed from the Second Bank.[48]

Though Duane had agreed with Kendall, Jackson, at a cabinet meeting on September 18th, had told his new treasury secretary that he should begin the process of removing the funds, and that the president would assume all the responsibility.[49] However, Duane, three days later on September 21st, wrote to the president, declaring that he refused to take the money from the Bank, not because he favored that institution; in fact, he stressed the point that he had always been opposed to the Second Bank, even though the House had "pronounced the public money in the Bank of the United States safe." He asserted that "a change to local and irresponsible banks will tend to shake public confidence and promote doubt and mischief in the operations of society."[50] Duane had accurately forecasted what would occur when the funds would eventually be removed from the Second Bank.

Jackson did not have the same confidence in the Bank as Duane and most of the cabinet. In fact, at the September 18th cabinet meeting, the general had tried to explain to his secretaries how the Bank had already mishandled the three percents the year before. Jackson told the story that in March 1832 the government had informed the Bank that it wanted to pay part of the national debt (paying off the debt was important to Jackson). The government wanted to redeem half of the three percents, approximately $6.5 million. However, Biddle was short on cash; he had made too many loans the year before. Therefore, Biddle wanted to postpone payment, and he was given a three-month extension. Later he was told that the government had planned to make a second payment on January 1, 1833, redeeming the other half of the three percents, and that it would need a total of $13 million within three months. Because Biddle could not afford to take so much money from circulation, he created a plan. He asked the holders of the three percents to give the securities to the Bank (about $5 million) which would send them to the government as evidence of payment. However, the Bank would not pay the principle; instead, it would borrow the principle for a year and pay the holders an interest of three percent. To do this, he sent his associate Cadwalader to England to consult with the financial firm of Baring Brothers. However, Cadwalader turned a legal scheme into an illegal one. Because he was unable to find enough holders to cooperate, he allowed the House of Baring to buy up the three percents for the Bank, with the securities remaining in the hands of the London bankers or in the possession of the original holders. This agreement was a violation of the Bank's own charter, because it was explicitly prohibited from purchasing the public debt, and Cadwalader had allowed Baring to buy the debt for the Bank of the United States. Biddle did repudiate Cadwalader's deal, but only after public opinion had forced him to take action. Jackson had used this episode as an example of Biddle and the Bank's irresponsibility, and in his opinion, the Bank could not be trusted with the government's money.[51]

When Duane had told Jackson that he would not remove the funds from the Bank, the general had asked him for his resignation. However, Duane had refused to resign, declaring that he would do nothing about the funds until the Congress convened.[52] The outraged Jackson, not wanting to fire his secretary of the treasury and fearing a cabinet rebellion, said, "But you said you would retire if we could not finally agree." Duane replied, "I indiscreetly said so, but I am now compelled to take this course." Jackson reminded Duane that "a secretary, sir is merely an executive agent, a subordinate, and you may say so in self defense." Duane responded that "in this particular case Congress confers a discretionary power, and requires reasons if I exercise it [removal of the funds]. Surely this contemplates responsibility on my part."[53]

Jackson could not allow Duane to continue to disobey him. He had to risk a cabinet revolt and fire him. On September 23rd, the general sent Duane a note stating that "your further services as Secretary of the Treasury are no longer required." Taney, the attorney general, was now appointed as secretary of the treasury, and Benjamin Butler became the new attorney general.[54]

Immediately after Taney had assumed office, he appointed Kendall as his special agent for the removal of the deposits. They joined with Levi Woodbury, the secretary of the Navy to begin the government's shift from national banking to deposit banking. They declared that beginning on October 1, 1833, all future government deposits would be put in the state banks selected by Kendall. These banks were the Girard in Philadelphia; the Commonwealth and the Merchants banks in Boston; the Bank of Manhattan Company, the Mechanics, and the Bank of America in New York; and the Union Bank of Maryland located in Baltimore. All seven of these state banks were considered Jacksonian, except the Bank of America in New York.[55]

To make matters worse for the Bank, the administration proclaimed that for daily operating expenses the government would begin to draw on its remaining funds until none existed in the Bank's vaults.[56] It is interesting to note that the government did not actually remove the funds from the Second Bank, desiring to deprive the directors of an excuse for contracting their business. Nonetheless, it caused a contraction in the money supply and an immediate decline of one and one-half percent in the Bank's stock.[57]

Deposit banking worked to the advantage of Jackson, providing him with almost complete control over fiscal matters. It created an increase of executive power, which remained in effect until the Congress abolished the president's power to select state banks in 1836.[58]

The opposition press referred to these initial seven state banks as pet banks, and by the end of 1833, their number increased to twenty-two. During the next three years, approximately ninety banks became pet banks or banks friendly to the administration. The Commonwealth Bank of Boston was run by David Henshaw, a fount of many valuable Jacksonian ideas. Taney had interest in another pet bank, the Union Bank in Baltimore. He was one of its stockholders, and he knew a good bank when he saw one. The president of the Union Bank, Thomas Ellicott, also provided the Jacksonians with many important ideas.[59]

It is interesting to note that some fourteen years before the creation of these pet banks, Chief Justice John Marshall had divested himself of the stock of the Second Bank prior to hearing the case *McCulloch vs. Maryland* that determined the Bank's constitutionality. Now Secretary of the Treasury Taney, soon to become the chief justice, acted more businesslike. While planning on where to place the public funds, he not only kept his state bank stock, but bought more as a nominee for his sisters and sister-in-law. Not wishing to appear to have a conflict of interest, Taney had refrained from choosing his own bank as a depository. The general did it for him.[60]

The allies of the administration, notwithstanding the criticism of the opposition, firmly supported the pet bank policy. Thomas Hart Benton declared that he "felt an emotion of the moral sublime at beholding such an instance of moral heroism."[61]

Taney had written the presidents of the original seven pet banks to explain the importance of these banks to the administration, and how the banks could benefit from the funds.

In selecting your institutions as one of the fiscal agents of the government, I not only rely on its solidity and established character, . . . but I confide also in its disposition to adopt the most liberal course which circumstances will admit towards other monied institutions generally. . . . The deposits of the public money will enable you to afford increased facilities to commerce and to extend your accommodation to individuals. And as the duties which are payable to the government arise from the business and enterprise of the merchants engaged in foreign trade, it is but reasonable that they should be preferred . . . whenever it can be done without injustice to the claims of other classes of the community.[62]

By December 1833, the public funds held by the Bank were almost drained, and both Jackson and Taney were responsible. The president's actions had caused a crisis in the market. The draining of the deposits left most of the financial interests in the nation worried about monetary affairs and caused a great shock to public confidence in the economy. The financial crisis was also influenced by the effects of the compromise tariff law, which led to another system of paying duties. Now the importers were forced to pay immediately rather than in six months time. This caused an increase in the demand for credit which was unavailable at the time.[63]

When the public funds were removed from the Second Bank, Biddle declared war on the administration by continuing to contract the money supply—a contraction that had begun prior to removal. Encouraged by the new deposits they received, the pet banks began to increase their loans. This put them in debt to the Second Bank, because when borrowers drew on their borrowed funds, the amount of notes and checks outstanding against the banks making the loans increased, and they eventually made their way to the Bank. It was now necessary for the lending banks to use the drafts that Taney had sent them to meet their obligations to the Bank. Taney's own bank in Maryland had already cashed in several of the drafts it had received from the secretary of the treasury. When Taney heard what had happened, he summoned the Union Bank's president to Washington to criticize his actions.[64]

If Jackson had not challenged Biddle by placing public funds in the pet banks, Biddle would have placed limits on the contraction. However, Biddle had to protect the Bank's reserves. Therefore, the more loans the pet banks made, the more pet bank notes ended up with the Second Bank, which then returned them to the pet banks for payment, causing a contraction of the money supply.[65]

According to Catterall, Biddle was protecting his Bank against a Jacksonian assault to destroy it. For example, in the fall of 1833, Catterall stated that a demand was made for $350,000 in specie "upon the branch at Savannah, which could be met only because, the suspicions of the board having been aroused by the failure of the bank to receive the notes of the Savannah branch, it had been sent large supplies of specie there."[66] Biddle had blamed Jackson for this attack on the Bank, and he showed his readiness to fight back in a letter he wrote to Joseph Hopkinson, a Philadelphia lawyer, on February 21, 1834. Biddle said, "This worthy President thinks that because he has scalped Indians and imprisoned Judges, he is to have his way with the Bank. He is mistaken."[67]

Biddle considered it his duty to counterattack. He was hoping that if he could bring enough pressure on the financial markets, he would force Jackson to restore the deposits. Perhaps, if the panic continued, the general might even recharter the Bank. On January 27, 1834, he wrote to William Appleton, the president of the Boston branch and declared that

My own view of the whole matter is simply this. The projectives of this last assault on the Bank regret, and are alarmed at it—but the ties of party allegiance can only be broken by the actual conviction of existing distress in the community. Nothing but the evidence of suffering abroad will produce any effect in Congress. . . . Our only safety is in pursuing a steady course of firm restriction—and I have no doubt that such a course will ultimately lead to restoration of the currency and the recharter of the Bank.[68]

Unfortunately, Biddle's little war against the Jacksonians in 1833 could not have come at a worst time. Businesses were in the midst of expansion, credit and cash were in demand, and tariff duties were due. The Bank was turning prosperity into potential disaster. Within two months from October 1833 to December 1833, the Bank reduced its loans by more than $5.5 million. In the next five months, loans had decreased by $18 million. To make matters worse, the Bank had demanded that all state banknotes be redeemed in specie, which put additional pressure on the state banks that now had to collect from their debtors while curtailing their own loans.[69] A recession had begun at the end of 1833 which lasted into 1834. Financial difficulties occurred in commercial and manufacturing centers throughout the country. By January 1834, every major city had its share of business failures.

The contraction of the money supply was causing serious banking problems in New York. The New York bankers owed the Second Bank nearly $1 million, and in December 1833, they informed Taney that the drafts they had received from the government were insufficient to deal with their financial problems. Taney responded by asking them to be more prudent in making loans, and not to cash their drafts under any circumstances.[70]

In Jackson's annual message in December 1833, he declared that removal of the public funds from the Second Bank had been successfully accomplished. He said, "The state banks are found fully adequate. They have maintained themselves and discharged all these duties while the Bank of the United States was still powerful and in the field as an open enemy, and it is not possible to conceive that they will find greater difficulties in their operations when that enemy shall cease to exist."[71]

Taney also gave his annual report to the Congress in December, defending the removal of the deposits. He told the Congress that he had asked the Bank to begin liquidating its business, but instead it began a process of loan restrictions that affected the economic welfare of the country. He found it difficult to believe "that such an institution as the Bank of the United States could bring itself . . . to bring general distress on the people." Taney remained critical of the Bank's policy of loan contraction, but in his opinion it was just as bad that the Bank had expanded its loans and discounts in late 1831 into 1832. For example, the Bank had increased its loans in 1831 from $42 million to $63 million, and in the first six months of 1832 to $70 million, all this while renewal was being considered by the Congress. In Taney's opinion, the Bank had "justly forfeited the confidence of the government."[72] It had no redeeming values and could do nothing right. Taney made some absurd statements in his report to the Congress. For example, he claimed that when the Bank lent money, it was to corrupt and enslave the people; if it failed to lend, it was to starve them. He even questioned the good credit that the Bank enjoyed throughout most of its years. He said,

It is well understood that the superior credit heretofore enjoyed by the notes of the Bank of the United States was not founded on any particular confidence in its management or solidity. It was occasioned altogether by the agreement on behalf of the public, in the act of incorporation, to receive them in all payments to the United States; and it was this pledge on the part of the government which gave general currency to the notes payable at remote branches.[73]

The Bank also had its defenders who spoke before the Congress in January 1834. Horace Binney, counsel for the Bank, and a director, told the members of the House on January 7th that the Bank proved indispensable in regulating the money supply. He then criticized Taney's "doctrine of an unregulated, uncontrolled, state bank paper currency." This would simply lead to inflation and panics.[74]

Several days after Binney, Calhoun spoke to members of the Senate. He reiterated what he had said in 1816, that the Bank was a vehicle used by the Congress to discharge the duties given to it by the Constitution to regulate the currency. He said, "So long as the question is one between a Bank of the United States incorporated by Congress and that system of banks which has been created by the will of the Executive, it is an insult to the understanding to discourse on the pernicious tendency and unconstitutionality of the Bank of the United States."[75] Calhoun emphasized that Taney did not have the authority to move public moneys from the depository provided by the Congress, unless he could prove they were unsafe. Even the Jacksonian supporters did not claim the funds were removed for safety reasons. Cambreleng, a Jacksonian, in December 1833, only one month prior to Calhoun's speech, had said that the shift in the deposits had nothing to do with their safety. In fact, he declared that the Bank "was a safe place for the public money."[76]

Clay had also attacked both Jackson and Taney. On the day after Christmas in 1833, before a packed gallery in the Senate, he said that "we are in the midst of a revolution, hitherto bloodless, but rapidly tending towards a total change of the pure republican character of the Government, and to the concentration of all power in the hands of one man." He discussed how the currency had been undermined and the charter vetoed. He was very critical of Taney, explaining that the duties of the secretary of the treasury were "altogether financial and administrative. He has no legislative powers; and Congress neither has nor could delegate any to him."[77]

Webster, the chairman of the Senate Finance Committee, was as critical as Clay in denouncing Taney and Jackson. Regarding Taney, he said, "It is no part of his duty either to contract or expand the circulation of bank paper." He went on to attack Jackson's veto message: "I see . . . plain declarations that the present controversy is but a strife between one part of the community and another. I hear it boasted as the unfailing security, the solid ground, never to be shaken, on which recent measures rest, that the poor naturally hate the rich." Webster then declared that those people evil enough to attack the Bank, "by arraying one class against another . . . deserves to be marked especially as the poor man's curse!"[78]

Clay sponsored two resolutions that passed the Senate by large majorities. On February 5, 1834, the Senate voted twenty-eight to eighteen, declaring that the reasons offered by Taney for the removal of the deposits were "unsatisfactory and insufficient," and on March 28th, it resolved to censure Jackson for the removal of the deposits, as an abuse of presidential power by a vote of twenty-six to twenty. Similar resolutions were rejected in the House, where the Jacksonian floor leader, James K. Polk of Tennessee, kept the discussion to the point.[79]

The censure resolution had stunned the general, and he protested to the Senate that it was incompatible with the "spirit of the Constitution and with the plainest dictates of humanity and justice." He said, "So glaring were the abuses and corruptions of the bank . . . so palpable its design by its money and power to control the Government and change its character, that I deemed it the imperative duty of the Executive authority . . . to check and lessen its ability to do mischief."[80]

Jackson defiance of the censure was a proclamation that he was the spokesman for the American people on the bank issue The president was sending a warning to the Congress that he would protect his office from congressional encroachment. He was reaching beyond the Senate and was addressing himself directly to the American people, telling them about a conspiracy against the executive branch. The general was the consummate politician, appealing directly to the public while arguing a defense against privilege and wealth.[81]

Clay, Webster, and Calhoun all tried to discredit Jackson's concept that the president directly represented the people, but failed to accomplish the task. The general was very popular among the electorate, and he both recognized this fact and used it to his advantage. Benjamin W. Leigh, a member of the new Whig party, which was made up of former National Republicans and others who opposed Jackson, declared that "Until the President developed the faculties of the Executive power [in the bank war], all men thought it inferior to the legislature—he manifestly thinks it superior; and in his hands the monarchical part of the Government has proved far stronger than the representatives of the States."[82]

Remini declared that Jackson's war against the Bank of the United States enhanced the power of the presidency and "liberated the President from the position of prime minister, responsible only to Congress. No longer was the chief executive simply the head of a coordinate branch of government . . . he could assert himself as the spokesman of the people and by skillful use of his powers force Congress to follow his lead."[83]

Throughout 1834, memorials and petitions for recharter were sent to the Congress, and distinguished citizens visited the White House to ask the president to restore the Bank's deposits. However, Jackson remained firm in his resolve to terminate the Second Bank. Some visitors even told the general that they were insolvent as a result of the downturns in the economy in 1833-1834. Jackson sarcastically declared: "What do you come to me for, then? Go to Nicholas Biddle. We have no money here, gentlemen. Biddle has all the money. He has millions of specie in his vaults at this moment, lying idle, and yet you come to me to save you from breaking."[84]

Jackson had blamed Biddle for the Panic of 1833-1834 and cursed his Bank. For the general, the Bank was not the solution to the economic woes that besieged the nation; it was the problem—a problem that he hoped would soon disappear.

NOTES

1. Ralph C. H. Catterall, *The Second Bank of the United States* (Chicago: University of Chicago Press, 1902), p. 215.

2. Robert V. Remini, *Andrew Jackson and the Bank War: A Study in the Growth of Presidential Power* (New York: W. W. Norton and Company, 1967), p. 77.

3. Ibid.

4. Ibid.; Catterall, *The Second Bank of the United States*, p. 223.

5. Remini, *Andrew Jackson and the Bank War*, p. 78.

6. Reginald C. McGrane, ed., *The Correspondence of Nicholas Biddle Dealing with National Affairs, 1807-1844* (Boston: Houghton Mifflin Company, 1919), pp. 171-172.

7. Catterall, *The Second Bank of the United States*, p. 225.

8. McGrane, *The Correspondence of Nicholas Biddle*, pp. 174-178.

9. Ibid., pp. 179-181.

10. Catterall, *The Second Bank of the United States*, p. 228.

11. Remini, *Andrew Jackson and the Bank War*, p. 78.

12. Bray Hammond, *Banks and Politics in America from the Revolution to the Civil War* (Princeton, NJ: Princeton University Press, 1985), pp. 393-395.

13. Catterall, *The Second Bank of the United States*, pp. 231-232.

14. Remini, *Andrew Jackson and the Bank War*, p. 80.

15. *Senate Journal*, 22d Cong., 1st Sess., 1832, p. 345; Catterall, *The Second Bank of the United States*, pp. 234-235.

16. *House Journal*, 22d Cong., 1st Sess., 1832, p. 1074; Arthur M. Schelsinger, Jr., *The Age of Jackson* (Boston: Little, Brown and Company, 1953), p. 87.

17. Remini, *Andrew Jackson and the Bank War*, p. 80; Catterall, *The Second Bank of the United States*, p. 235.

18. McGrane, *The Correspondence of Nicholas Biddle*, pp. 192-193.

19. *Senate Journal*, 22d Cong., 1st Sess., 1832, pp. 451-453; Catterall, *The Second Bank of the United States*, pp. 235-236.

20. Catterall, *The Second Bank of the United States*, p. 239; Hammond, *Banks and Politics in America*, p. 405; Remini, *Andrew Jackson and the Bank War*, pp. 81-82.

21. Hammond, *Banks and Politics in America*, p. 406.

22. Ibid.

23. Remini, *Andrew Jackson and the Bank War*, pp. 82-83.

24. Ibid., p. 84.

25. Ibid., p. 85.

26. *Senate Journal*, 22d Cong., 1st Sess., 1832, p. 463.

27. McGrane, *The Correspondence of Nicholas Biddle*, p. 196.

28. Remini, *Andrew Jackson and the Bank War*, p. 98.

29. Ibid., pp. 98-99.

30. Ibid., p. 99.

31. Ibid., pp. 100-101.

32. Ibid., pp. 105-106.

33. Ibid., p. 106.

34. Ibid., p. 110.

35. Catterall, *The Second Bank of the United States*, p. 285.

36. Ibid., p. 286.

37. Ibid.

38. Ibid.

39. Ibid., p. 287.

40. Remini, *Andrew Jackson and the Bank War*, p. 111.

41. Ibid.; Hammond, *Banks and Politics in America*, p. 412.

42. John Spencer Bassett, ed., *Correspondence of Andrew Jackson*, Vol. 5 (Washington, DC: Carnegie Institution of Washington, 1931), pp. 52-54.

43. Remini, *Andrew Jackson and the Bank War*, pp. 111-112.

44. McGrane, *The Correspondence of Nicholas Biddle*, p. 202.

45. Ibid., p. 205.

46. Bassett, *Correspondence of Andrew Jackson*, Vol. 5, p. 101.

47. Remini, *Andrew Jackson and the Bank War*, p. 115; Hammond, *Banks and Politics in America*, p. 413.

48. Remini, *Andrew Jackson and the Bank War*, p. 117; Catterall, *The Second Bank of the United States*, p. 293.

49. Hammond, *Banks and Politics in America*, p. 417.

50. Ibid., pp. 417-418.

51. Remini, *Andrew Jackson and the Bank War*, pp. 120-121.

52. Ibid., p. 123.

53. Ibid., pp. 123-124.

54. Bassett, *Correspondence of Andrew Jackson*, Vol. 5, p. 206; Remini, *Andrew Jackson and the Bank War*, p. 124.

55. Remini, *Andrew Jackson and the Bank War*, p. 125; Hammond, *Banks and Politics in America*, p. 419.

56. Remini, *Andrew Jackson and the Bank War*, p. 125.

57. Catterall, *The Second Bank of the United States*, p. 295.

58. Frank Otto Gatell, "Spoils of the Bank War: Political Bias in the Selection of Pet Banks," *American Historical Review* 70 (October 1964): 36.

59. Hammond, *Banks and Politics in America*, p. 419.

60. Ibid.

61. Ibid., pp. 419-420.

62. Ibid., p. 420.

63. Catterall, *The Second Bank of the United States*, pp. 297-298.

64. Hammond, *Banks and Politics in America*, p. 421.

65. Ibid.

66. Catterall, *The Second Bank of the United States*, p. 299.

67. McGrane, *The Correspondence of Nicholas Biddle*, pp. 221-222.

68. Ibid., pp. 219-220.

69. Remini, *Andrew Jackson and the Bank War*, p. 127; Thomas P. Govan, *Nicholas Biddle: Nationalist and Public Banker, 1786-1844* (Chicago: University of Chicago Press, 1959), p. 247.

70. Hammond, *Banks and Politics in America*, p. 422.

71. Ibid., p. 423.

72. Ibid., pp. 423-424.

73. Ibid., p. 424; *Register of Debates*, 23d Cong., 1st Sess., 1833, p. 2352.

74. Hammond, *Banks and Politics in America*, p. 428.

75. *Register of Debates*, 23d Cong., 1st Sess., 1834, pp. 217-218.

76. Hammond, *Banks and Politics in America*, p. 429.

77. *Register of Debates*, 23d Cong., 1st Sess., 1833, pp. 59-94.

78. Ibid., 23d Cong., 1st Sess., 1834, pp. 439-442.

79. Ibid., 23d Cong., 1st Sess., 1834, pp. 59, 220; Remini, *Andrew Jackson and the Bank War*, p. 141; Richard Timberlake, *Monetary Policy in the United States: An Intellectual and Institutional History* (Chicago: University of Chicago Press, 1993), p. 45.

80. Remini, *Andrew Jackson and the Bank War*, p. 142.

81. Ibid., p. 144.

82. Ibid., p. 147.

83. Ibid., pp. 147-148.

84. Ibid., pp. 148-149.

9

The Last Years of the Second Bank

THE DECLINE OF THE BANK

Andrew Jackson actually began the weakening of the Bank with the withdrawal of the public funds from its vaults in 1833. From then until the Bank's charter expired in 1836, the president did all that he could to undermine Biddle and the Bank.

In January 1834, Jackson ordered Secretary of War Lewis Cass to instruct Biddle to surrender all funds, information, and accounts concerning pensions to the War Department's commissioner of pensions. Biddle ignored the order, claiming that Jackson's action was illegal. Cass then ordered the immediate suspension of pension payments, which angered the veterans and their congressmen.[1]

The pension issue went to the House Ways and Means Committee, which returned a report criticizing the Bank and not the president, for the suspension. However, in the Senate, a pro-Bank body, the majority supported the Bank for refusing to comply with what it called an improper order.[2]

The Democratic newspapers used the pension issue to their advantage, as they condemned Biddle for challenging the president's order and refusing to surrender money that did not belong to him. No one could believe that the general was responsible for withholding money from veterans, many of whom had served under his command. It was much easier to blame the aristocratic Lord of Chestnut Street who many blamed for the panic of 1833-1834. Even Daniel Webster, Biddle's supporter in the Congress, urged him to yield to the president on this matter. He wrote to Biddle on February 12, 1834, declaring that "pensioners will not believe [that Jackson] is the cause of keeping back their money." However, Biddle proved a stubborn man and refused to listen to Webster to give up the pension money held by the Bank. The result was a decline in the popularity of the Second Bank.[3]

Jackson now had Biddle on the defensive and intended to keep him there. What the president wanted to do now was to repudiate Biddle's contention that the banks in New York, under the influence of Van Buren, were jealous of the Second Bank, and were conspiring to replace it with a bank of their own. The president wanted this issue discussed in the Congress, and asked Vice President Van Buren to find the appropriate person for the job. The vice president asked Silas Wright of New York, who was on the board of the Mechanics and Farmers Bank in Albany, a company operated under the umbrella of the Albany Regency, a political machine created by Van Buren, to make a speech in the Senate that would end the conspiracy rumors for good. Wright made a convincing speech, proclaiming, "I go against this bank and against any and every bank to be incorporated by Congress, whether to be located at Philadelphia or New York, or any where else within the twenty-four independent States which composed this Confederacy upon the broad ground which admits no compromise, that Congress has not the power, by the Constitution, to incorporate such a bank." His speech denied any attempt to create a new bank favorable to New York and caused many Democrats to understand that Jackson was not just against Biddle's bank, but opposed to any national bank.[4]

By the end of February 1834, public opinion had turned against the Second Bank and became very pro-Jackson. The pro-Bank governor of Pennsylvania, George Wolf, in his annual message to the state legislature, publically condemned Biddle for bringing "indiscriminate ruin" upon the state. The upper house of Pennsylvania passed a resolution denouncing the Bank for its contractionary policy that contributed to the panic in 1833-1834. Meanwhile both U.S. senators from Pennsylvania stated publicly that they could no longer support the actions of Biddle and the Bank.[5]

In New York, Governor William Marcy denounced the Bank in his annual message for doing little to assist the New York banks, and he stated that he would help by asking the state legislature to loan them state stock. In April 1834, the New York state legislature made available $6 million of five percent state stock for loans, calling it the Marcy mortgage.[6]

Biddle fought back by denying that the Bank was responsible for the panic of 1833-1834. In a letter to his friend Joseph Hopkinson on February 21, 1834, he wrote

You may rely upon it that the Bank has taken its final course and that it will be neither frightened nor cajoled from its duty by any small drivelling about relief to the country. All that you have heard on that subject from New York is wholly without foundation. The relief, to be useful or permanent, must come from Congress & from Congress alone. If that body will do its duty [the restoration of the public funds and rechartering of the Bank], relief will come—if not, the Bank feels no vocation to redress the wrongs inflicted by these miserable people.[7]

By 1834, Biddle knew that most Jacksonian Democrats were opposed to the Bank, but what made recharter even more difficult for him was the division over the issue among his most popular Whig supporters. For example, Webster favored a compromise with the Jacksonians, calling for a charter of either three, four, or six years beyond 1836, a deal Biddle was willing to accept. However, Clay, who personally despised Jackson, wanted no compromise. It was either another twenty-year charter or nothing. Therefore, Webster was unable to secure the full support of the Whigs. Meanwhile, Calhoun lost interest in recharter, and he supported a system that would put the United States exclusively on the gold standard.[8]

In April 1834, the Democrats pushed through the House, the anti-Bank chamber, four resolutions that would permanently block the rechartering of the Bank. They were submitted to Polk's House Ways and Means Committee and adopted by the full House on April 4, 1834. On the first resolution, the House decided by a vote of 134 to eighty-two not to recharter the Bank; it then voted 118 to 103 not to restore the public deposits; then, by a vote of 117 to 105, it supported the state banks as places of deposit of the public funds; finally, by a vote of 175 to 42, it overwhelmingly called for the formation of a committee to investigate the affairs of the Bank, and to determine the causes of the panic of 1833-1834. This last resolution passed so convincingly because most of the Congress firmly belie-ved that Biddle's polices were responsible for the economic downturn.[9]

The general was overjoyed with the passage of these resolutions, for it marked the end of the Bank for all intents and purposes. He knew that it was only a matter of time before the Democrats would prove that Biddle had destroyed the economy to win his charter. He wrote to his son Andrew Jackson, Jr., on April 6, 1834 and said that "the overthrow of the opposition in the House of Representatives by a vote on the reso[lu]tions of the committee of ways and means was a triumphant one, and puts to death, that mamouth [sic] of corruption and power, the Bank of the United States."[10]

Biddle could do little about the first three resolutions, but he refused to open his books for his enemies. Furious, the investigators returned to Washington and demanded a citation of contempt. Taney and several members of the Kitchen cabinet had supported the citation, but the majority of House Democrats refused to cooperate with them for good reason. Many in the Congress had dealings with the Bank, and had written private letters to Biddle. The Bank president had shrewdly observed that it would have been ironic if he went to prison "by the votes of members of Congress because I would not give up to their enemies their confi-dential letters."[11]

Realizing that his defiance condemned him in the eyes of the public, Biddle had asked the more friendly Senate to conduct the same investigation. His request was referred to the Senate Finance Committee, and John Tyler's written report, praising Biddle and the Bank's operations, was made public in December 1834. However, it was too late to help Biddle and the Bank, as the November elections had already taken place. The Democrats had increased their strength in the House, and now had a majority in the Senate.[12]

By the end of February 1834, a group of New York businessmen, friendly to the Bank, formed the Union Committee—a committee to end the Bank's policy of contraction. The members of the committee wanted to speak to Biddle and the management of the Bank to convince them that the reduction of the money supply was wreaking havoc on the economy. Biddle was not happy with having to deal with his supporters from New York. In fact, he really didn't know who his real supporters were anymore. He was still smarting over the betrayal of Governor Wolf of Pennsylvania. In a letter to Samuel Breck, a member of the Pennsylvania legislature, on March 1, 1834, Biddle said that he was distressed by the actions of Wolf, and that this caused him to deny giving any relief to New York.

A Committee from New York has been visiting the Bank for the purpose of procuring some relief for that city which would of course have reacted on our own State. Yesterday the Board was to have decided it, & I have no doubt that the Bank would have made an effort to give relief—but when we saw the Governors [*sic*] message—saw how totally useless the efforts of the Bank had been to sustain the credit of the State in appeasing the spirit of the party—and how little reliance could be placed on the men in power, we determined that it was in vain to make an effort—and accordingly, instead of sending the relief expected, we wrote to the New York Committee that the conduct of the Governor of Pennsylvania obliged the Bank to look to its own safety, and that therefore we declined doing any thing at present.[13]

Biddle did not get off the hook so easily. The Union Committee led by James G. King told Biddle that his reasons for failing to help the New York banks were unacceptable, and that if he continued to refuse aid, he would lose whatever support he had in New York state. Albert Gallatin, a long-time supporter of the Bank and a member of the committee, declared that the Second Bank should make every effort to help the New York banks. Finally, at the end of March 1834, Biddle and the Bank's management offered relief, but it was too late, for Governor Marcy, as mentioned above, recommended a loan to the banks. The Bank's cause was now ruined among its closest friends in New York.[14]

Biddle continued to contract the money supply into the spring of 1834, and became even more resolute when the House had passed the four resolutions against the Bank in April. However, when the Congress finally adjourned without restoring the public funds or giving hope of recharter in June 1834, Biddle decided to end his contraction policy. A committee was chosen in June to determine a course of action. In a letter to William Appleton, the head of the Boston branch, Biddle explained his course of action. He said that as long as the Congress was in session, the Bank would have continued its contraction policy, hoping to pressure the Congress and the Jackson administration to recharter the Bank or at least to restore its public funds. However, now that the Congress had adjourned, without granting the Bank its rightful demands, it was now necessary to reassess policy. On July 11, 1834, the Bank Management Committee finally determined to ease its policy of contraction, noting that the reason for change was the adjournment of the Congress.[15]

Seven days later, Samuel Jaudon, the owner of the *United States Gazette*, wrote to Biddle that the press had accused the Bank of contracting the money supply for political reasons, and that the recent expansion would last only as long as the Congress remained adjourned. The country was bracing for another contraction in the autumn.[16]

Emboldened by the Democratic victory in the congressional elections in November 1834, Jackson indicated that the government would stop accepting branch drafts in the payment of taxes. The general was trying to show the country that the Bank was unnecessary, and he promised to provide the nation with a "sound and portable currency."[17]

Though everything pointed to the demise of the Bank at the end of 1834, Biddle refused to believe it. He was now alone in hoping for its recharter before the next election. The Whigs were no longer supporting the unpopular Bank, realizing that to back recharter was to court political disaster. Thurlow Weed, the Whig party leader in New York, explained that any candidate connected with the Bank was committing death. He said that it would be "suicidal [to] carry politics into business. The poor were almost all against before, and this course will make them unanimously so. My feeling, and judgment say, make war against the Banks."[18]

Webster, who remained a friend of the Bank to the end, had written Biddle in the spring of 1835, despairing the state of the Whig party. He wrote, "It appears to me that our political affairs are taking a very decided turn, & that if nothing be done to check the current, Mr V. B. will be elected President, by a vast majority." Webster was upset about the splintering of the Whigs into the Northern and Southern Whigs, feeling that it would cost them the election in 1836. He was hoping that Biddle could unite the Whigs in Pennsylvania, as Webster was trying to do in Massachusetts, behind a national issue to save the party in 1836. He said, "You can judge whether any thing can be usefully done. For my part, I confess, it looks to me as if the whole Whig Strength in the Country was either to be frittered away, or melt into support of Mr. V. Buren."[19]

As the power of the Bank eroded, the president's control over the financial operations of the country increased. Using his treasury secretary, Jackson initiated a policy that became known as deposit banking—the movement of large amounts of money in and out of state banks. The general believed that deposit banking, together with a return to specie currency in place of paper notes, would provide the country with a sound banking system, making a national bank unnecessary.[20]

In April 1834, Jackson sent to the Congress a number of measures to change the currency and banking system which became known as the Deposit Act. It became part of a report submitted by Taney to the House Ways and Means Committee, and it proposed the following: the treasury secretary should have the power to select the pet banks; he should be allowed to remove the deposits from any bank, after explaining his reasons to the Congress; banks would provide monthly financial reports; the government would have the right to examine all financial books and records of the pets; gold be revalued to bring it slightly above silver at the mint; and deposit banks could not issue notes under five dollars. Later this prohibition against paper would apply to notes under twenty dollars. The idea was to make specie the country's currency for regular transactions whereas banknotes would only apply to commercial purposes.[21]

Both Jackson and Benton had wanted to restore specie as the major currency of the country. Taney had written to Polk in 1834 that "the first step towards a sound condition of the currency is to reform the coinage of gold . . . As this general paper currency [notes of the Bank of the United States] is gradually retiring from circulation the gold should be prepared to take its place."[22] Benton had already made several speeches on this subject in the Senate, and he pointed out that devaluation would end the need for any paper currency.[23]

In 1834, gold was undervalued at the mint relative to silver. Fifteen ounces of silver was equal to one ounce of gold. In other countries, such as France, the ratio was 15.5:1. If Taney had his way, he would overvalue gold at the mint by establishing a new ratio of 16:1. By increasing the mint value of gold, the government was making its exports more competitive in the market. Both the Whigs and Democrats knew that the country needed a boost out of the recession in 1834, and they put partisan politics aside to pass the antideflationary Gold Coin Act in April 1834.[24]

However, the other measures of the Deposit Act remained stalled in the Congress when the Senate refused to approve Taney's nomination as secretary of the treasury. He had committed the unpardonable act of removing the public funds from the Second Bank. Jackson now turned to Attorney General Levi Woodbury, one of the few cabinet members who had approved the removal of the funds, and nominated him to be the next treasury secretary. The Senate acted quickly to confirm his nomination, and he remained in office throughout the remainder of Jackson's term and all of Van Buren's.[25]

After two years of wrangling in the Congress, the Deposit Act was finally passed in June 1836. This act represented a distant compromise of the Taney recommendations of 1834, and the general reluctantly signed it because he felt it would help Van Buren win the presidency in 1836.[26]

The provisions of the Depository Act put limits on the selection of pet banks by the secretary of the treasury. A deposit bank had to be found in every state, as long as certain conditions were fulfilled. Funds could not be transferred from bank to bank unless the Treasury Department required it, and if transferred, the funds would be sent to the nearest bank, and not one at the other end of the country. The Act also established limitations on the quantity of public funds held by the bank, by stipulating that no bank could hold public funds in excess of a sum equal to three-fourths of its capital. Unfortunately, this created an increase in the number of pet banks from twenty to ninety, which now made them more difficult to control.[27]

The Deposit Act also called for the redemption of all pet banknotes in specie, and prohibited the issue of notes for less than five dollars after July 4, 1836. The pets were also denied from receiving any notes under five dollars in payment of a debt owed to the United States. Later the amount was raised to ten dollars, and by March 3, 1837, it was twenty dollars.[28]

The deposit banking system was meant to replace the Second Bank of the United States, which officially went out of business in March 1836. It might have worked if the number of banks had been kept small. However, the Congress wanted guarantees that each state would have pet banks, and that they could only hold a limited amount of public funds. This forced the government to create too many pet banks and, without the proper regulatory machinery, it would lead to economic disaster for the nation.[29]

THE CLOSING OF THE SECOND BANK

The Second Bank of the United States died slowly. Its popular support rapidly decreased due to the belief that Biddle and the Bank had caused the panic of 1833-1834 by rapidly contracting the money supply. The public, among them many former supporters of the Bank, remained irritated with Biddle for refusing to surrender the pension money and later declining to submit to a House investigation into the Bank's affairs. Finally, the remaining Bank's supporters lost all hope that the institution could be saved after the Democratic victory in the November 1834 congressional elections.[30]

Though all of the above events were important in weakening the Bank, it was the removal of the public funds that marked its end as an effective central bank. Biddle wrote to Charles Hammond, a lawyer and well-known journalist of Cincinnati, on March 11, 1834, that Jackson, "by removing the public revenues has relieved the Bank from all responsibility for the currency, and imposed upon it a necessity to look primarily to the interest of the Stockholders committed to our charge. Our friends must therefore bear with us, if in the midst of the present troubles, we should endeavor to strengthen the Bank so as to make it able here after to interpose effectively for the relief of the Country."[31]

Generally speaking, the Bank's directors managed their affairs in a praiseworthy manner throughout 1835. They transferred funds to the east from distant offices in the interior of the country, and they began selling out branches.[32] With the sale of the offices came the disposal of the active debt, the suspended debt, and the real estate, which included all the banking houses. This covered everything that the Bank owned in these branches, which was a much easier way of settlement than for the Bank to attempt to collect all its debts itself. This method also made it much easier for the community, allowing those who purchased the debt to continue the business and prevented, in many cases, the loss of jobs and other economic disruptions when major businesses close in a community. The Bank's property was mostly sold to local banks in the cities and towns where the branches were established.[33]

The Bank began selling its offices as early as March 1835 when orders were issued to the branches at Fayetteville, Cincinnati, Savannah, Richmond, Utica, and Lexington to stop making new loans. In the next few months, all the other branches were told to prepare to close. By November 30, 1835, nine of the Bank's branch offices had disposed of its debt, and by April 3, 1836, the number had reached eighteen.[34]

In August 1835, Biddle wrote to his friend Silas M. Stilwell of New York that the Bank "is winding up its affairs, quietly and certainly. The nature of its operations which consist mainly in selling out its debts on long credits, is calculated to ease the debtors, and our great object is to close its concerns in such a manner as to avoid all pressure."[35] On January 23, 1836, loans ceased being made in New York City, and none were undertaken at any of the other branches.[36]

The stockholders held their last meeting on February 19, 1836, when they voted to give Biddle "a splendid service of plate, with suitable inscriptions in token and commemoration of the gratitude of the stockholders for his faithful, zealous, and fearless devotion to their interests." Unfortunately, the plate was not ready at the time, and it was presented to Biddle several years later.[37] John Sargeant, one of Biddle's closest friends, spoke at this meeting about how the Bank and its president were always at the beckon of the country. He said,

When danger threatened, when credit was trembling, when confidence was shaken, whenever, in a word, a revulsion was threatened, with its disastrous train of consequences, this Bank, strong in its power, stronger in its inclination to do good, anticipated and averted the crisis. By judicious liberality, it prevented or relieved the pressure, it encouraged by its example and support, it cheered by its countenance. . . . Hereafter, if search should be made among the rubbish of the years that are past, some things may be found in wanton license of the press, which, unexplained, or falling into the hands of persons unacquainted with the times, might lead to the belief that this was indeed a strange sort of Bank, and the President of it a very strange sort of man. The record of this day's proceedings will be their triumphant contradiction . . . [the gift to Biddle] a grateful trophy of victory, won at last by integrity and truth over unmerited and unmeasured calumny.[38]

The charter of the Second Bank of the United States officially expired on March 4, 1836. However, Biddle would continue to lead the Bank under a state charter for three more tumultuous years.

NOTES

1. Robert V. Remini, *Andrew Jackson and the Bank War: A Study in the Growth of Presidential Power* (New York: W. W. Norton and Company, 1967), p. 160.

2. Ibid.

3. Ibid., p. 161.

4. *Register of Debates*, 23d Cong., 1st., 1834, pp. 399-402.

5. Remini, *Andrew Jackson and the Bank War*, p. 164.

6. Ralph C. H. Catterall, *The Second Bank of the United States* (Chicago: University of Chicago Press, 1902), p. 341.

7. Reginald C. McGrane, ed., *The Correspondence of Nicholas Biddle Dealing with National Affairs, 1807-1844* (Boston: Houghton Mifflin Company, 1919), p. 222.

8. Catterall, *The Second Bank of the United States*, p. 341; Remini, *Andrew Jackson and the Bank War*, p. 165.

9. Remini, *Andrew Jackson and the Bank War*, p. 166; *Register of Debates*, 23d Cong., 1st Sess., 1834, pp. 3474-3477.

10. John Spencer Bassett, ed., *Correspondence of Andrew Jackson*, Vol. 5 (Washington, DC: Carnegie Institution of Washington, 1931), p. 259.

11. Remini, *Andrew Jackson and the Bank War*, p. 167.

12. Ibid.

13. McGrane, *The Correspondence of Nicholas Biddle*, pp. 224-225.

14. Catterall, *The Second Bank of the United States*, pp. 343-344.

15. Ibid., p. 347; McGrane, *The Correspondence of Nicholas Biddle*, p. 237.

16. Catterall, *The Second Bank of the United States*, p. 348.

17. Remini, *Andrew Jackson and the Bank War*, p. 168.

18. Ibid.

19. McGrane, *The Correspondence of Nicholas Biddle*, pp. 250-251.

20. Remini, *Andrew Jackson and the Bank War*, pp. 168-169.

21. Ibid., p. 169.

22. Richard H. Timberlake, *Monetary Policy in the United States: An Intellectual and Institutional History* (Chicago: University of Chicago Press, 1993), p. 46.

23. Ibid.

24. Ibid.

25. Ibid., p. 47; Remini, *Andrew Jackson and the Bank War*, p. 169.

26. Remini, *Andrew Jackson and the Bank War*, pp. 169-170.

27. Ibid., p. 170.

28. Ibid.

29. Ibid., p. 171.

30. Ibid., pp. 173-174.

31. McGrane, *The Correspondence of Nicholas Biddle*, p. 226.

32. Catterall, *The Second Bank of the United States*, p. 365.

33. Ibid.

34. Ibid., p. 366.

35. Ibid., p. 368.

36. Ibid.

37. Bray Hammond, *Banks and Politics in America from the Revolution to the Civil War* (Princeton, NJ: Princeton University Press, 1985), p. 440; Walter B. Smith, *Economic Aspects of the Second Bank of the United States* (Cambridge, MA: Harvard University Press, 1953), p. 176.

38. Smith, *Economic Aspects of the Second Bank of the United States*, p. 177.

10

Conclusion

THE UNITED STATES BANK
OF PENNSYLVANIA

Throughout most of 1834, Biddle gave no indication that he was interested in doing anything other than preparing the closing of his Bank. It wasn't until November of that year that we have the first indication of interest in a state charter by Biddle. On November 13, 1834, Biddle received a letter from his friend and fellow bank supporter R. L. Colt, stating that "the more I have thought about the Bank, the better I like your idea of applying to your State for a Charter for 35 Millions." In fact, Colt made it clear to Biddle that he would probably have no difficulty in applying to any state, with the exception of New York, for a charter.[1] For more than a full year, very little appeared in the Biddle correspondence denoting continued interest in a state-chartered bank. Then from December 4, 1835, his correspondence becomes rife with interest. Obviously, from 1834 until the end of 1835, Biddle had stilled hoped for the recharter of the Second Bank.

On December 4, 1835, Jasper Harding, Biddle's Pennsylvania colleague and good friend, wrote to him about the climate of opinion in the Pennsylvania capital toward a prospective new bank. He wrote,

I have just returned from Harrisburg—every thing looks as favourable as could be expected, through the kindness of the Speaker, Mr. Middlesworth I obtained last evening a copy of the committees of the House in confidence, not to show it in Harrisburg to injure him, before it was announced from the chair, I send you a proof slip—Pennepacker the chairman on Banks is a very clever country member I think not disposed to throw difficulties in the way.[2]

Two days later in a letter to Biddle, Charles Davis wrote, "The opinion rapidly obtains here that Pena. will grant you a Charter if Congress declines acting in the matter." He told Biddle that the state of Pennsylvania would love to have him preside over a state bank, but most people believed that Biddle only wanted to close the Bank of the United States and then "devote [him]self to higher pursuits than the Story of Banking."[3]

Biddle began negotiations with the Pennsylvania authorities in earnest at the end of December 1835. He applied for a charter as a citizen of Pennsylvania who was "devotedly attached to her interests and fame."[4] Though he had the support of most of the leaders in both political parties in the state, he had opposition from the Democratic leaders in Washington, who made it clear to their party associates that if the Bank of the United States were continued, "it would break the president's heart." Since Jackson was leaving office in a little more than a year, and Van Buren did not want to risk losing the votes of the state of Pennsylvania in the next election, there was no serious opposition to the charter in the state.[5]

The bill to charter, introduced on January 19, 1836, was called "An Act to Repeal the State Tax on Real and Personal Property and to continue and extend the improvements of the State by Railroads and Canals, and to charter a State Bank to be called the United States Bank." On February 19, 1836, the stockholders of the Second Bank of the United States, with the exception of the federal government, met and agreed to accept the new Pennsylvania charter. They then permitted the transfer of the assets of the Second Bank to the United States Bank, and then approved the payment to the American government for its twenty percent interest in the Second Bank. The old stock became exchangeable for the new on a one-for-one basis. The charter had cost the Bank almost $6 million, but it was worth every penny to preserve the established credit and former connections, and to avoid the losses that liquidation of the institution would incur. The Bank was now officially called the United States Bank of Pennsylvania.[6]

It should be noted that the United States Bank of Pennsylvania had nothing in common with the Second Bank of the United States, except the same management. The Second Bank was a corporation under federal charter with specific powers and responsibilities, while the United States Bank was a corporation under state charter with no unique powers, and having the same duties as any other state bank. The First and Second Banks of the United States had much more in common than the Second Bank had with the United States Bank. However, some students of history believe that since Biddle and the stockholders of the Second Bank formed a new bank, they see a continuation of the Second Bank in the United States Bank. Nothing could be further from the truth.[7]

Biddle wanted the world to know that he was still in the banking business. He sent a copy of his new charter to Baring Brothers and Company of London with the following statement: "Substantially however it is a very good charter, better in many respects than the present. It has one extraordinary merit. It is a triumph of good sense over the idle prejudice against foreign capital . . . and no further action is necessary on the part of the foreign stockholders who will come in of course for as many shares in the new Bank as they hold in the present."[8]

However, the charter had important limitations on the powers of the Bank.

The Bank could only deal in bills of exchange, gold and silver bullion, "or in the sale of goods really and truly pledged, for money lent and not redeemed in due time, or goods which shall be the proceeds of its lands." The Bank could only purchase its own stock, treasury notes, or public stocks created by the government of the United States or the State of Pennsylvania. It could also purchase the "stock of, or loans to any of the incorporated companies of this state, for the construction and improvement of roads, bridges, canal or inland navigation, or other stocks which may be bona fide pledged as security for debts to the bank, and not duly redeemed." The total amount of debts that the Bank may owe, "whether by bond, note or other contract, excepting the amount of money due to the depositors, shall not at any time exceed double the amount of capital stock actually paid in."[9]

Other provisions of the charter disallowed note issue of less than ten dollars, and fixed the maximum rate of interest on loans made in Pennsylvania at one-half percent a month. It also stated that all notes, bills, and deposits were redeemable in gold and silver. If the Bank could not redeem its notes in specie immediately, it would incur a twelve percent penalty, and the charter would suffer forfeit if the irredeemability lasted more than three months.[10] The charter was amended in the spring of 1836 to allow the institution to purchase other bank stock. In September 1836, it acquired the Merchants' Bank of New Orleans and in November the Insurance Bank of Columbus, Georgia. They now became active agents of the United States Bank of Pennsylvania.[11]

The main office at Philadelphia did mostly general banking business, and the offices located at Pittsburgh, Erie, and New Brighton operated similarly, but on a smaller scale. Outside the state, the Bank conducted business through offices called agencies. They were located in New York, Boston, Mobile, Natchez, and New Orleans. These agencies dealt mostly in domestic and foreign bills of exchange, and a few loans on personal security were made. The ownership of the Bank was mostly Pennsylvanian and European.[12]

The new Bank owned about $15 million of claims on other banks as a result of the sale of its branches and other assets. It hoped to receive payment of these claims in one to four years. It had a $35 million capitalization which was considered large for a state bank.[13]

The Bank had begun its career in a prosperous economy beginning on March 4, 1836. There was a large accumulation of wealth in the western states, resulting from land speculation and the building of roads, canals, and railroads. This growth economy would come to an end in the spring of 1837, and with it the United States Bank of Pennsylvania would begin its decline which would lead to failure and liquidation in 1841.[14]

THE PANIC OF 1837

From 1834 to 1836, the government's receipts from public land sales increased dramatically. In 1834, there was only $4,900, an increase of only $900 from the year before. However, in 1835, the receipts totaled $14,800 and in 1836, an astounding $24,900. Public land sales would take a steep fall to $6,800 in 1837, the year of the panic.[15]

Public land sales became an important medium of speculation, as they stimulated the American economy. Most of these lands that the government sold were located in the Mississippi and Ohio river valleys. The soil here was rich for farming, and the sites held potential for both urban and industrial development. The government sold its land for $1.25 an acre. The price was kept low to benefit the poor settlers, but it mostly helped the professional speculators and their banks.[16]

After 1833, the state banks showed little restraint when it came to lending money. They were permitted to count the notes of other banks as reserves and expand their loans accordingly. Unfortunately, there was no reserve requirement the banks had to maintain before 1837, which meant that banks could lend their entire legal reserves. To make matters worse, the only restraint on the banks, the Second Bank of the United States, no longer performed a regulatory role, after the public funds were taken from its vaults in 1833. (Before the removal of the funds, the Second Bank would gather state banknotes that came into their possession, and return them to the state banks for payment in specie.) These lending institutions were forced to make loans more prudently to keep enough specie available for redemption.[17] The total number of banks in 1836 was six hundred, and one third of them were established since 1833. Banknote liabilities increased greatly throughout the nation. In the eastern half of the United States, the banks increased their note issue by fifty percent from 1833 to 1836; in the western sections, it rose by one hundred percent, and in the south by one hundred thirty percent.[18] The nation was accumulating a very large debt, but few cared, as assets were purchased and wealth was being made.

With the passage of the Deposit Act in 1836, the government was able to rid itself of its huge surplus. The surplus was caused by four factors: the paying off of the national debt, land sale revenues, the general prosperity of the nation, and tariff revenue.[19] The only question the Congress had was how to dispense the surplus. The general refused to allow it to be pumped into the states for fear of inflation. So the Congress, with an ear to their constituents, distributed the surplus among the states. As of January 1, 1837, all surplus in excess of $5 million was to be deposited with the states in proportion to their respective representation in both the House and Senate. The money would come in four installments in the first month of each quarter in 1837. This was the first step that led to the downturn in the economy in 1837.[20]

On July 11, 1836, the general took the second step that contributed to the panic. He directed Secretary of the Treasury Levi Woodbury to issue the Specie Circular. It stated that land agents could only accept gold and silver in payment for public lands. Though the act was meant to prevent "frauds, speculations, and monopolies in the purchase of public lands," it came too late to do any good. Its purpose was to protect the destitute settlers and curb the speculators, but it accomplished neither. Instead, it made it more difficult for the settlers to buy land, as specie was hard for them to find. On the other hand, the speculators, who already owned many acres of land, had more access to specie. Now they would also benefit from fewer land sales, which would increase the market value of their real assets.[21]

With the passage of the Specie Circular, the government appeared to be distancing itself from the state banks, which it could no longer effectively control. Now the Specie Circular and distribution of the treasury surplus had caused total disorder in the economy. Biddle, in a letter to John Quincy Adams, in November 1836, explained what was happening:

The commercial community were taken by surprise. . . . The creditor States, not only receive no money, but their money is carried away to the debtor states, who in turn cannot use it, either to pay old engagements or to contract new. By this unnatural process the specie of New York and the other commercial cities is piled up in the Western States—not circulated; not used, but held as a defense against the Treasury—and while the West cannot use it—the East is suffering for the want of it. The result is that the commercial intercourse between the West and the Atlantic, is almost wholly suspended, and the few operations which are made, are burdened with the most extravagant expense."[22]

Biddle was blaming the federal government for poor planning in the distribution of the surplus. The Jackson administration had caused a flow of funds against the tide of normal trade. Specie supposedly flowed westward to further the sales of public lands in compliance with the Specie Circular, but was needed in the east to provide for the surplus distribution.[23]

Though the Specie Circular and the distribution of the treasury surplus contributed to the Panic of 1837, there were international causes too. Financial relations between Great Britain and the United States during this period caused problems in the foreign exchange market. England was a major financial and industrial power in the world. The British commercial interests discovered in the United States a premier market for its goods and capital, and a prolific source of cotton for its mills. The United States, on the other hand, found in England a market for its cotton and securities to pay for the British goods.[24]

In June 1836, British specie reserves were falling rapidly, and the Bank of England had decided to raise its discount rate from four to four and one-half percent; in August, it was raised again to five percent. When the Bank of England had heard about the Specie Circular, it sent a letter to its Liverpool agent, instructing him to reject the paper of specific English banking houses that were tied to American financial interests.[25]

The consequences of this curb on credit and the effort to stop the export of gold caused a serious crisis in the American foreign exchange market in the spring of 1837. American cotton exporting firms failed, and the cotton market found itself in a serious crisis, as cotton prices fell to new lows. The Bank of England, by raising its rates and refusing credit to American interests, had changed the direction of specie movements. For the first time in several years, American specie exports to England were more than imports by $2.3 million.[26] The British had stopped buying from American firms and had ceased lending to them, and, at the same time, they demanded payment from these American firms who owed large sums of money.[27]

In the spring of 1837, it proved difficult for American firms to make foreign remittances. Sterling bills sold for a premium of twelve and one-half percent, and even at that rate, they were hard to secure. In New York, merchants had asked Biddle and the United States Bank of Pennsylvania to send specie to Europe to alleviate the crisis there. Unfortunately, Biddle had less than $2 million of specie at the Bank, and he could not afford to send any of it abroad. Finally, on May 10, 1837, all specie payments were suspended in the United States.[28]

After the suspension of specie payment, the economy experienced some financial relief when stock prices rose. However, there was little change in internal trade, which continued to decline, as southern and western merchants could not do business in the eastern commercial centers, due to the reluctance to accept their banknotes and drafts. The recession continued, but there was at least a decline in business and bank failures. It appeared that the Panic of 1837 was less disastrous than the one in 1819.[29]

In March 1837, Biddle and other bankers attempted to convince the newly elected president, Martin Van Buren, to repeal the Specie Circular. They were sure that it was the major cause of the panic. However, Van Buren, ever loyal to Jackson, refused to consider repeal. Finally, on May 31, 1838, good sense prevailed, and a congressional resolution abolished the Specie Circular. Once again, people could buy public land without having to pay in gold or silver.[30]

In February 1838, the tight money policy of the Bank of England was relaxed. It reduced the discount rate on bills of exchange and notes to four percent. There was no need to maintain the four and one-half percent, as Britain's specie reserves were at 10 million pounds as compared with 4 million a year earlier. This stimulated a demand for American stocks and corporate security issues. The reduction in the Bank of England's discount caused an increased flow of specie to the United States and led many branches to support the resumption of specie payment.[31]

Though Biddle's United States Bank no longer had debt on its short-term foreign accounts, and the Panic of 1837 appeared to have ended, Biddle wanted to play it cautiously, and he refused to support the resumption of specie payment in the spring of 1838. In a letter to John Quincy Adams, he advised the delay on resumption, as he talked about time as "the great restorer, time to settle; time to adjust accounts; time to send the debtors' crops to the market; time to dispose of his property with the least sacrifice; time to bring out his resources to pay his debts."[32]

However, the New York bankers, under Gallatin's leadership, held a meeting in April 1838, and they decided to resume specie payments on May 10th. They would be the only bankers to do so that early, as everybody else remained cautious about financial conditions. Even the specie conscious Boston bankers had refused to resume payment, which led Gallatin to remark "that they hated Van Buren more than they loved the gold standard."[33] It should be noted that this decision by the New York bankers to resume specie payment by May 10th enhanced its image as a responsible money center. The prestige of the New York banks grew in London, and by the late 1830s, New York replaced Philadelphia, once and for all, as the leading financial center in the United States.[34]

By August 1838, all the state banks had resumed specie payments, and many believed that America's financial problems were a thing of the past. Commodity prices began to rise between August 1838 and April 1839, and American exports, once again, exceeded imports.[35]

Toward the end of 1838, Biddle had announced that he would retire from banking at the end of March 1839. On February 26, 1839, a month before retirement, he was invited to the White House as an honored guest of President Van Buren. According to James Hamilton, who was also in attendance, all went well. Hamilton remarked, "This dinner went off very well, Biddle evidently feeling as the conqueror. He was facetious and in intimate converse with the President."[36]

On March 29, 1839, at the age of fifty-four, Biddle officially resigned from the presidency and the board of directors of the bank, leaving he said, "in a state of great prosperity and in the hands of able directors and officers."[37] His resignation was primarily due to his state of health and his desire to pursue other interests in his life.[38]

Thomas Dunlap was chosen as Biddle's successor. He was a trained lawyer and had been second assistant cashier of the bank before assuming its presidency. Thomas Wren Ward, an agent for Baring Brothers and Company in the United States, characterized Dunlap as a "lawyer of second rate standing . . . worthy, upright, and indolent." Ward had little doubt that he would become Biddle's spokesman.[39]

THE PANIC OF 1839 AND THE END
OF THE UNITED STATES BANK

The economy took a sharp downturn in 1839, causing the United States Bank's specie reserve to decline from $4 million in January to only $1.5 million in October.[40] This time events in Great Britain were the primary cause. Between January and October 1839, bullion in the Bank of England decreased from over 9 million pounds to 2.5 million, and it looked like the central bank of England would suspend specie payments.[41] Commercial houses had collapsed in Canton, Calcutta, Le Havre, and Brussels, caused by severe shortages of specie. Financial conditions had declined rapidly in Great Britain, which influenced the sale of cotton. British exports to Europe had declined due to the business recession, and British imports, valued at 10 million pounds, were paid for with a loan from the Bank of France.[42] These events effected the demand for cotton in the United States and the credit of the United States Bank.

Though cotton prices had recovered briefly in 1838, they declined rapidly throughout 1839, as England's demand for cotton declined. At the same time, the Bank of England's rising discount rate had discouraged new business with the United States. As with cotton, American securities were no longer welcome in Great Britain.[43]

To acquire specie and remain solvent, the United States Bank had issued postnotes and foreign drafts. The postnotes were short term promissory notes due in six months, paid interest and sold at a discount. They became bank liabilities that were sold as investments. They were offered at high yields and ended up crowding out other types of investment. These securities became popular because they were affordable to small investors. They were issued in denominations as low as ten dollars and sold to yield as much as twenty percent per annum.[44]

The United States Bank's postnote issues had increased from about $5.5 million in June 1839 to over $9 million in September 1839. The postnotes made the United States Bank a creditor of the state banks in New York, Boston, and elsewhere, and this caused animosity and distrust toward it.[45]

American financial interests were blamed by the English press for causing the financial crisis in Great Britain by reducing the British gold supply through the sales of their securities in 1838. This provided the United States with a $9 million net inflow in specie that year. It forced the British to raise rates and reject American bills founded on corn, cotton, and stocks, and that caused the specie net inflow to the United States to fall to only $750,000 in 1839.[46]

On October 9, 1839, the United States Bank suspended specie payment once more, as its specie reserves had declined rapidly. Banks in Philadelphia, Rhode Island, and about one-third of the banks in Ohio followed the same course. However, many banks in New England, New York, and elsewhere continued to pay in specie.[47] Biddle, realizing that his Bank was in trouble, briefly came out of retirement and rushed to its defense. He declared that the Bank had no choice in suspending specie. It was either that or force the community to pay its obligations immediately to the Bank, which would cause sacrifices of its property just to collect specie to ship to Britain. He asserted that the resumption of specie in 1838 came too quickly, as many banks still had low specie reserves. He blamed the recession in England on bad weather conditions, causing poor crops, and resulting in heavy losses of the Bank of England's gold reserves.[48]

While Biddle was busy blaming the international events for the panic of 1839, the banks in New York and Boston were accusing the United States Bank for starting the economic crisis. They condemned the Bank's cotton operations and Biddle's failure to reduce credit and deflate prices. As a result, the United States Bank's stock had declined in 1839 from $100 a share to $79 at the year's end. It briefly revived in early 1840, but then declined continuously until the Bank's end in 1841, when it was selling for $3 a share.[49]

The money markets of New England and New York were calm, and loans were easy to acquire, as the rates remained low in 1840. This was not the case in

New Orleans and Mobile, where the financial situation remained critical, as specie
was hard to find. The quantity of American stocks sold in Europe in 1840
was small compared with the previous year.[50] Meanwhile, the United States Bank
was having serious problems in the foreign exchange market. In February 1840,
its bonds sold at a price that caused it to pay ten percent for money in London.[51]
The crisis of 1839 was much more serious than the one in 1837, especially in
Great Britain. The loss of bullion suffered by the Bank of England in 1839 made
for a longer recovery time than in 1837. England's specie reserves finally began
increasing in 1842.[52]

On April 3, 1840, the Pennsylvania legislature declared that all banks were
obligated to resume specie payments by January 15, 1841 or forfeit their charter.[53]
This did not bode well for the United States Bank, whose condition in the spring
of 1840 was questionable. Its officers were viewed as "poor stuff," and many experts in the banking business did not believe that it would ever resume specie
payments. The Bank's loans and discounts had contracted from November 1839
to January 1841 from $39 million to $21 million. On June 16, 1840, the Bank's
directors stated that "no loans now running to maturity, shall be renewed; and that
upon all loans, whether on accommodation paper, upon stock, or upon other
security, a payment of at least ten percent will be required, when due, and the
balance to be settled by notes at from one to seven months." Also the salaries of
the Bank's officers were reduced, bringing a saving of $40,000 a year.[54]

As January 15th approached, the date that the Bank had to resume specie
payments, it found itself with $7.5 million in circulating notes and $1.6 million
of postnotes outstanding. It had exported large quantities of specie in the last
quarter due to international obligations.[55] The Bank had no recourse other than
borrow from other state banks in Philadelphia. The Philadelphia banks, with the
aid of the banks in New York, Boston, Providence, and Hartford, had loaned the
United States Bank $5 million. However, even with this loan, the Bank could not
resume payments, and it had to borrow from abroad.[56]

The state of Pennsylvania pressured the banks within its borders, including
the United States Bank, to resume payment in specie before they were ready. On
January 14th, the eve of resumption, the United States Bank was obligated to
redeem $2.6 million of its notes. In the next three weeks that it stayed open, it
paid out $6 million in specie, and note redemption took over $4 million. Pressure
was put on the Bank to meet all its obligations, as large drafts from New York and
Philadelphia were presented.[57]

At the time that the demands on the United State Bank had seemed insur-
mountable, the state of Pennsylvania had asked for a loan of $400,000, which it
had every right to do under the law, to meet the interest on the state's debts, due
on February 1, 1841. As soon as the loan was granted, the state demanded payment in specie. All of the demands on the Bank had finally drained its supply of
specie. On February 4, 1841, the United States Bank of Pennsylvania closed its
doors forever.[58]

Nicholas Biddle, president of the Second Bank from January 1823 to March

1836, and then president of the United States Bank of Pennsylvania from March 1836 to March 1839, did not enjoy a peaceful retirement. He worried about the Bank's fate during the economic crisis of 1839-1840. He was sued for $250,000 by angry stockholders, and he was later arrested on criminal conspiracy charges. However, he was freed by the court, only to face more litigation. All of this ceased when Biddle died on February 27, 1844, at the age of fifty-eight, from severe bronchitis and dropsy.[59]

THE VALUE OF THE BANK OF
THE UNITED STATES

In July 1836, Andrew Jackson issued the Specie Circular which stated that all government land purchases had to be made with specie. Most historians agreed that it was one of the causes of the Panic of 1837. The issuance of the Specie Circular proved that deposit banking as an alternative to central banking had failed. In 1832, Jackson vetoed the renewal of the Bank charter, and in 1833, he had removed government funds from the Bank's vaults, and placed them in state banks called pets. Within three years, the number of pets increased dramatically, with a conspicuous absence of government regulation. This led to an increase in lending by the pets, which fueled the land speculation, leading to the Specie Circular and the Panic of 1837.

It is difficult to predict what would have happened if the Second Bank had its charter renewed. We do know that Biddle understood the importance of the Second Bank as a central bank. He had expanded the money supply in the early 1830s to stimulate the economy, and he had contracted it in 1833-1834 while the Bank's deposits were being removed. It is the opinion here that Biddle would have used the power of the Bank in 1835-1836 to mitigate the conditions that led to the Panic in 1837; he did not have that opportunity, and the economy suffered as a result.

The destruction of the Second Bank of the United States marked the end of central banking until the birth of the Federal Reserve Banking system in 1913. From 1837 to 1863, the nation had two kinds of banks: the state banks, which were chartered by the state governments, and private banks incorporated under free banking laws. The adjective free meant that any individual or group could start a bank after complying with certain regulations. These banks existed in about eighteen states (New York being one of them). Some of these free banks were fly-by-night organizations that literally opened up one day and closed the next, without ever intending to pay their depositors in specie.[60]

The national government removed itself from all banking with the creation of an independent treasury. It was originally passed in 1840, repealed in 1841, and reestablished in 1846 until the advent of the Federal Reserve. By the terms of this Act, all public money was to be kept in the treasury rather than in the state banks, where it was considered unsafe.[61] This proved the folly of removing the funds from the Second Bank in 1833.

During the Civil War, serious inflation forced the government back into banking. It passed the National Banking Act in 1863, which allowed the government to charter national banks that issued national banknotes.[62] The creation of the national banking system was no substitute for a central bank and in no way resembled the Bank of the United States. The treasury still held the government's funds, and there was still no bank that could control the money supply.

The absence of a central bank became even more critical after the Civil War. From the end of the war until the first decade of the twentieth century, the money supply grew erratically, causing long periods of deflation with intermittent intervals of serious inflation, resulting in recessions in 1873, 1882, 1893-1895, and 1907.[63] During these downturns, banks ceased to pay out cash in any form, not just specie. It is interesting to note that before the Civil War, when banks suspended payment, it usually applied to specie only. In the recession of 1907, suspensions were longer than in any of the previous ones. Sometimes banks would wait as long as two months before paying out any cash to its depositors. It could be said that the recession of 1907 was caused by a severe deficiency in the money supply.[64] This led to the passage of the Aldrich-Vreeland Act in 1908 which established "national currency associations" composed of ten or more banks to issue emergency banknotes. It also created the National Monetary Commission, which reported in 1912 that the banking system in the United States suffered from serious weaknesses. It called for the creation of a central bank which would provide an elastic money supply for the banking system and act as an agent of the treasury. In December 1913, President Woodrow Wilson responded to the commission by signing the Federal Reserve Banking Act.[65]

It was unfortunate that it took the American government so long to recognize the need for a central bank. From the withdrawal of public funds from the Second Bank of the United States in 1833 to the creation of the Federal Reserve in 1913, there was no central bank to regulate the money supply or act as a fiscal agent of the government. As a result, the economy suffered from an inelastic money supply, and the government found it difficult to collect taxes and disburse revenue.

NOTES

1. Reginald C. McGrane, ed., *The Correspondence of Nicholas Biddle Dealing with National Affairs, 1807-1844* (Boston: Houghton Mifflin Company, 1919), pp. 245-246.

2. Ibid., p. 257.

3. Ibid., pp. 257-258.

4. Thomas P. Govan, *Nicholas Biddle: Nationalist and Public Banker, 1786-1844* (Chicago: University of Chicago, 1959), p. 284.

5. Ibid.

6. Walter B. Smith, *Economic Aspects of the Second Bank of the United States* (Cambridge, MA: Harvard University Press, 1953), pp. 178-179.

7. Bray Hammond, *Banks and Politics in America from the Revolution to the Civil War* (Princeton, NJ: Princeton University Press, 1985), p. 440.

8. Govan, *Nicholas Biddle*, pp. 284-285.

9. Smith, *Economic Aspects of the Second Bank of the United States*, p. 180.

10. Ibid.

11. Ibid.

12. Ibid., p. 181.

13. Ibid., p. 183.

14. Ibid.

15. Hammond, *Banks and Politics in America*, pp. 451-452.

16. Ibid., p. 452.

17. Ibid., p. 453.

18. Ibid.

19. Ibid., p. 455; Robert V. Remini, *Andrew Jackson and the Bank War: A Study in the Growth of Presidential Power* (New York: W. W. Norton and Company, 1967), pp. 170-171.

20. Hammond, *Banks and Politics in America*, p. 455.

21. Ibid.

22. Smith, *Economic Aspects of the Second Bank of the United States*, p. 185.

23. Richard H. Timberlake, *Monetary Policy in the United States: An Intellectual and Institutional History* (Chicago: University of Chicago Press, 1993), pp. 53-54.

24. Hammond, *Banks and Politics in America*, p. 457.

25. Ibid., pp. 457-458.

26. Ibid., p. 459; Smith, *Economic Aspects of the Second Bank of the United States*, pp. 187-188.

27. Smith, *Economic Aspects of the Second Bank of the United States*, p. 188.

28. Ibid., pp. 191-192.

29. Ibid., pp. 193-194.

30. Ibid., p. 195.

31. Ibid., pp. 203-204.

32. Ibid., p. 204.

33. Ibid.

34. Ibid., p. 205.

35. Ibid., p. 209.

36. McGrane, *The Correspondence of Nicholas Biddle*, p. 337; Hammond, *Banks and Politics in America*, p. 501.

37. Hammond, *Banks and Politics in America*, p. 501.

38. Smith, *Economic Aspects of the Second Bank of the United States*, p. 213.

39. Ibid.

40. Hammond, *Banks and Politics in America*, pp. 502-503.

41. Ibid.

42. Ibid., p. 503.

43. Ibid.

44. Ibid., p. 505.

45. Smith, *Economic Aspects of the Second Bank of the United States*, p. 214.

46. Ibid., p. 217.

47. Ibid., p. 219.

48. Ibid., pp. 219-220.

49. Ibid., p. 220.

50. Ibid., p. 221.

51. Ibid., p. 222.

52. Ibid.

53. Ibid., p. 223.

54. Ibid.

55. Ibid., p. 225.

56. Ibid., pp. 225-226.

57. Ibid., p. 226.

58. Ibid., p. 227.

59. Remini, *Andrew Jackson and the Second Bank of the United States*, p. 175.

60. Gary M. Walton and Hugh Rockoff, *History of the American Economy* (New York: Harcourt Brace Jovanovich, 1990), pp. 252-254.

61. Ibid., p. 251.

62. Ibid., pp. 407-408.

63. Ibid., p. 405.

64. Ibid., pp. 412-413.

65. Ibid., p. 413.

Bibliography

PUBLIC DOCUMENTS

U.S. Congress. *Annals of Congress*. Selected volumes.
U.S. Congress. *House Journal*. Selected volumes.
U.S. Congress. *Register of Debates*. Selected volumes.
U.S. Congress. *Senate Journal*. Selected volumes.

NEWSPAPER

National Intelligencer. 1814.

BOOKS

Adams, Henry. *The Life of Albert Gallatin*. New York: Peter Smith, 1943.
Adams, Henry, ed. *The Writings of Albert Gallatin*. Vol. 3. Philadelphia, PA: J. P. Lippincott and Company, 1879.
Bassett, John Spencer. *Correspondence of Andrew Jackson*. Vol. 4. Washington, DC: Carnegie Institution of Washington, 1929.
Bassett, John Spencer. *Correspondence of Andrew Jackson*. Vol. 5. Washington, DC: Carnegie Institution of Washington, 1931.
Blackford, Mansel G., and K. Austin Kerr. *Business Enterprise in American History*. Boston: Houghton Mifflin Company, 1986.
Catterall, Ralph C. H. *The Second Bank of the United States*. Chicago: University of Chicago Press, 1902.
Chown, John F. *A History of Money from AD 800*. London: Routledge, 1996.
Dewey, Davis R. *The Financial History of the United States*. New York: August M. Kelley Publishers, 1968.
Ferguson, E. James. *The Power of the Purse: A History of American Public Finance, 1776-*

1790. Chapel Hill, NC: University of North Carolina Press, 1961.

Ferguson, E. James, ed. *The Papers of Robert Morris, 1781-1784*. Vol. 1. Pittsburgh, PA: University of Pittsburgh Press, 1973.

Ferguson, E. James, ed. *Selected Writings of Albert Gallatin*. Indianapolis, IN: The Bobbs-Merrill Company, 1967.

Fite, Gilbert C., and Jim E. Reese. *An Economic History of the United States*. Boston: Houghton Mifflin Company, 1973.

Frisch, Morton J., ed. *Selected Writings and Speeches of Alexander Hamilton*. Washington, DC: American Enterprise Institute for Public Policy Research, 1985.

Gordon, Thomas Francis. *The War on the Bank of the United States*. New York: B. Franklin, 1967.

Govan, Thomas P. *Nicholas Biddle: Nationalist and Public Banker, 1786-1844*. Chicago: University of Chicago Press, 1959.

Gunther, Gerald, ed. *John Marshall's Defense of McCulloch v. Maryland*. Stanford, CA: Stanford University Press, 1969.

Hammond, Bray. *Banks and Politics in America from the Revolution to the Civil War*. Princeton, NJ: Princeton University Press, 1985.

Hendrickson, Robert. *Hamilton I*. New York: Mason/Charter, 1976.

Hepburn, A. Barton. *History of Currency in the United States*. New York: Macmillan and Company, 1915.

Holdsworth, John, and Davis R. Dewey. *The First and Second Banks of the United States*. Washington, DC: U.S. Government Printing Office, 1910.

Jensen, Merrill. *The New Nation: A History of the United States during the Confederation, 1781-1789*. New York: Alfred A. Knopf, 1967.

Jones, Alice Hanson. *Wealth of a Nation to Be: The American Colonies on the Eve of the Revolution*. New York: Columbia University Press, 1980.

Knox, John Jay. *United States Notes*. New York: Charles Scribner's Sons, 1899.

Kutler, Stanley I., ed. *The Supreme Court and the Constitution: Readings in American Constitutional History*. New York: W. W. Norton and Company, 1977.

Lebergott, Stanley. *The Americans: An Economic Record*. New York: W. W. Norton and Company, 1984.

McGrane, Reginald C., ed. *The Correspondence of Nicholas Biddle Dealing with National Affairs, 1807-1844*. Boston: Houghton Mifflin Company, 1919.

Mitchell, Broadus. *Alexander Hamilton: The National Adventure, 1788-1804*. New York: Macmillan Company, 1962.

Myers, Margaret G. *A Financial History of the United States*. New York: Columbia University Press, 1970.

North, Douglass C. *The Economic Growth of the United States, 1790-1860*. New York: W. W. Norton and Company, 1966.

Nuxoll, Elizabeth M., and Mary Gallagher, eds. *The Papers of Robert Morris, 1781-1784*. Vol. 8. Pittsburgh, PA: University of Pittsburgh Press, 1995.

Redlich, Fritz. *The Molding of American Banking: Men and Ideas*. New York: Hafner, 1951.

Remini, Robert V. *Andrew Jackson and the Bank War: A Study in the Growth of Presidential Power*. New York: W. W. Norton and Company, 1967.

Robinson, Raymond H. *The Growing of America: 1789-1848*. Boston: Allyn and Bacon, 1973.

Rockhoff, Hugh. *The Free Banking Era: A Reexamination*. New York: Arno Press, 1975.

Rothbard, Murray N. *The Panic of 1819: Reactions and Policies.* New York: Columbia University Press, 1962.

Schlesinger, Arthur M., Jr. *The Age of Jackson.* Boston: Little, Brown and Company, 1953.

Smith, Adam. *The Wealth of Nations.* Edited by Edwin Cannan. New York: Random House, Modern Library Edition, 1937.

Smith, Walter B. *Economic Aspects of the Second Bank of the United States.* Cambridge, MA: Harvard University Press, 1953.

Smith, Walter B., and Arthur H. Cole. *Fluctuations in American Business, 1790-1860.* Cambridge, MA: Harvard University Press, 1935.

Studenski, Paul, and Herman Krooss. *Financial History of the United States.* New York: McGraw Hill, 1952.

Summer, William G. *A History of American Currency.* New York: Putnam's Sons, 1878.

Syrett, Harold, ed. *The Papers of Alexander Hamilton.* Vol. 2. New York: Columbia University Press, 1961.

Syrett, Harold, ed. *The Papers of Alexander Hamilton.* Vol. 3. New York: Columbia University Press, 1962.

Syrett, Harold, ed. *The Papers of Alexander Hamilton.* Vol. 7. New York: Columbia University Press, 1963.

Syrett, Harold, ed. *The Papers of Alexander Hamilton.* Vol. 8. New York: Columbia University Press, 1965.

Taylor, George R., ed. *Jackson and Biddle: The Struggle over the Second Bank of the United States.* Boston: D. C. Heath, 1949.

Temin, Peter. *The Jacksonian Economy.* New York: W. W. Norton and Company, 1969.

Timberlake, Richard H. *Money, Banking, and Central Banking.* New York: Harper and Row, 1965.

Timberlake, Richard H. *Monetary Policy in the United States: An Intellectual and Institutional History.* Chicago: University of Chicago Press, 1993.

Unger, Erwin. *These United States.* Englewood Cliffs, NJ: Prentice Hall, 1989.

Ver Steeg, Clarence L. *Robert Morris Revolutionary Financier.* Philadelphia: University of Pennsylvania Press, 1954.

Walton, Gary M., and Hugh Rockhoff. *History of the American Economy.* New York: Harcourt Brace Jovanovich, 1990.

Wilburn, Jean Alexander. *Biddle's Bank: The Crucial Years.* New York: Columbia University Press, 1967.

Young, Eleanor. *Forgotten Patriot Robert Morris.* New York: Macmillan Company, 1950.

ARTICLES

Adams, Donald R. "American Neutrality and Prosperity, 1798-1808," *Journal of Economic History* 40 (1980): 713-737.

Calomiris, Charles W. "Institutional Failure, Monetary Scarcity, and the Depreciation of the Continental," *Journal of Economic History* 48 (1988): 47-68.

Engerman, Stanley. "A Note on the Economic Consequences of the Second Bank of the United States," *Journal of Political Economy* 78 (July/August 1970): 725-728.

Frass, Arthur. "The Second Bank of the United States," *Journal of Economic History* 34 (1974): 447-467.

Gatell, Frank Otto. "Spoils of the Bank War: Political Bias in the Selection of Pet Banks,"

American Historical Review 70 (October 1964): 35-58.

Hammond, Bray. "Jackson, Biddle and the Bank of the United States," *Journal of Economic History* 7 (1946): 1-23.

Redlich, Fritz. "American Banking and Growth in the Nineteenth Century," *Explorations in Economic History* 10 (spring 1973): 305-314.

Rezneck, Samuel. "The Depression of 1819-1822, A Social History," *American Historical Review* 39 (October 1933): 28-47.

Scheiber, Harry N. "The Pet Banks in Jacksonian Politics and Finance, 1833-1841," *Journal of Economic History* 33 (1963): 196-214.

Temin, Peter. "The Economic Consequences of the Bank War," *Journal of Political Economy* 70 (March/April 1968): 257-274.

Walters, Raymond, Jr. "The Origins of the Second Bank of the United States," *Journal of Political Economy* 53 (1945): 115-131.

Index

Adams, John, 32, 38
Adams, John Quincy, 64, 90, 97-98,
    103, 116, 123, 155-156
Albany Regency, 142
Allison, David, 101-102
American Revolution, 1, 3-7, 12, 14-15
Ames, Fisher, 23
Appleton, Nathan, 123-124
Appleton, William, 133, 144
Armstrong, John, 81
Articles of Confederation, 8, 12, 15-16
Astor, John Jacob, 32, 41, 43-46, 81,
    106

Bank of England, 7-9, 21, 26-27, 89,
    155-159
Bank of Massachusetts, 14
Bank of New York, 14, 21-23, 26-28,
    32
Bank of North America, 1, 10-14
Bank of Pennsylvania, 11-12, 27, 32
Bank of Stephen Girard, 33
Bank of the United States. *See* First
    Bank of the United States; Second
    Bank of the United States
Bank of the United States vs. Deveaux,
    28, 71
*Bank of the United States vs. Planters
    Bank*, 75
Barbour, James, 52
Barbour, P. P., 87-88

Baring Brothers, 56, 90, 131, 152,
    157
Barker, Jacob, 44-46
Battle of Saratoga, 5
Benton, Thomas Hart, 68, 102-
    104, 121-123, 132, 146
Biddle, Charles, 80
Biddle, Nicholas, 75, 82-83, 97-
    102, 121-124, 126-131, 141-
    145, 147-148, 155-156, 158;
    attacked by Jacksonians, 105-
    116; banking policies, 84-93;
    contracts the money supply,
    133, 136; his death, 159-160;
    early years, 80-82; election as
    Second Bank president, 79-
    80; forms United States Bank
    of Pennsylvania, 151-153; his
    resignation, 157. *See also*
    Second Bank of the United
    States; United States Bank of
    Pennsylvania
Bills of exchange, 2, 13, 41
Binney, Horace, 135
Blair, Francis P., 106, 112, 121,
    128-129
Blount, William, 101
Boudinot, Elias, 24
Breck, Samuel, 144
Brown, Alexander, 89
Brown, Ethan Allen, 70

Buchanan, James, 62-63
Burr, Aaron, 20
Butler, Benjamin, 131
Butler, Pierce, 22

Cadwalader, Thomas, 100, 102,
    123-124, 131
Calhoun, John C., 44-45, 50-55, 98-99,
    105, 110, 112-114, 128, 135-136,
    143
Calhoun-Webster-Lowndes bank bill,
    52
Calomiris, Charles, 4
Cambreleng, Churchill C., 106, 123,
    135
Campbell, George W., 44-46, 98, 102
Cass, Lewis, 141
Catterall, Ralph C. H., 60-63, 111, 133
Chauncey, Elihu, 80
Cheves, Langdon, 51, 64, 69, 71-72,
    79-80, 82-83, 85-87; as president of
    the Second Bank, 73-75. *See also*
    Second Bank of the United States
Church, John B., 14
Clay, Henry, 30, 32-33, 53-54, 82, 91,
    97, 103, 106, 115-116, 121-128,
    135-136, 143
Clayton, Augustine S., 122
Clayton resolution, 123
Clinton, George, 31
Colt, R. L., 79-80
Commonwealth Bank, 106
Continental bills, 3
Continental Congress, 1, 3-4, 6, 9-10
Craig, John, 81
Crawford, William, 37, 58, 60-61, 73,
    80
Cryer, Hardy M., 128

Dallas, Alexander, 43-46, 49-54, 60
Dallas, George, 122
Dallas-Calhoun national bank bill, 54
Davis, Charles, 151
Deposit Act, 145-146, 154
Deposit banking, 145, 147
Dickens, Asbury, 100
Donelson, Andrew, 124
Duane, James, 8
Duane, William J., 130-131

Dun, Walter, 108
Dunlap, Thomas, 157

East Pennsylvania Banking and
    Trust Company, 13
Eaton, John, 104, 114
Eaton, Peggy, 114
Election of 1832, 97, 115,
    121-122, 126-127
Ellicott, Thomas, 79
Ellsworth, Oliver, 22
Embargo of 1807, 39, 41
Eppes, John W., 50

Findley, William, 45
First Bank of the United States,
    37, 40-41, 43, 49-50, 53-54,
    56, 58, 71, 79, 112; as a cen-
    tral bank, 28-29; Congress
    and the Constitution, 22-25;
    failure to recharter, 29-33;
    organization and operation,
    25-28. *See also* Hamilton,
    Alexander
First National Bank of Boston, 14
Fisher, James C., 64
Fisk, Jonathan, 31
Floyd, John, 127
Force Act, 129
Franklin, Benjamin, 12

Gales, Joseph, Jr., 88
Gallatin, Albert, 29, 37-38, 40-41,
    43-44, 75, 79, 109, 112, 144
Genesee Agricultural Society, 67
Girard, Stephen, 33, 41, 44-45,
    56, 58, 93
Gold Coin Act, 146
Gouge, William, 64
Govan, Thomas P., 98
Green, Duff, 105, 112
Greene, Nathanael, 7
Greene, William, 70
Grundy, Felix, 45, 110-111

Hamilton, Alexander, 1, 6, 10-11,
    13, 23-31, 50, 55-56, 71-73,
    109; and the Bank of New
    York, 14; on the bank plans

of 1779 and 1781, 7-9; on a
national bank, 21-22; on his plan
for America, 19-20; on revision of
the Articles of Confederation, 16.
See also First Bank of the United
States
Hamilton, Alexander, Jr., 109
Hamilton, James A., 109-110, 121, 157
Hammond, Bray, 32, 58, 103
Hammond, Charles, 147
Hanson, Alexander, 40
Harding, Jasper, 151
Hemphill, Joseph, 113
Henshaw, David, 107
Hill, Isaac, 99-100, 105-106
Hoffman, George, 98
Holdsworth, John, 32
Hopkins, Samuel, 67
Hopkinson, Joseph, 133, 142

Ingersoll, Charles J., 122
Ingham, Samuel, 99-100, 105, 111

Jackson, Andrew, 93, 104-107,
    121-124, 127-136, 141-147;
    early attitude toward banks,
    97-103; bank veto message,
    124-126; leads opposition to
    Second Bank, 107-116. *See
    also* Jacksonians
Jackson, James, 22
Jacksonians, 97-99; propaganda, 103-116.
    See also Jackson, Andrew
Jaudon, Samuel, 144
Jefferson, Thomas, 19, 24-25, 29-32,
    38-39, 50, 55
Johnson, Richard M., 98, 103-104, 123
Jones, William, 44-46, 49, 57-58, 69,
    71, 74; Jones and the Second Bank
    of the United States, 59-63. *See also*
    Second Bank of the United States

Kendall, Amos, 98, 104, 106, 111, 116,
    121, 124, 130-131
King, James G., 144
King, Rufus, 50-51, 54
King William's War, 7, 9
Kitchen Cabinet, 99, 105-106, 111,
    116, 143

Land banks, 9, 14
Laurens, John, 12
Lawrence, Isaac, 85
Leigh, Benjamin, 136
Lennox, David, 26
Lenox, Robert, 83-84, 99
Lewis, William B., 98, 101, 104,
    107-108, 111, 113
Livingston, Edward, 114, 122
Livingston, Robert R., 14
Lowndes, William, 50-52

Madison, James, 20, 23, 31-32,
    37, 39-41, 44-46, 49-50, 52-
    54, 57
Malthus, Robert, 81
Marcy, William, 126, 142, 144
Marshall, John, 71-72. *See also*
    McCulloch vs. Maryland
Martin, Luther, 71
Mason, Jeremiah, 99-100
McCulloch, James, 58, 62-63, 71,
    74
McCulloch vs. Maryland, 28, 71-
    73, 107, 125, 132. *See also*
    Marshall, John
McDougall, Alexander, 14
McDuffie, George, 110-111, 121-
    123
McLane, Louis, 114-116, 123,
    128-130
Mechanics and Farmers Bank,
    142
Meeker, Cochran and Company,
    101
Meredith, William, 80
Monroe, James, 46, 80-82, 90
Morris, Gouverneur, 10
Morris, Robert, 1, 7, 9-14, 19,
    22

Nichol, Josiah, 112

Ordinance of Nullification, 129
Osborn, Ralph, 72
*Osborn vs. the Bank of the United
    States*, 72
Overton, John, 98, 101

Panics: 1819, 67-71; 1833-1834,
    141-143, 147; 1837, 153, 155-156,
    160; 1839, 157-158
Parish, David, 41, 44-46
Period of the Confederation, 14
Pet banks, 132-133
Pickering, Timothy, 6
"Piece of Eight," 2
Pinkney, William, 71-72
Planters Bank, 74-75
Polk, James K., 101, 136
Postnotes, 158-159
Pryor, Norman, 101

Randolph, Edmund, 24-25
Randolph, John, 54, 115
Relief party, 101
Remini, Robert V., 113, 136
"Report on Manufactures," 20. *See also*
    Hamilton, Alexander
"Report on a National Bank," 20-22. *See*
    also First Bank of the United States;
    Hamilton, Alexander
"Report on Public Credit," 20. *See also*
    Hamilton, Alexander
Ricardo, David, 81
Rice, Joel, 101
Roberts, Jonathan, 45
Rush, Richard, 98, 105-106

Safety Funds Act, 105
Sargeant, John, 88, 126, 148
Second Bank of the United States, 37,
    43-46, 67-71, 79-93, 97, 99, 101-
    102, 104-107, 109, 111-116, 151-
    152, 154, 159-161; its closing, 147-
    148; creation of, 49-55; decline of
    141-147; investigation into, 63-64;
    organization of, 55-59; recharter
    bill in Congress, 121-124; specu-
    lation and fraud, 61-63; and the
    Supreme Court, 71-75; removal
    of government funds, 127-137. *See
    also* Biddle, Nicholas; Cheves,
    Langdon; Jones, William
Shays's Rebellion, 15
Smith, Adam, 21
Smith, Dennis, 62
Smith, Samuel, 32, 98, 110-111,

    121-122
Smith, William, 23
Specie Circular, 154-156, 160
Spencer, John C., 63, 82
State Bank of Georgia, 74-75
Stilwell, Silas M., 148
Strong, Caleb, 22

Taney, Roger B., 106-107, 115,
    121, 124, 129, 131-135, 143,
    145-146
Tariff Act of 1816, 68
Thomas, Francis, 123
Toland, Henry, 107
Treaty of Ghent, 52
Trevett vs. Weeden, 15
Tyler, John, 143

Union Bank, 131-133
Union Committee, 143-144
United States Bank of Pennsylva-
    nia, 151-153, 156; its closing,
    157-159. *See also* Biddle,
    Nicholas

Van Buren, Martin, 81, 98, 105-
    107, 109-110, 113-114, 126-
    127, 142, 146, 152, 156-157
Virginia and Kentucky Resolu-
    tions, 73

War of 1812, 37-38, 44, 68, 82,
    87; financing, 39-42
Washington, George, 4, 7, 19, 24-
    25
Watmough, John, 123, 128
Wayne, Anthony, 7
Webster, Daniel, 51-54, 60, 71,
    99, 116, 125-126, 129, 135-
    136, 141, 143, 145
Weed, Thurlow, 145
White, John, 79
Williams, George, 62
Willing, Thomas, 11-12, 26, 30,
    79
Wirt, William, 71, 127
Wolcott, Oliver, 27-28
Wolf, George, 142, 144
Woodbury, Levi, 131, 146, 154

About the Author

EDWARD S. KAPLAN is Professor in the Department of Social Science at New York City Technical College of the City University of New York. He has co-authored *Prelude to Trade Wars: American Tariff Policy, 1890–1922* (Greenwood, 1994), authored *American Trade Policy, 1923–1995* (Greenwood, 1996), *U.S. Imperialism in Latin America: Bryan's Challenges and Contributions, 1900–1920* (Greenwood, 1998), and has written several articles on U.S. economic history.

ISBN 0-313-30866-7